'One of the most feared villains in London's underworld.'

Time Out

'. . . chillingly unrepentant story.'

The Times

'. . . evokes a vanished era . . .'

Independent on Sunday

'. . . colourful . . . chilling . . .'

Sunday Express

'. . . fascinating . . . reads like a Who's Who of the British criminal class.'

Coventry Evening Telegraph

'. . . pulls no punches . . . compelling reading.'

Kent Today

'. . . the full, violent story. Read it if you have the stomach.'

Glasgow Evening Times

'Macabre, malignant and malevolent, Mad Frank is an incredible phenomenon . . . fascinating.'

Scallywag

MAD FRANK

Memoirs of a
Life of Crime

by Frankie Fraser

as told to
James Morton

TIME WARNER
BOOKS

TIME WARNER BOOKS

First published in Great Britain in 1994
by Little, Brown and Company
This edition published by Warner Books in 1995
Reprinted 1995 (five times), 1996 (twice), 1997, 1998,
1999 (twice), 2000, 2001
Reprinted by Time Warner Paperbacks in 2005
Reprinted by Time Warner Books in 2005 (twice), 2006

A CIP catalogue record for this book
is available from the British Library.

ISBN-13: 978-0-7515-1137-6
ISBN-10: 0-7515-1137-4

Typeset by Hewer Text Composition Services, Edinburgh
Printed in England by Clays Ltd, St Ives plc

Time Warner Books
An imprint of
Time Warner Book Group UK
Brettenham House
Lancaster Place
London WC2E 7EN

www.twbg.co.uk

Contents

Prologue	ix
Chapter 1	1
Chapter 2	26
Chapter 3	55
Chapter 4	66
Chapter 5	96
Chapter 6	109
Chapter 7	144
Chapter 8	166
Chapter 9	191
Chapter 10	208
Chapter 11	216
Chapter 12	232
Chapter 13	248
Chapter 14	270
Chapter 15	285
Chapter 16	319
Index	331

For my sister, Eva,
with my thanks and love

Prologue

The *Independent* had it wrong when their reporter said I'd been shot dead outside Turnmills Night Club in 1991. I was only in hospital for two days that time. He'd have been nearer right about me after I was shot in Mr Smith and the Witchdoctor Club in Catford in South London in March 1965. I was charged with murder over that one and it was Henry Botton – he's long dead now – who shopped me for it. I don't know why he did it. Earlier in the evening he'd had £25 off me because he was on bail for a receiving charge. He'd come across and asked me for a loan. That'd be £200 in today's money.

Mr Smith's was in Rushey Green, Catford. The premises at one time had been a cinema and then a bingo hall, and they did them up very tastefully. It was a night-club where you could eat and dance to a band, and a casino. It had a cabaret and the chorus girls from the Astor in Berkeley Square used to have a coach bring them over to do the floor show. The owners, Paddy McGrath and Owen Ratcliffe, were from Manchester and Owen had a bit of a reputation up there. There's a story that he fired a gun into the ceiling of a club when he went to collect a gambling debt off Dominic, the son of Jack Pye, the wrestler. Owen and Paddy had a club in Stoke-on-Trent and another, the famous Cromford Club, in the centre of Manchester. Both of them were very successful, especially the one in Manchester. So, like so many people, they wanted to open one in London. And that's where they ran into difficulties. Even though they knew London well enough they were out of their depth. There was problems going on in the club almost from the start. There were drunks causing trouble, messing up the casino side of the business and spoiling it for the customers who came with their wives. So they approached Billy Hill and Albert Dimes to ask them for their advice. They'd known Billy and Albert for years, and they asked them the best way to run a club in London. Billy and Albert give them sensible advice and recommended they be introduced to me and Eddie Richardson as people who might be able to help them. In fact I'd met them years before at the Cromford. We met them on 7 March 1966 – it was a Monday – in Billy Hill's flat in Moscow Road near Paddington and came to an arrangement. They didn't exactly specify what had gone wrong but they wanted us to get some doormen, bouncers you'd call them nowadays. They didn't mention any names and, although the police have always said the fight was a quarrel with Harry Hayward and his family for control of the club, we didn't even know he was using the club. In fact that night Harry wasn't in the club at all. There was no problem in providing bouncers and so we went on to discuss the financial arrangements. As the club had just started and wasn't making money we agreed they, the owners, should pay the doormen's wages and, once it was on a firm footing, Eddie and me would have a share. At the time Eddie and me had a company, Atlantic Machines, which put one-armed bandits in clubs, and part of the agreement was that we would put a couple of our machines in Mr Smith's.

When the business side was all settled the owners said we should go down to the club and have a drink and some supper, and that's what we did. This was about 7 or 8 in the evening. We told them we couldn't stay on because we had some business up West. They said, 'Come back afterwards for a social drink.' We said we'd be pleased to, but we might not be back until 10 or 11 or even later.

There was a benefit of me and Eddie being there and being seen having a drink. We were a protection against trouble, but there again with hindsight it could have been like the red rag to the bull. You don't know until it actually happens. Mostly it only does good, but it can rebound if people feel it's a sort of challenge. Anyway we got back about 10 that night with some friends. There must have been about five or six of us including Harry Rawlings and Ronnie Jeffreys. I noticed Billy Hayward, Harry's brother, was there having a drink with Henry Botton and Peter Hennessey, one of a number of brothers.

We started earning our money right away because Jimmy Moody, who worked with us at Atlantic, came in with another man and came over to our table. He told us what he was there for. He was planning to do the casino and had come in to have a look at it.

I thought he was joking and anyway, I said, 'If you're serious you can't do it. We're going to be employing the doormen and we'll be helping them not hindering them – forget about it.' And Jimmy said, 'Of course, forget it.' To this day I'm not sure if he was serious or just joking. I'll never know now because he was shot dead last June.

Anyway, it now seems as though when Billy Hayward and his friends seen Jimmy and his friend join us for a drink, they didn't know what Jim was in there for really. They thought, 'What is this?' and that we were ganging up on them, which we weren't in any way whatsoever. Having made a deal with the club to see there wasn't no trouble, the last thing we'd have done is kicked off with trouble the first day. Billy's lot, they sent out for guns including a shotgun. One of the people drinking with Billy was Dickie Hart and he had a gun with him, but we didn't know it at the time.

What I heard years later, and I think it's right, is what they were afraid of was really a domestic matter. Roy Porritt had worked for us, me and Eddie, on the machines. He was a great mechanic. He'd left us to go on his own but we were still friendly. Billy Hayward had been having it off with Roy's wife. Roy had found out and told her to drop it out otherwise he'd tell us, and there's no doubt we'd have been cross with Billy.

The owners had gone by 1 a.m. and we were all happy staying on and having a drink. We were two separate groups, but we chatted to each other and that's when Botton had the £25 from me. Then about

3.30, just as we were about to go, the manager, a burly Scot, pointed out to us that Billy Hayward and his friends were still drinking. By now they were the only other people left in the club besides ourselves. The club only had a licence until 3 a.m. Now we had an interest we didn't want it breaking the licensing rules, and the manager asked Eddie to have a word with Billy and the others.

Over he went, but they took umbrage and wouldn't go. At this stage I was still talking to the manager and so I never heard exactly what was said. Eddie and Peter Hennessey walked on to what was the dance-floor and were having a straight, fair fight, and suddenly all hell broke loose. Dickie Hart had produced a gun and slipped away from the raised dais where the tables were, and from a distance of about thirty feet he's firing a 45 revolver at random more or less. He could have hit anybody – friend or whoever. One bullet hit a chair leg and another the roof, and a third hit Harry Rawlings in the shoulder and arm and busted an artery. In seconds Harry was bleeding to death. Literally seconds, you could see it. I told Hart, who was still waving the gun, that Rawlings was very seriously injured and we had to get him to hospital. He said all right, but then he went and fired another shot. Jimmy Moody went over to Rawlings and tied a handkerchief around his arm in a tourniquet which must have saved his life. Then he and Ronnie Jeffreys carried Harry out. I walked in front of them and Dickie Hart followed on behind still pointing the gun.

I was absolutely beside myself with what Hart had

done. There was no cause for it whatsoever. Eddie had gone on the dance-floor to have a fair fight with Peter Hennessey. We hadn't gone there for trouble of any kind. As far as we were concerned we were friends; I wouldn't have given Botton £25 if we hadn't been. I was infuriated with the unfairness of it, and as Hart came through the door leading to the back entrance I hit him as hard as I could in the mouth with my fist. With my other I grabbed his hand and held the gun, but he shot me in the thigh smashing my thigh-bone completely, although I did manage to knock the gun away on to the floor.

I've only a vague idea of what happened next because my leg just collapsed and I went down in a heap, but I do remember Botton slinging a tonic bottle and shouting, 'You're fucking mad, Frank.'

We was outside now and someone lifted me up. I was half on his back and I hopped on my right leg about 300 yards up the road. My left was gone; it was just swaying about. Then we heard the police siren going. I told the people who were helping me to go, and I half dived and half fell over a small privet hedge into someone's front garden. That's where the police found me. They were local and, of course, they knew exactly who I was. I was put in the same ambulance as Hart and he and I were in beds side by side in Casualty at Dulwich Hospital. That was when he died.

1

Now I'm seventy, I think if I'd come from a criminal family things might have been different. Certainly I wouldn't have done my sentences the hard way I did. Of course I listened to my parents, but it's not the same as having an Uncle Jim who's been inside to come and tell you, 'Do it this way, son', and you listen and respect him because he's been through it himself. But by the time I'd even thought about it, I had a reputation and it was too late. Every screw was lining up to teach me a lesson.

Even though my mother once told me my father had served eighteen months for manslaughter in Canada, my family were straight people. My father's father married a Red Indian woman. Originally the family was from Scotland, but my grandparents on my father's side never came back to England. That grandfather was born in Canada and lived on the Great Lakes. I don't really know what he did there. My father used to buy all the American papers, all the comics, but he never talked about his life. He never said and we never asked him. It's not like today when television has put the world on your doorstep. Now you could say,

'Look, Dad, there's Canada, what part were you in?'
But in them days it didn't arise. I do know my father
ran away when he was about ten years old. He was in
the Merchant Navy. He did his two years before the
mast. We're talking about over a hundred years ago.
He joined the American navy and had seven years in
that service. I believe he was in their war with Spain
at the end of the 1890s.

My father came to London as a merchant seaman
and he must have met my mother during the First
World War. My mother originally lived in Ponsonby
Terrace on the Embankment. It's quite grand today
but it wasn't then. The family moved to Waterloo and
most probably he met her when he was staying in one
of the clubs or hotels they had round there. He would
have been about thirty-five then. He died during my
trial on the Isle of Wight in June 1970, but they never
told me until I reached Wakefield Prison. He was
about eighty-eight years old. My mother died in 1982,
twelve years later. She was then about eighty-five.

I was born in 1923. I don't know how I got my
middle name of Davidson; my father was just James
Fraser. My mother's father was a Norwegian who
made hats, and her mother was Irish from Cork.
Later my mother's father was a watchman for Stuart
Surridge on the docks. I remember him breaking his
leg, and I used to wheel him to Guy's Hospital for
treatment. My brother and sisters and me were all
born in Cornwall Road, and my grandparents stayed
there until my grandfather died.

The eldest of the family is Peggy, who is about five
years older than me. She married Georgie Harwood

who was a Communist. His brother Harry Harwood was high up with Harry Pollitt, and they did their best to get me to be a Young Communist before the War. When it started they couldn't get in the Army quick enough to fight fascism. Harry Harwood was taken prisoner at Dunkirk. George did very well and ended up a Warrant Officer. He stayed in the Army for the next seventeen years and came out with a pension. He was never in any trouble at all, but he never turned his nose up at me. He'd come from a more rough and ready background than me; his family were more criminal than me. They came from the same street as Alfie Hinds, and that made him understand.

Kathleen and Jim are twins. They are three years and four months older than me. Kathleen went to America and now lives in a village near Cleveland. Her daughter, Della, is a very well qualified nurse. Jim works for a firm of publishers in the Grays Inn Road and doesn't live that far from the old house. My other sister Eva has been the closest to me, and she of everyone has stood by me through my troubles. She married Jimmy Brindle, one of the family who came from Camberwell.

My father worked for the same South London firm, Stuart Surridge, as my grandfather. He was a very honest man; very honest and very, very poor. He worked seven days a week turning on the boilers. My mother used to have three cleaning jobs. One was at I.C.I., a brand-new building at Millbank just over Lambeth Bridge, the second was in a little hotel in Waterloo Road, and then it was back to I.C.I. in the evening. I began stealing early on and bringing it home, saying I'd found £1 or £2. My mother would say she had the luckiest children, but she would not tell my father because he would have made me take the money down to the police station. I'm sure it would simply have been divided up by the coppers there.

We lived in a terraced house in Howley Place, later it was called Howley Terrace. It was two-up, two-down with a scullery at the back. The toilet was in the yard and of course there was no bath. I shared my room with my elder brother, and the girls shared the back room upstairs. The front room was my parents' bedroom which looked out over the street. If there was a birthday party for the children, the bed was tucked up into a corner. The front room downstairs was a sort of kitchen which had wooden shutters.

There was also a little corner shop. Now it's been torn down. The street was bombed in the War, it took a terrible pounding. But then it was a terrific street. There was a muffin man on a Sunday; jellied eel men came round. There was always something going on – fights and things. It was alive. There were also some interesting people lived in the district. One of them was Liz English, who was known as 'Lumps-and-bumps' because of the whacks she got on the head from the police when she was drunk. She'd come into a pub and stand in front of the open fires they had then and lift her skirts before the fire. She didn't wear knickers, and she'd stand and shift her bum so one cheek and then the other got warmed. Her son 'Mile Away' Johnny English was the look-out for local people; he was called that because when he was meant to be a look-out that's where he'd be. Liz had the flower pitch by Waterloo Station which Buster Edwards has now. There was also 'Dartmoor Annie' who had the paper stall opposite, and used to give everyone who was released from Dartmoor a quid as he came off the train. Though I had no help family-wise, I did know people. 'Lumps-and-bumps' would mark my card about any vans which might have good parcels on the concourse, and I could sell 'Dartmoor Annie' the bits and pieces I'd nicked.

Another character was Chopper Sims, the all-in wrestler, who lived with his yard backing on to ours. I used to see him at the Ring at Blackfriars. Later he was involved somehow in the Chalkpit murder case when the former Australian M.P. was convicted and sent to Broadmoor. I think Chopper give evidence for the prosecution.[1]

Right opposite the house were all arches with doors on them, and over the top were little hotels in Waterloo Road leading to Waterloo Bridge. As the road went up higher, so did the arches. In some of them were Covent Garden baskets which porters put on their heads, and then in others there would be scenery for West End theatres. Further down the Civil Service Association, which had a shop in the Strand, had its store. Right at the end – it was cul-de-sac – there was a hotel. And

---

[1] Thomas Ley had once been the Minister of Justice in New South Wales but had been convicted of bribery. He became obsessed with the idea that John Mudie was having an affair with his mistress. Mudie was kidnapped and taken to a chalk-pit in Surrey where his body was found. In March 1946 Ley was convicted but declared insane, and died after a month in Broadmoor. Smith, who had helped him, had his death sentence commuted to life imprisonment.

round the corner there was the famous tattooist, Birch I think he was called, in the Waterloo Road. The hotels would sling all their rubbish out into our yards and so there was rats coming out of the arches. On a Sunday people would fetch their bull terriers and have races to get the rats. The terriers would catch some of the rats, sling them up in the air, and everyone would cheer.

At the top of the turning was Belvedere Road, and a bit further down was the London Wastepaper Company. The women who worked there came to the top of our street when they had their fights. Our street was perfect because there was no traffic. There was posts one end and coming from the other direction was the river. The women and the men would come and watch, stand round in a ring just where the Festival Hall is now. There were some terrific fights, both women and men. No one interfered but it was real blood and thunder. Today people would be absolutely shocked but then – sixty years ago – it was like just par for the course.

If it was a spur-of-the-moment argument then the people who worked in the area would come, a circle would be formed, they would strip off and fight there and then. If they'd come out of the factory or the London Wastepaper Company, the girls would still be wearing the sacking around their legs to keep the rats away.

But if it was a long-standing argument then it would be an arranged fight, with the local street bookmaker there and all and sundry from far and wide; people who didn't know the participants but who would be there to watch and have their bets on. On occasion this applied to the women when a long-standing quarrel turned into an arranged fight. They were knock-down fights until the end, when someone said they'd had enough or they were knocked unconscious. They were really boxing rather than wrestling – kicks, punches, elbows, heads. If they wrestled on the ground they would be pulled apart and stood up. It was a sort of mutual understanding and there was often a sort of referee, a dominant personality in the crowd who would take it upon himself to make them stand. It was a different way of life than today. In that sense people were more disciplined then. If a dominant personality came along, the crowd would defer to him. The crowds and everybody were very honourable. No one else participated. If the fighters crashed into the ring of onlookers they would be pushed back into the middle but nobody, whichever side they supported, would give a sly dig either. It was honourable but it was extremely bloodthirsty. There were no breaks for rounds, they just fought and fought. Of course that was understandable. Remember in 1933 men were doing twenty rounds legitimate boxing; people who had had only three or four bouts behind them. If a man turned professional, his first fight could be ten rounds. So when they had fights at the top of our street, because it was a bare-knuckle fight there was no such thing as a breather. The women's fights were absolutely ferocious – they tore into one another.

I never saw a copper break up a fight. It was a part of life. If he had told people to disperse in them days they would have done, but if it was a fair fight, in his opinion, he would leave it alone. Of course it wasn't fair by today's standards. There were no breaks, and if blood was pouring from a gash over an eye no one stepped in and wiped it away. But if there was just the two of them, then as far as the copper was concerned that was all right.

Betting could go to pounds, which was an awful lot of money then. It was mostly two shillings or half-a-crown, but with the big, arranged fights it could be pounds with the big punters who'd come especially for the fight. In the summer it was like a festival; there was a carnival atmosphere. On the Sundays as I say they'd also have the pit bull terriers after the rats – tempting them out the arches where the dossers now sleep.

One Sunday, I had a fight with one man in the morning which continued after dinner and then in the evening after tea. It was just an ordinary disagreement between two young lads. It was so unimportant that I can't remember what it was about. I think he came from another part of the district, from Broad Walk near the old Ring in Blackfriars, and there was animosity between their street and ours. I can't remember what his name was now. I ended up with a face out to here. A pal of mine went to Boots and got some leeches to put on my eyes to draw the blood; they stayed until they were so fat they fell off me. Three good fights they were. He never give in and I never give in. Everyone sort of acknowledged we should call it a day.

My father was at work all day on a Sunday, so he didn't know about my fights. My mother also worked and they were timed so she didn't see them. Even if she saw a crowd she wouldn't want to watch. She never dreamed that I'd be fighting. If they saw my face, then I'd say I'd been in a fight and leave it at that. Black eyes and cuts were a part of life in them days. But there's no way she would have stood to see me fighting at the top of the street. Eva and the rest of my family, me sisters and brother, would be watching. That was part of the environment, a natural thing. There was nothing unusual in it. In many ways the street was perfectly respectable for the district but that part, the fights at the top, was accepted.

When I was five I had a bad accident. I used to collect those cigarette cards with footballers and boxers on the back of them. I was at the top of Howley Street and there would be great big lorries going back and forwards over the cobblestones, a very rutty road. Because they couldn't go too fast over the cobbles I used to run alongside and ask the drivers to chuck out their cigarettes cards. They'd sling them out and I'd run into the road and collect them. This day I did it and another lorry come along and smashed right into me. Remember the brakes in them days were not like the brakes of today. Ran over my head. Eva, my sister, found me lying in the road. She screamed for help and I'm told I was put on the tailboard of a lorry and rushed to hospital. I was in a terrible state. I was in St Thomas's Hospital on and off for years. It developed into meningitis and all the spin-offs that go with it.

Later, when I came out of hospital, me and Eva would take a pillow-case down to Godden & Hanken in Great Newport Street to be filled with second-day bread. They would fill it for threepence or sixpence and sometimes sling a few cakes in and all. Dad had to be at work at 3.30 a.m. and as soon as he'd gone Eva and I would go with Tim, the Airedale we had. Mother worried about loss of face and Dad would have stopped us if he'd known. He was far too proud. We had to get there early to beat the other kids to it. My other brother and sisters wouldn't have come; Eva and me were the rebels. Off we went across Waterloo Bridge, making sure Tim didn't put his head through the little pillars and get wedged. Then straight up Bow Street, left into Long Acre and over to Great Newport Street. Although in those days she didn't have to worry about filthy men, Mum would hang on for us to get back before she went to work.

In the summer the family went off hop-picking down to Paddock Wood and Marden. It was a busman's holiday. You got paid for working on your holiday. We all picked but we kids ran about. It was really wonderful for Tim. Each family had a little hut, with a communal toilet for about four families. No one thought anything about it. Then at Christmas our treat was for a friend of my mother, Mrs Smith, who had two daughters Rose and Eva – my sister was named after her – to take us over Waterloo Bridge to the Lyceum to the pantomine. Mrs Smith used to make a seed cake, and we'd eat it whilst we watched the panto. There aren't too many photographs of us as children. Photographs cost sixpence, and if we had our photographs took we'd have had to dress up and that meant new gear; it was an unbelievable luxury. We did go to Southend once. That was when my father lost a finger in an accident at work and they give him £100 compensation. We went with some of the money he got and we had our photos took then. When I see photos of Charlie and Eddie Richardson, and Ronnie and Reggie Kray, I realize by comparison their people had plenty of money. We were dirt poor; dirt poor, but the family was honest.

I was brought up Catholic and when I went to communion I used to cover the hole in my boot with the other foot so it didn't show when I knelt down. It didn't occur to me that the other boot had a hole, or that all the other kids had the same. I used to serve at Benediction on Sundays, but I got the sack and a clip to go with it when I put the chalice in the wrong place. It did me a favour, I didn't have to do it any more. Funnily, the only thing I ever won a certificate for was religious instruction, but then they used to give them out like toilet paper at R.C. schools in those days. Eva's got it somewhere.

All the local children used to swim in the Thames and you'd see the rats swimming with you. Until I was about twelve we went in with nothing on. When the pleasure boats passed sometimes we'd climb on to the posts by the bank and we'd call out 'sling your mouldies out'. The people would throw pennies and we'd catch them.

It was about then I saved Bill Murray from drowning. The tide was just about going out, but there was a little mud beach by the Oxo building so you could walk into the water. You'd walk in and start swimming. He didn't realize there was a current taking him out. He shouted out, and though I wasn't much better a swimmer I went after him and pulled him out. We just took it for granted. It was only when we got older we realized the significance. I was talking to his son, Michael, the other day about saving his father's life, and he knew about it.

I was always keen on sport. I was captain of the football at school, St Patrick's Catholic School, Cornwall Road, the street where I was born. I was captain from about ten until I left. They gave you your shirt and that was faded from washing. You supplied the boots if you could afford them. Mostly you played in anything – street boots, plimsolls. I was picked for Lambeth Schoolboys and South London Schoolboys. We played at Dulwich Hamlets ground. I was inside right, I wasn't big enough for any other position. Bill Murray's in the photo taken of the team. He did a bit of bird early on and then worked hard for the rest of his life. He died in 1988. His eldest son, Billy, is now serving life for the murder of a security guard in Scotland.

In The Cut right opposite us was a market where there was a store called, I think, Pegry, quite famous, cheap and cheerful. They used to have plimsolls hanging outside on a rail. Mine were tattered because I had to play football and box in them. I couldn't ask my mother to buy me a new pair because if she'd known it was for boxing she would've stopped me – and anyway they cost 11d which was more than she could afford. I never had enough to buy them myself. I went up and dragged a pair off which I knew would fit. I pulled the lot down. There was such a clatter it caught the assistant's attention. I was chased – in those days everyone had a go to catch you. I was chased round to where London Weekend TV is now, and I was caught by a man from a family called Hearns who were very good at boxing. They never nicked me but they took the plimsolls back. When I boxed that night one of my plimsolls came off, but I did win. You had three bouts in an evening, and in the last bout the other one came off too. They were just worn out and I was left in my socks. I won on a casting vote, maybe they had sympathy. The result was in the paper and my mother found out; she put a stop to my boxing after that.

I was about nine when I met the Sabinis, who controlled the racecourses and the clubs during the Thirties. There were six brothers led by Charles who was known as Derby, or 'Darbo' by his real friends. They fought for the control of the racecourses, getting rid of Billy Kimber and his team from Birmingham and then another firm called the Cortesis. This was before my time of course. Now they ran the bookmakers on the courses in the south of England. If the bookmaker wanted a pitch he had to pay the Sabinis. They sold him the tissues on which he put up the names of the runners, they sold him chalk to write the odds, and they had little bucket boys who brought a sponge round to wipe off the odds. Of course the bookmaker could have done it just as easily himself, but he wasn't allowed to. It was good for the Sabinis' image for the punters to be able to say, 'Aren't they good, looking after that little boy?'

I went to school with some boys called Murray (no relation to the Bill Murray I saved from drowning) whose mother had a flower pitch at Charing Cross

Station. I used to carry the flowers over Hungerford Bridge with one of her sons. They were much more alive to the ways of the world. It was through them I was took to racing. I was a bucket boy. My mother would think I was having a day out and I wouldn't tell her the full SP. Depending how the day went, I got 2/6d or 7/6d. But I'd come and say I got this at the day's outing and she'd just accept it. She didn't have a wicked thought in her head. It was as if there was some golden tree I'd shaken; it wasn't hard to convince her. For me it was a nice little white lie. If she had've tumbled she'd still have clapped her hands and said, 'Thank God for it.' If my father had known I was getting money from what was a protection racket, he'd have taken the belt to me. You must remember he wasn't a brutal, evil man but he was a hard man. You didn't run away to sea where they knocked them from pillar to post at ten years of age without becoming hard. He didn't think for one moment he was being brutal or anything like that. It was a way of life for your good, and you'd have to do something to deserve it and all. He was a fair man though hard, just as his life was. He'd have certainly tanned the life out of me if he'd even had a suspicion. He never knew I went to the races. He didn't gamble; he had a drink but he could hold it, but as for gambling that was the evil of evils.

'Darbo' would tap me on the head and say, 'Take this home to your Mum,' and I'd say 'Thank you, Darbo.' He took a chuckle from it because he knew I was copying what I had heard; saucy little kid, but with the right style. 'Darbo' didn't have a menacing sort of style, just a nice man, but he didn't look a mug either. To me, even then, I could tell he was something special.

At the age of twelve I was replaced. I was too old – they wanted younger kids to get the sympathy of the punters. It was not long after that I was caught thieving for the first time. That was when I started my criminal career proper. I'd nicked three packets of cigarettes – I remember they were Players – from a little shop in Stamford Street, I think it's a restaurant now, and I was sent to approved school. Well, I'd been nicking things – fruits, cigarettes, cash, anything I could lay my hands on – for years, but this time was the first time I was caught. I think it was poverty drove me to crime in the first place.[2]

I remember the driver of the Black Maria the first time I was nicked was Thomas Meaney. He was a police driver who lived near us at 78 Stamford Street. He took me boxing at Scotland Yard, something my mother didn't like because of the fractured skull and meningitis. I'd also had concussion and a loss of memory whilst playing football in the school yard. He was a horrible man, at the same time as being a great practical joker. Instead of being decent, perhaps not even mentioning it, he had great pleasure in telling my mother I'd been in his van. Anyway, in December 1950 he goes out drinking with an Irishman from the same flats and they have a skinful. The Irishman goes

---

[2] Fraser's C.R.O. form shows that on 1 August 1939 he was discharged for the cigarette offences, and it was five months later that he was sent to an approved school for warehousebreaking and stealing electrical fittings.

home, sees a lump in the bed, thinks it's a dummy and stabs it. But it was Meaney. The man got three years for manslaughter; the murder got chucked. I can't say I was sorry.

I never even got to St Benedict's, the Catholic approved school I was sent to. I escaped on the way and so I ended up in another approved school, Arndale in Grays, Essex, a much tougher one. I escaped from there with Jimmy Essex and another boy, Jackie Barrett from Clerkenwell, but we got caught after a few miles and got the cane on our bums from the headmaster. My parents didn't come and visit me. I wouldn't have taken the liberty of asking them. I wouldn't have dreamed of it. Nobody like us had cars, and fares were expensive down to Essex. I was in the approved school for about four weeks and then me and Jimmy Essex got away again.

Whilst I was out I worked at Boots the chemist as a delivery boy. I got the job from Patsy Fleming when I bumped into him in Ludgate Circus. I'd met him at Arndale and he'd escaped a few weeks after me. I had a bike with a big heavy basket on the front and used to ride all round Soho. I used to see the men standing on the pavements in little groups talking, because Soho was really a village then. Of course I knew Albert Dimes from going to see the Italian processions and playing football, one Catholic school against another. Albert loved both sport and the parades, and I would see him on the corners. He was an outstanding man, you couldn't miss him, 6'2". It was a very interesting job delivering the medicines to clubs, flats, hotels, houses all over London, as far away as Wapping to a ship's captain. I delivered to 'Hutch',[3] the night-club singer, and to Winston Churchill. Service then meant what it said. I was earning twelve shillings a week and stealing on the side. No one I knew had to buy a shaving brush except from me. I lasted quite a while until I turned it in. I had the intelligence to realize that a stocktaking might occur, so I then got a job with Odhams Press on their bike. This one didn't have a basket, just a little despatch bag. It had no brakes, you braked on the pedal. After the great big Boots one it was like a proper bike. Of course, then I'd be thieving from the offices I'd been delivering to, creeping back later. I don't mean a petty thief; I wouldn't steal from ladies' handbags, that was taboo. I'd creep back for the safes, which were often left unlocked. Soho was where I really grew up.

By now it was early 1940 and the War was on. When we weren't working Patsy and I'd go out at night in the blackout, nick a car, smash a window and nick some suit lengths. But he got a bit adventurous and said one day, 'Let's do some daylight ones.' So we did Bravingtons which was on the corner at King's Cross. There were no traffic lights there then. There was a policeman on point duty and he and a colleague commandeered a taxi and chased us. Patsy did well and we lost them. I said, 'Let's get out,' and as we did, wallop, there's the taxi. There was another chase and we climbed an alleyway wall. Patsy got over but the barbed wire on top caught me in the leg. Patsy's pulling one leg saying, 'Give me the rings,' and the

---

[3] Leslie Hutchinson was a long-time favourite of royalty and nobility whose career lasted well into the 1960s.

police are pulling the other. Eventually they got me down, but by then Patsy'd got away. It's silly because I was identified as the driver. Since I was pleading not guilty to everything, I couldn't say they were wrong and I was the passenger. I was disqualified for ten years and sent off back to the approved school. I didn't stay there very long; I escaped again.

Finally in April 1941, so I'd be 18, I was arrested with Johnny Barry and two other boys. We were caught on the premises breaking into the Waterloo Hosiery in The Cut to get ladies' stockings. In the night I climbed over the top of the shop and smashed the window. The people who lived opposite must have had a phone and called the police. I couldn't get out the back; there was only one way out, and that was the way I come in. That's how I was captured. Johnny Barry got probation. He did about six weeks inside before he got it, and the food on remand was so revolting he came out like a rasher. Years later, in about 1945, I bumped into him in Wandsworth. He said, 'I'm eating now, I'm used to it.' I think the other boys got nine months each. They were a year or so older than me. I got Borstal because I was too young to go to prison.

First of all I was in Brixton for a short time. Wormwood Scrubs was really the remand prison, but that had been taken over by MI5 or MI6 and Black Marias were going in and out in an attempt to fool people into thinking it was still a prison. Of course, any con in London could have told it wasn't. From Brixton I was sent to Feltham, not that far from London Airport.

One day we were being marched back from chapel, just as though we were in the Army. About four of us, including Dickie Miller and a boy named Maloney, simply made a run for it. The wall in that part in those days was just like a Borstal wall, about 12–15 feet high. We were all fit and you could reach the wall, jump on one another's back and pull the next one up. Away we went. Of course they were never short of prison officers. There were almost more prison officers than prisoners, and although it was a good try we were too far away to get out. There was a good fight, but when they put us down the punishment block they put us through it. There was nothing unusual in that; it's what you expected before you even started. Then there was the usual remand to the Visiting Magistrate, the usual bread and water, loss of mattress and P.C.F.O. (Penal Class until Further Order). After a couple of months I came up from the punishment block, and then I was sent to Rochester Borstal which was a closed one. That's when I was convicted of doing a screw, 'Holy Joe' O'Connell, in the bathhouse.

Previously I'd got bread and water three days (Number 1 diet), seven days' Number 2 diet, which was only a bit better, and P.C.F.O., for being abusive to a Borstal officer. I'd sworn at him. In those days they put you on report at the slightest excuse. I was down the punishment block for about a fortnight – they called it the separate cells at Rochester. Every night between 6 and 7 you came out and were locked in your cells for what they called silent hour where you could read or write a letter.

I hadn't had a bath or anything down the punishment

block – in the wing you got a cold shower every morning and a bath once a week. I pointed this out to the screw in charge, 'Nippy' Hurst. They called him 'Nippy' because he was always diving about. He said, 'All right, in silent hour I'll have you opened up and you can have a bath but you mustn't be too long.' And he kept his word.

Whilst I was having my bath there was a couple of what they called leaders. Prisoners usually had brown jackets but then if you improved in your behaviour you got blues, though I never did. Then you became a leader with a little ring round the sleeve of your blue jacket. These were hanging about to make sure I didn't abuse this bath privilege. Whilst I was having me bath 'Holy Joe' kept coming in. He was called that because he was one of those types who punished the body and saved the soul. I realize now that it was a farce, and by today's standards he was kinky. I was young and he kept coming in: 'Hurry up, hurry up, lad.' I was out of the bath inside ten minutes and it was still, 'Come on, hurry up, hurry up.' He must have been in half a dozen times. It wouldn't seem natural now, but in them days no one thought of things like that. I lost me temper and I swore and said, 'Bollocks.' I shouldn't have said it but that was the state he'd got me in. He was a tall man, 6'1" or so, in good shape, 35–40, and with that he gave me a tremendous right-hander. But I was young and fit and although it staggered me I just flew at him. I had him over and had him in the dirty bath water forcing his head underneath. With that the two leaders dragged me off and shouted for help. Other officers arrived and sticks were out. To assault an officer in them days was sacrilege, and they really put me through it. I was taken down the separate cells and they really paid me. That was when I got the birch plus 15 days' No. 1 diet, 42 days' No. 2, the maximum you could get, 14 days' no mattress, and P.C.F.O.

At the end of that I was transferred to Feltham and then on to Portland Borstal on the Isle of Wight. It had been another Dartmoor, but in about 1922 it had been changed to a Borstal. Of course, when I went there was still screws who had been in the place when it was a penal servitude prison. Portland was where John Lee, the man they tried to hang,[4] had done his sentence. His name was still cut in the wall of the punishment cells.

This would be in 1941. The Governor was a man named Fidler who later went to Maidstone where he was regarded as a progressive man, but when he was in Portland he seemed to me more like a Hitler. Portland was where I was on the pounding. It was one of the most dreadful forms of punishment you could meet. It was a semi-circle with little cubicles, say half a dozen.

---

[4] In 1885, nineteen-year-old John Lee was convicted of the murder of Emma Keyse, an elderly and wealthy spinster, who had been maid to Queen Victoria. She was found in her home in Devon with her throat cut on 15 November 1884. The room in which she was found had been set on fire. Lee was the prime suspect. She had reduced his wages as her footman over some trivial piece of bad behaviour and he had spoken out against her. Sentenced to death on mainly circumstantial evidence, he was to be hanged by James Berry. Every time Berry pulled the lever the trap-door failed to open. When he then tested it, the trap worked. After three attempts the hanging was abandoned and Lee, who said he had dreamed this and who always protested his innocence, was reprieved. He was released in December 1907 and died in America in 1933. Following this, and another bad experience in which he decapitated a client, Berry gave up his trade as hangman, took up religion and eventually committed suicide.

In each was a pounder. It was lead or iron at the base, then an iron pole with a knob at the top. You had to pound flintstone all day long until it was dust. At the end of the day a screw came out with a box, a shovel and a sieve, and you had to have filled the box. He shook the sieve and only the powder could get through. If you didn't fill the box to a line, then you were down there longer. This was only in the punishment block. Your elbows were shattered. It was freezing cold in the winter. The screws sat in sentry boxes in front of you about ten foot away. It lasted from 7.30 in the morning until 6 in the evening except for a break for dinner. It was hell.

When it came to it I refused to do the powdering. I just wouldn't come out of my cell. I told them I wouldn't. I'd realized it was an absolutely cruel and pointless punishment because they were granite stones you had to pound into dust. Afterwards when they'd been sifted to powder it was then slung away. It wasn't to any purpose; the warders were gloating and they threw it away in front of you. I just said, 'No, I ain't doing it.' The sheer audacity of what I had done was such they couldn't handle it and so I was sent to Wandsworth Prison. The Governor then was a Major Grew, and I believe he had witnessed more executions than any other Governor in the country. He was a tall, debonair military man; they were all alleged to be majors or captains in the Navy. He always wore an Anthony Eden hat. The Governor was all-powerful.

My record followed me. That was the trouble. Life could be made so difficult. You could be put on report for the slightest thing. For example, you weren't allowed to put your bed down until 8 o'clock at night when a bell went dead on. It was a mattress with a bedboard, and the mattress had to be stacked against the wall until then. The blankets had to be neatly folded and hanging down from the bedboard. The furniture in your cell was hard wood and a lump of wood concreted into the wall as a table. Most prisoners would be tempted to sling a blanket on the floor. If the screws – and they made it their business – saw you doing that before 8 p.m. then you were on report. And by the time your door was opened at 7 in the morning your bed had to be up. So you stood to get on report every second of the day.

Then I was moved to Chelmsford. It was there I met Billy Hill. He'd come out the day War was declared from a four-year stretch he'd got in 1936. If you were a prisoner and had less than three months to do, you were released immediately. If you had done six months of a Borstal sentence it was the same. He'd only been out a couple of months when he was caught in a smash-and-grab raid in Conduit Street in 1940 with Harry O'Brien and a man called 'Little George' from Camden Town, I can't think of his other name. The raid was in full daylight and the car stalled. Bill got away from the motor and was caught in New Bond Street about two or three hundred yards away. Billy managed to straighten a copper out and he was only charged with conspiracy, for which the maximum in those days was two years. The others were charged with shopbreaking and they got three years.

Billy was the prison barber at the time, though what he knew about haircutting I'm not sure. I was in trouble the whole time, on bread and water, and Bill was very kind to me. He took me in the cell they used for haircutting and told me to try and keep my head down. I got on with him marvellous. We had the same birthday, December 13th, although of course he was twelve years older, and he liked a rebel. He never got into trouble in prison himself. Before I settled down at Chelmsford I got into such a lot, and in a way he admired that.

And after a bit I did settle down and got a job as a cleaner. This was far better than being in the mailbag shops. I saw quite a bit of Bill, even though as a young prisoner you weren't supposed to mix with anyone over twenty-one. But as a cleaner I had more of a licence to move around.

Part of my job was to go to the kitchen every morning with a bucket, where I'd get hot water for the other prisoners to have a shave. They'd put their beakers in the bucket and that was all the water they could have. When I'd go back to the kitchen I'd have to take the empty cans and I'd return with another bucket. This time it would be grub from the kitchen which the guy there had laid on for us, a bit of meat and bread, cheese, things like that which were incredibly hard to get in prison. We were literally starving on the diet. I'd give it to Bill; he'd distribute it to his mates and give me something with which to treat my pals. I loved it. That was really how our friendship started.

Then I went back to Wandsworth and on to Chelmsford, where I met Bill again when he got his four years' penal servitude for an attack on an Islington postmaster in August or September 1942.

Teddie Hughes – who later got twelve years for the London Airport job in 1948 – and Jock Wyatt, who was very friendly with the Whites, were with him. Before that Bill had had a month as a suspected person. He'd given the Law a few quid not to put him under the Vagrancy Act. If they had done, he could have got up to twelve months.

I'd never come across anyone like Bill before. He was one of the top thieves in the country and a top villain as well. He came from a family who lived in Seven Dials, which was a really rough part of London then. Now it's quite smart with the Cambridge Theatre and restaurants. His sister Maggie was a good-class shoplifter. She got four years' penal servitude at the Old Bailey for stabbing a copper in the eye. The judge says, 'Take her away,' and she says, 'You didn't say that last night when you were making love to me.'

2

In about November 1942 I was taken in handcuffs to Southend for my medical for the Army, and then back to the nick. When I came out in January 1943 I'd done every day of my time.

The War organized criminals. Before the war thieving was safes, jewellery, furs. Now a whole new world was opened up. There was so much money and stuff about – cigarettes, sugar, clothes, petrol coupons, clothing coupons, anything. It was a thieves' paradise. I was a thief. Everyone was a thief. People who I'd known before the War at the races who were villains but who weren't thieves – now they were. They'd been called up and didn't fancy the Army so they were on the run. They couldn't make money at the races because that was the first place people would look for them, and so they'd turned to thieving. And some of them turned out to be very good thieves and all. So it was a whole new world.

Before the War some people wouldn't grass on you, but they wouldn't take part in villainy. In criminal terms they were honest, but now everyone was crooked. Mums, they'd want to buy extra eggs for

their children and a bit of extra meat. If you nicked
anything you could sell it through your buyer. Say
you nicked a load of tea. They were in chests then,
there weren't such things as tea-bags, and you'd nick
sixty or seventy of them, a lorry-load. Then you'd sell
the tea to a man, and he'd sell it to shops, and the
shopkeepers would sell it to the customers without
taking their coupons. Everyone was involved. It was
wonderful.

You could nick a car, take the back seats out, take it
into the West End, do a job, and the chances of getting
caught were just about nil. I'll never forget one in
Hanover Square. It was a gentleman's tailor's, a very
high-class one at that. We had on wardens' helmets
with the letters 'A.R.P.' on them, and armbands. We
smashed the windows in with the car and when people
came looking asked them to stand back, saying,
'Control, please stand back.' People were helping
to load the car up.

If there was an air raid going on then better still.
Of course all the headlights of cars were blanked out
so only a fraction of the light showed, and this meant
the police had near enough no chance of being able
to see a licence plate in the dark. There weren't that
many cars about because of petrol rationing, but then
there weren't that many police cars about either.

I'd only been home a week or less when my
calling-up papers came through the registered post.
We'd been bombed out of Howley Place and we were
living in Old Buildings, Long Lane, off Tabard Street
in the Borough. My mother answered the door and
signed for them. When I see what they were I slung

them on the fire. So from that moment onwards I was an absentee.

A couple of weeks later we were in a taxi, me, Johnny Reynolds (he'd done five years' penal servitude for a smash-and-grab), Lennie Garrett and Jimmy Davies, who was known as 'South American Joe'. He was a good-looking man who always wore an Anthony Eden homburg. He was a good driver but he could turn his hand to anything. We went by a big brown van at the Oval near the cricket ground. Johnny, who was older and more experienced, said, 'That's the Flying Squad.' We said, 'Go away' meaning 'you're wrong', and we all looked at the van parked on a kerb. That was our mistake; we should have ignored it. Right away they chased us. The cab driver pulled in and Jimmy and I ran. Johnny Reynolds and Lennie Garrett were not on the run and so they stayed. In those days, as I say if there was a hue and cry everyone would join in, not like today when you've got a bit of a chance, and we didn't get that far.

I was taken to the barracks in Whitehall at Great Scotland Yard, and then an escort from Norwich came to pick me up and take me to the Gibraltar barracks which were then part of the prison. I had nothing on me when I was arrested – no bent gear or nothing – and so at Norwich when I went in front of the C.O. he said I'd start clean and to go over to the general stores and get uniform and everything. This was about 4 in the afternoon. The stores were closed and the guard said he'd show me how to draw my clothing in the morning. I was left alone again and I caught the next train back to London.

This time I lasted about three weeks. I had a crooked van rung with false plates in a garage in Camberwell, and one day when I went to collect it the Law was hiding and they caught me.

Before that, in February or early March 1943, I'd been over in a place in Notting Hill, which was one of the places where we went when we were on our toes, when the police led by Ted Greeno raided it looking for deserters. Greeno spotted Garrett, who wasn't a deserter but who'd been a professional boxer before the War, and he just called him out. 'Come on,' says Greeno, 'you're the boxer, come on.' He was quite high up in the hierarchy then. They had a straightener, a fair fight with their fists. It was in a sort of mews where there were a lot of totters – rag-and-bone men. Greeno and Garrett went outside and we made a ring for them. If it had been scored on points then Garrett would have won, but at the end they were both standing and they just shook hands. No one was nicked. The fight just seemed to be enough. That's how arrogant the Law was, although I'm not complaining on this occasion. Today no one would believe it.

However, when I was nicked this time I was a deserter. I got three months in prison for the van and I did every day. When I'd finished an escort came to take me back to Norwich. I was handcuffed inside the prison and off we went. When we arrived at Norwich Station there was a big crowd making its way to the barrier, I was handcuffed in front and I managed to become separated from the guards by about two feet. When I got to the ticket office I nodded and said they'd got the tickets, and bosh I was away.

The cuffs were very old-fashioned and they literally slid off. The wartime Derby was being run at Newmarket at the time, and I managed to make my way over there with a couple of lifts in lorries, and from there it was down to London. I never saw the race, but I remember it was a lovely summer's day. I couldn't go home, of course, but there was plenty of people I could go to. I stayed in London, but I was in touch with my mother and Eva and it never occurred to me that they'd catch me. You had to think you were uncatchable – immune – if you didn't your life would be hell.

I was only out another three weeks when I was arrested for shopbreaking, George Carters, a clothing store in Southwark. George Smith, who later got eight years for the London Airport robbery,[1] was in on it with me along with Charlie Williams whose mother, Lou, had her eye put out with a hat-pin by Billy Hill's sister, Maggie. It was one of the first places that had an alarm wired to a police station. People spoke about these alarms but no one believed it could possibly happen. No one realized that technology was forging

---

[1] The 'Airport job' was a raid in 1948 on London Airport said to have been organized by Jack Spot. It ended in disaster when the police discovered the plot in advance of the raid. Detectives were substituted for the baggage handlers who were to be robbed, and a battle took place. Several men were convicted and received up to twelve years' imprisonment. Teddy Machin escaped, as did Franny Daniels who held on to the chassis of a lorry and received severe burns whilst doing so.

ahead and a burglar alarm could be fixed straight to the local police station. You went through the panelling to the shop; but in the panelling were the alarms which we didn't see or even take any notice when we saw them. We thought they were electricity wires. All you would hear would be a very quiet whirring. We did hear it as we were tunnelling through from a store in the yard, but the next thing we heard was the police cars arriving.

Because I was so small George and Charlie pushed me under an old-fashioned sink and I nearly got away with it. I was there two hours and I actually crept out once, but as I saw the only way out was the way we'd come in and there was still police about, I crept back in again. I was still under the sink when they eventually found me. George Smith got probation that time. Charlie Williams got fifteen months and so did I.

Around this time, whilst I was on the run, I met up with a girl, Katie, who was about six years older than me and whose husband was away fighting for King and Country. She'd already had a child by him. She'd been a friend of a number of guys who I'd been out thieving with. During the fifteen months she was writing me letters. You never got them unless you sent out a letter, and then you could have one in reply. Unauthorized letters were just given to you on the morning of your discharge. After I came out we got together and we had three children. But it didn't work out really. When it came to it we stayed together until around 1951. Then when I went away in 1952 it finished finally. When the boys got older they looked me up.

It was in 1943 at Wandsworth that I met 'Ruby'
Sparks.[2] I got the fifteen months on the Tuesday at
the County of London Quarter Sessions and was sent
to Feltham to sew mailbags. You sat inside your cell
with the door open. If I do anything I do it properly.
The regulation was eight stitches to an inch. I wasn't
a cheat. A screw complained I was doing the stitches
too far apart. I took umbrage and protested and he
gave me one whilst I was sitting down, and so I did
him. Within seconds I was overpowered and down the
punishment block. It's a fact of life, no big deal. In
front of the Governor and remanded to the Visiting
Magistrates. That didn't take long. Fifteen days' No.
1 diet, twenty-eight days' No. 2, fifty-six days cellular
confinement, ninety days' loss of remission and off to
Wandsworth.

There were sandbags at the windows of E1, which
was the usual punishment wing, so I went on E2 and
it was there that I met 'Ruby'. At that time he was
doing twenty-three weeks for having a false I.D. card,
and it meant he automatically had to do five years'
penal servitude because his ticket of licence for a
prior offence had been revoked. That meant twenty
months with remission.

'Ruby' was very good to me. He gave me a little

[2] John 'Ruby' Sparks was one of the great pre-war burglars and
smash-and-grab raiders. He acquired his nickname following the
burglary of a Maharajah's flat in Park Lane. Sparks sold the £40,000
of rubies he had stolen thinking they were imitation. He played a
principal part in the Dartmoor Prison Riot of 1932. He also escaped
from the Moor. After he had written his memoirs, *Burglar to the
Nobility*, in 1961 he retired and later opened a corner shop. He
died in 1991.

parcel with some bread and butter and the screws swallowed it – letting him give it me, not the bread and butter. This was like gold when you're a kid of nineteen.

'Ruby' had two bits of luck. The M.P. Sidney Silverman's brother, Wally, who was a con man and who knew a bit about the law, was in the nick with 'Ruby'. He was doing time for fraud. I think that the reason why Silverman was so much against capital punishment and so much in favour of prison reform was that his brother was inside. When 'Ruby' Sparks got extra bird for the mutiny he was doing five years' penal servitude plus five years' preventive detention. He got another five years' penal servitude. Then he was transferred to Parkhurst. Whilst he was there he bumped into Wally Silverman, who was an old solicitor's clerk, doing time for fraud. He told him this wasn't right. 'You can get more P.D. than P.S. but not the other way around. Why don't you petition?' 'Ruby' did. He won and came out better. His sentence was changed to nine years' penal servitude in all. Old Jim Turner, who got the same as 'Ruby' but who took no part in the mutiny, got longer because there was no remission on preventive detention.

The next time 'Ruby' got penal servitude was in 1938 when he got a five. He got out after forty months and in 1942 picked up twenty-three weeks for having a false I.D. during the War, and the remaining twenty months of his ticket got added on. This time when he was in Wandsworth he met a little red-haired guy, Jimmy Boyle, another solicitor's clerk also doing time for fraud. Now, Jimmy said, the twenty-three weeks plus five years wasn't legal. The licence shouldn't have been revoked. 'Ruby' had got his ticket before the War and you couldn't get a sentence on a wartime measure. So 'Ruby' got a special release. I was on the landing when I saw him going out. He was in his civvies and he went to give me his wrist-watch. I said, 'It's no good to me in here.' I didn't smoke so it wasn't worth it for me to sell it. He burst out laughing and went on his way under escort.

I met up with Jimmy quite often over the years, and it was him who told me one day in Bedford that whilst you had an appeal in against conviction you couldn't lose your remission. Appeals were up very quickly then but it helped. So when I was due to come up before Visiting Magistrates, if I could I would lodge appeal papers. I would then abandon the appeal when the magistrates had dealt with me, and if I got into more trouble I'd try to appeal out of time. That way I could only be sentenced to bread and water and so on and I kept my remission. They changed the law eventually, but it was good fun whilst it lasted.

Whilst I was in Wandsworth I got into a lot of trouble and the doctors decided there was something wrong with me mentally. The Senior Medical Officer and his junior said they were sending me to Wormwood Scrubs, where once or twice a week I was to go to Banstead for electric shock treatment. It was a last resort and could do you more harm than good. With the head injuries I'd had it was not going to do me any good. When I went to Wormwood Scrubs to the prison hospital there, I met Ivor Novello.[3] He'd been sent to prison for petrol rationing offences. I spoke to him several times. He seemed quite a pleasant man and everyone made a fuss of him. I suppose he was one of the most famous people who'd been in Wormwood Scrubs. He was a household name. Now we know he was a raving poof, but in those days people didn't believe those type of things ever went on. He didn't flaunt it like they do today. I never realized he was; it never entered me head. The prison officers were falling over themselves to get in with him. He was there when I had a row with another officer and was sent back to Wandsworth. As it happens, it was the best thing that could have happened because I never got the electric shock treatment.

At Wandsworth there was a basement landing and in air raids officially we were all supposed to go down to it, but the prison officers soon got the hump about that and left you in the cells. In October 1943 the blitz was over, but what the Germans were doing was sending over half a dozen hit-and-run planes. My punishment was finished but they still kept me on the landing right bang opposite the condemned cells the other side of E2. There was a Canadian in the cells, I think he was the first person to be convicted of a machine-gun murder.[4] The night before he was due

---

[3] Writer of, and star in, a number of musicals including *Perchance to Dream*. Perhaps his best-known song was the patriotic 'Keep the Home Fires Burning'.

[4] Although the hanging of a Canadian for a murder such as this does not appear in Rocky Stockman's comprehensive *The Hangman's Diary*, cases involving Allied servicemen were sometimes hushed up.

to hang he was kicking up in his cell and you could hear the screws rushing in, so I started smashing up in my cell in sort of sympathy with him – a token for him. The air raid was on at the same time. I took me blackout curtain down. It shows you how daft the screws were – it's unbelievable, this – they're telling me to put me blackout curtain up while I'm smashing the windows and the furniture and trying as best I can to barricade the door. All they had to do was turn off the electric light switch which was just outside the cell, and here they were telling me to put me blackout curtain up. Eventually they come in. I was knocked unconscious and dragged down to the strong cells on H1. The next day I was on report for assaulting an officer, the usual thing, and again I refused to leave the cell, I was just lying there. So they brought the Governor down, it was most unusual to do this in them days. They put a table down and he took the evidence and remanded me to the Visiting Magistrates. They gave me some more bread and water.

I did every day of that fifteen months and came out under escort in the autumn of 1944. And the same thing happened again. This time I was taken to Bradford. As we reached the barracks I was let out of the van, and straight away I ran into a park on one side of the camp where there was a fair. I was still in civvies, quite smart, but I got no money, not a penny on me, and I was walking this fair when, by a miracle, there were two Londoners, Johnny Lane and 'Little George' with their wives. I'd done bird with them at Borstal. They'd come up North to get away from the doodlebugs. I stayed with them that

night and we done a bit of villainy, bust a shop window
and took some ladies' dresses. It was quite easy in the
blackout. They'd already made a contact up there to
sell the gear and they gave me a few quid, and the
next day I just caught the train back to London.

Whilst I was on the run I was half fancied for a
murder. A man was run over by a lorry. As I couldn't
drive at the time they were quite wrong about it. I kept
out of the way, but the man had convictions and it died
the death.

I stayed out until January 1945 and it was during
this time I had a run-in with Ken Drury's father.[5]
He'd nicked me when I was about fifteen, and about
four years later I met him in the Temple Bar pub
known as The Doctors in the Walworth Road. It was
Christmas and I was on the run from the Army. He
was as crooked as anything. He had another copper
with him, and I could see he wasn't after nicking me
this time. I give him a score[6] and he could have licked
my boots. He must have taught his son. Then one
night I was in the Dorset Arms, Clapham Road, and
I wasn't so lucky. The police and the Army police
had a joint enterprise to round up deserters and they
surrounded the pub. I got out through the lavatory
on to the roof but as I dropped down there they were
waiting. Two days later I had a very big escort from
Great Scotland Yard. This time I was handcuffed to
another deserter – he was the best tailor in London

5 In July 1977 Commander Kenneth Drury was found guilty in the
Porn Squad case and sentenced to eight years' imprisonment, reduced
on appeal to five years.
6 £20.

and a fantastic gambler. We'd met in the cells together in Great Scotland Yard. He told me he'd done quite a few escorts and would be bang in trouble, and he would have to try to do a runner. He asked if I was handcuffed with him whether I'd go with him, and I said of course I would. When we got to King's Cross Station he said, 'Let's have a go?' and we did. We steamed at the screws and made a run for it. Didn't do us any good. There was snow on the ground and we had a hard time in it. The police commandeered a taxi and caught us going up a hill.

This time we were put in the guardhouse at Bradford. It was packed; there must have been thirty deserters, and there was a big balcony where guards walked around with baseball bats. There was quite a few London faces there including Eddie Raimo, who I thought was called Rainbow – he'd glassed Billy Hill in a pub in Clerkenwell – and my old mate Patsy Fleming. That was a Saturday. Nothing happened until the Monday morning when I was taken in handcuffs to see a doctor. On the way I had a row with one of the orderlies and he went in to tell the doctor about it. I followed, was uncuffed and with that I just dived straight through the window. It was on the ground floor and only about four feet high. I didn't mind, I was twenty-one and fit. They was out and after me and heads rolled because of it but I was taken to the cells at Belle Vue, Bradford, and I had a tear-up in them.

Two days later they brought a psychiatrist in to see me, and although I didn't know it at the time I was certified and sent to North Riding Mental Hospital.

And there were a number of people I knew in there. One was Alf Lucy, who was just about the 'Guv'nor' of West Ham at one time. He'd run off with Jack Spot's first wife. And there was Bert Rogers, uncle of the comedian Ted. He and Ted's father had been caught in a funny way. They'd done a bank in London somewhere with a third man. The manager had been in the First World War and he kept his gun in the bank with him. As Ted's Dad and Bert and the third man got in the back of the van, the manager ran out on to the pavement and took a shot at them, hitting the third man. Ted's Dad and Bert took him to hospital, but he was dead when they got there. That's how they were traced.

A month later I was sent to Edinburgh where they had an electro-psychograph machine – it was one of the first places to have one. They put it on your head. It didn't do me any harm. In the April I was called in front of a military doctor and was told that there'd been a court-martial in my absence. I had been found guilty and given two years' hard labour and 900 days loss of pay, but owing to my mental condition I was unfit to serve it and so I was being discharged medically. I couldn't believe it.

So in April 1945 I got my ticket. I had eight weeks or more medical discharge and an escort took me home. My mother had to sign for me and then every week money was sent to her to look after me. She was thrilled. When it stopped she was really upset.

I never even put on a uniform. The stores were always closed at the weekend when I arrived. On the other hand my brother, James, was a good soldier and was decorated. He thinks if they'd got me abroad it would have been the making of me because I would have had to be there and do some proper fighting.

Of course when I got out I went straight back to thieving. I was working literally every day and spending it at an alarming rate as it came. I was good to my family and my friends. I didn't smoke and I didn't gamble. I had a drink, nothing foolish, but I did go out to the clubs because that was all you did in them days. I was a good spender – foolish really,but that was all you did in that period. So I had to go out really to get money to support the way I was living. I was hardly ever out; when I was I earned good money, but it never lasted me. My friend John Parry, to his credit, did sensible things with his money.

In 1945 he and I did a job together and John never looked back.[7] In fact he left £6 million when he died. He ended up with a string of betting shops and God knows what else. He was in Borstal with me and two years later I put him on the road. We did a robbery at James Clarke's, the very big glass manufacturers. The firm put in windows blown out by the doodlebugs and V2s, and made a fortune. The man whose son worked for them, Billy Stubbs, stuck the robbery up for us. Johnny Parry drove the car and me and another got the cash – £280 or so each which was quite a bit of dough in those days. He never did another robbery, put his money to work and went on from there.

I think the only other time he was arrested was in 1953 when he and some others had a Post Office guy

[7] His son Gordon Parry received ten years for his part in the Brinks-Mat robbery.

straightened. When diamonds were sent through the post the man would weed them out and let Johnny know. Eventually the man from the Post Office was caught and convicted, and he then shopped Johnny and the others. I was in Wandsworth at the time and they approached Billy Hill, who in turn asked me to get in to the Post Office man to get him to alter his evidence. When he gave evidence at the Old Bailey the Post Office man said there was a man named Parry involved, but he wasn't in court. I got £500 for it. Parry came to Broadmoor with Eva to confirm my money was there after they were all found not guilty.

As I said, the War had made criminals out of a lot of people. One of the things then was smash-and-grab. The streets weren't as full of traffic and the police didn't have as many cars and certainly no hand-held radios. I remember doing one at Ealing, it was fairly typical of what went on. About 2 o'clock in the afternoon we just pulled up in the car. The pavement wasn't really wide enough for the car to be on the pavement so we pulled up at the kerb. I just jumped out, smashed the window, moved people out of the way and got the trays of jewellery, got back into the car and away. We dumped the motor and jumped on a tube coming back to central London. If you did it at night you'd stick out like a sore thumb.

Sometimes you could get a safe. You would literally just take it out of the shop. You'd be surprised how many people kept the safes by the door. If you were south of the Thames the safe went in the canal at Camberwell or in the Thames by the Oxo buildings. If you were in North London it went in the Regent

Canal or up Paddington Basin. I can honestly say there must have been three or four safes of mine in the canal at Camberwell. I wouldn't have minded being a scrap-metal merchant.

My mate, Patsy Lyons, got five years' penal servitude in 1945. I was with him on the robbery at the end of 1944 which earned it. In a little courtway from Victoria Street to Caxton Street there was a series of shops, and one of them was a jeweller's. Me and another man went in the jeweller's and held them up with a bar of iron. Patsy stayed with the car. I started smashing the display counter and we cleared about £12,000 from the window; it was quite a lot in those days. All the people came running out – those were the 'have-a-go' days – but we got away in the car, got back to Bermondsey and realized there wasn't as much there as we thought, we must have dropped things on the way to the car, and so we went to do another jeweller's in Bond Street. We must have been crazy. Someone had obviously taken the car number, and as we went through the Rotherhithe Tunnel to work our way through to the West End we heard police cars after us and we were chased. At the junction of Old Street and City Road we were hemmed in and crashed. We all jumped out and made a run for it. I ran behind a bus, stopped, and took my gloves and scarf off, then I turned round and just walked along back towards the police. The police had thought I'd run straight on and I got clean away. Patsy and the other man, who got Borstal, weren't as lucky.

It must seem pushing our luck to go out again after

we'd had £12,000 of tom in the morning, but it doesn't work out quite that way. On the £12,000 we wound up getting peanuts for it. The loser always inflates the loss and also there is a tremendous mark-up even on a shop sale. So if you buy a ring for £100 and try and sell it the next day, you might be lucky to get a tenner. And that's a legitimate purchase. The people who most probably do better out of jewellery is the kids who break into homes and steal their bits and pieces. They then sell it individually to other working and middle-class people who don't know where it's come from. That way they'll get a better price. That person would happily pay £300 for something which would cost £1,500 in a shop. The prospect of being caught with the jewellery they bought is minimal. The loser probably had it for years, has lost the receipt and can't give a proper description. That type of thief does better on value for money than the professional. Today, every member of the public would buy without asking too many questions if they thought they had a bargain.

A few years ago a pal of mine did a jeweller's, a tie-up, and I believe officially it was said that nearly £2 million pounds' worth of jewellery was stolen. I think about five of them were engaged on this endeavour and my friend who took a leading part, which meant that he would have at least an equal share, he received £7,500 altogether. That was getting it in dribs and drabs as well. They just couldn't sell the tom.

Whoever you go to to sell, it will always be, 'Oh how difficult this particular jewellery is. It will require resetting and cutting and this will devalue it because there's been such a hue and cry about it.' And there's no challenge to this type of market. The thief has to put up with whatever price comes up unless he finds someone who personally fancies a piece or pieces of the jewellery for his own personal use, and that man would have to go to the expense of having it altered. If you're not lucky enough to find that person you're lumbered. But jewel raids will always go on. It's easy to carry away and you might be lucky to get that particular diamond or two which could come to a lot of money. That's the chance you're looking for. It is a very precarious commodity to sell. Sometimes you can get a commission, that's the better thing because you know exactly what you're going for and what you're going to get for it.

In January 1945 on the day before Eva was due out from finishing her six-month sentence for shoplifting, Patsy (who'd got bail for the Victoria robbery) and me went to do another robbery, a lovely little jeweller's just off Bond Street. It was to be another smash-up. 'Harry Boy' Jenkins, who was later hanged for the de Antiquis murder, was with us. 'Harry Boy's' brother, Tommy, and Bobby Headley were nicked for the murder of Captain Binney but 'Harry Boy', who was with them, wasn't charged. When they took 'Harry Boy' in to the police he had this brilliant idea and he chinned the police sergeant, knowing full well he'd be mercilessly beaten up. As a result everyone on the ID parade had to be plastered up with tape and so he wasn't picked out. He eventually got Borstal for the assault on the copper. Headley was convicted of murder and sentenced to death but then reprieved;

Tommy got eight years for manslaughter and breaking and entering.[8]

We couldn't do this jeweller's because there were police all over the place and when we saw them we left it. On the way back, however, we saw a van distributing cigarettes to corner shops, so we held it up with the bars we'd taken for the jeweller's, and unloaded as many cartons as we could into the Railton motor car we had. So when Eva came out the next day I could make life a lot more pleasant for her. I took her out shopping to get some new clothes without her having to nick them.

Billy Hill came out the end of June 1945 and I met up with him again then, but at the time I was on bail to the Old Bailey. That was for a raid on the Town Hall at Benfleet where we were after clothing coupons; we'd also knocked a copper about but he never picked me out on the ID. They saw our van in the grounds with their torches, but we steamed into them and knocked them down. They got the number of the van and we were picked up at Roding Bridge, Barking. We were slinging everything out the back of this van, boxes, jemmies, at the police cars. They chased us all through the East End. We wanted to get to the south side of the Thames where we knew several turnings where we could lose them, and in the middle of Rotherhithe Tunnel of all places we ran out of petrol. There was six of us in the motor. Three

[8] Captain Ralph Binney R.N. was knocked down whilst trying to prevent the escape of the jewel thieves. A medal, the Binney Medal for gallantry, was struck in his honour. Alec de Antiquis was shot dead in Charlotte Street on 29 April 1947 whilst trying to prevent the escape of robbers who had raided a jeweller's shop.

got away. They knew that somewhere there were stairs which were beyond the river. I didn't know that and to my luck there were police cars blocking the southern end. Those who went up the stairs got away which was good. Three of us were arrested – me, Charlie Ransford and 'Spindles' Jackson. His real name was Clawson but he answered to 'Spindles'. In 1942 Charlie Ransford had been done for murder with Jimmy Essex. They were both found not guilty of murder but guilty of manslaughter. He got eighteen months and Jimmy three years' penal servitude.

I then got bail after about a fortnight in custody, and after another two weeks my trial was up. I pleaded not guilty just as a matter of giving it a run. When it came to it Spindles got two years, Ransford and I got twenty months' hard labour each. I went to Wandsworth, and then I was transferred to Shrewsbury where I did the Governor. It was after that I first got the Cat.

After I'd been at Shrewsbury for about ten days I was put on report for a completely fictitious offence. I was said to have been abusive to a prison officer. If I had've been I wouldn't have minded, but when I was marched in to the Governor the next morning to answer the charge and he asked me what I had to say, like the fool I was on many other occasions, I said the screw wasn't telling the truth and the first chance I got I'd give him one. The Governor, who was one of the very first men who'd risen from being an officer to the Governor class, was with prison officers all the way. Laconically he went, 'My officers can look after themselves. They'll see who gets beaten up.' Quite blatantly. I was still only twenty-one and on his table was an ebony ruler like a little truncheon. I was young and fit and I pushed the screws aside. I grabbed the ruler off the table and hit him with it over the head. With that the sticks rained on me and I was knocked unconscious. I'm not grumbling about it. It was par for the course.

Whilst I was in the punishment cells there I was in a body belt. After a day or so I was put in a shirt and the body belt put over it again. In the body belt your wrists are handcuffed to each side of the belt and all you can do is waggle your hands. You can't lift the body belt up or down. I was kept in it then until I saw the Visiting Magistrates. There was no question of asking to go to the lavatory. Remember this was 1945. If you wanted to urinate you just pissed on the floor. If you wanted to go worse than that, you just had to bottle it. If they felt like it, then they would let you go to the toilet. If you asked, then they wouldn't let you go. They took enjoyment in not letting you. I'd already learned from previous experience not to give them the satisfaction of asking.

My brother James came back from Italy and came to see me in Shrewsbury with my mother. I was in a terrible state. They went to the *Daily Mirror* about it. It was the campaigning newspaper of the day, but they didn't do anything. It was a bit much for them. Nobody took the establishment on then like they would today. There were no MPs who would listen to you. What I am telling must have happened to many prisoners up and down the country. I was weighed off at Shrewsbury, and as it was such a little prison I was moved to Liverpool.

In the past when you got the Cat, men's nipples had been ripped off when the ends of the lash had gone round, and so now you put your head through a leather hood which protected your chest and your kidneys as well. Like everything else the build-up was the worst. Sometimes the Visiting Magistrates didn't even tell you your punishment. The Chairman would say, ' You'll be advised at a later date,' and then if you knew anything about prisons you knew it would be the Cat. From the moment you were sentenced by the Visiting Magistrates you could wait only up to a fortnight. You always got it after breakfast or dinner when the prison was locked up. In those days there were no prisoners running about. You never knew when you would be getting it, so there you'd be in the cell down the punishment block and you'd hear the heavy boots. 'Ready?' Keys rattled and then nothing would happen. It was all part of the procedure to unnerve you. Nothing would happen that day at all. They would do this quite regularly and then just as you thought it would be another false alarm, the door would be opened and there would be a mob of them. You'd be wearing your prison slippers and be marched to the laundry or workshop, somewhere big enough to put the tripod up. Your hands were tied above you and the smaller you were the harder it was because you were stretched more. Your head was forced through a slit in the canvas. I'm told that if you got it for robbery it wasn't as severe, but when you were given it for an attack on a screw they really give it you. And in those days gross personal violence didn't have to amount to much, sometimes not much more than a push. Remember, you didn't have a barrister or solicitor to ask questions for you in front of the Visiting Magistrates.

The doctor, a Visiting Magistrate, Governor and various screws would be there. The Governor would read out, 'Francis Davidson Fraser, you've been sentenced to eighteen strokes of corporal punishment – in your case the Cat.' Sometimes it would be a silent count and sometimes a verbal count. 'Stroke One' Whooosh. 'Stroke Two' and so on. Sometimes they would pause after six. It depended on who the Governor was, but mostly it went straight on. And it was up to you. Your pride wouldn't let you show any fear or hurt and that gave them great pleasure to go straight on. Your back was cut to ribbons and the thud knocked the air out of you. Some men ended up with consumption after they'd had the Cat.[9]

Of course it hurt terrible, but the Cat was better than the birch. It was across your back and it was somehow more manly, but the birch was across your bare bottom; it was very humiliating and it hurt much, much worse. The sound of the swishing of the birch was unbelievable and the twigs really hurt. I'd already had that at Maidstone when I was sent there from Rochester Borstal. The Cat had little knots tied on the end but you never see it or who was doing it, although at Wandsworth it was always a screw called Nicholls. He was down the punishment block for twenty-five years, from 1928 to 1953, and was

[9] One of them was Alfie Hinds Snr who received four years and the Cat for his part in a theft of about £23,000 at Portsmouth in about 1927.

always the extra officer in the condemned cell. A giant of a Yorkshireman; he loved his work.

I remember first seeing him when I was nineteen and I was in Wandsworth. I came in late off exercise to get me dinner and as I went by this very end cell on E2, the punishment landing which was used as an office, there was Nicholls with a tin which you had your porridge in. It would have been prepared two or three days before and made your punishment on No. 2 diet even worse. It was like cement and there he was scooping it down with a spoon thoroughly enjoying it. You had to see it to believe it.

There were always plenty of screws watching you get the Cat. They didn't have to be there but they loved it, just hoping they would see you crying or showing you were hurt. No man worth his salt would let them have that satisfaction. That was the most important part – not to let them see hurt or fear.

After you had the Cat they just put some ointment on you and nature took its course and you went back to your bread and water in the punishment block. It was no big deal. If you did the Governor you got the Cat.

I was dead lucky in Liverpool because I did the top villain up there and got away with it. The Governor at Liverpool was Horricks, who'd been Governor of Chelmsford, and about six weeks before I came out I got outdoor work. I was given a job knocking down the old women's hospital. Harry Bass had given me the idea to get a bit of colour in my cheeks, so I didn't let everybody know I'd been in prison by my pallor. Horricks used to have a notice on his desk: *Be brisk,*

Be businesslike, Be off. So I was brisk and businesslike and Horricks said he'd consider my request to work outside in the grounds.

Harry Bass, known as 'Harry the Doctor', worked with an Italian known as 'Johnny No Legs' who suffered from a wasting disease. 'No Legs' was a brilliant locksmith and he and Bass worked a scam along the following lines. They would look at a jeweller's which was not quite top class and watch the manager lock up and switch on the burglar alarm. They would watch again the next morning when he came to switch off the alarm and open up. By the evening 'No Legs' would be in his electric wheelchair and when the manager locked up once more he would say, 'Excuse me, could you help me, I've lost the keys to my tool-box.' Now there's no man on earth could refuse such a request. 'Oh, all right, my man' and he'd give him the bunch of keys. Then round would come Harry with an Anthony Eden hat and a stethoscope round his neck. 'Excuse me, sir, could you tell me the way to Acacia Avenue?' And the manager would say, 'Oh yes, doctor, if you go down there . . .' Meanwhile 'Johnny No Legs' would have taken an impression of all the keys he wanted. Harry would say, 'Thank you very much, sir', and off he would go.

They'd wait about six weeks and they'd completely unload the shop. How Harry came to take a tumble was that there was a conference of jewellers or something like that and they got to saying how they'd all been robbed but there hadn't been a moment when the keys had been out of their sight; 'Well, the only time was when I lent a man . . .' And another said,

'That's funny, that happened to me', and so did another. So when it happened again at Blackpool they were waiting. Harry got three years' penal servitude and Johnny two years, I think. I suppose people were more naïve and trusting in those days.

Years later I met Harry again in prison. Johnny was dying and sold his story to a newspaper. He and Harry had just continued their scam. Although he didn't name Harry, it didn't take the police too much brains to put two and two together and arrest him a second time.

First day I was out on the working party, Harry Bass had this row with this local villain, a big docker who was doing time for some sort of protection racket. He gave Harry a clump with a shovel and called him a Cockney bastard. So I found a sort of bar of iron which had come from the building we were knocking down, and really done him with it. He was a big powerful man. He didn't go out and he somehow managed to claim me, but Harry got the bar of iron and when the screws appeared they caught us rolling round on the path. He was in hospital with a fractured skull and I was charged with fighting. I was asked how he got this injury and I said I didn't know; he'd just attacked me and he must have got it rolling around on the ground with all these stones about. To his credit when the police questioned him he said he didn't remember. Harry had a crooked screw at Liverpool and he got the bar cut up in the engineering shop and took it out with him in pieces so they never found it. It made the story that the man'd hit his head on the rocks plausible, and I got out of it completely. When he came back from hospital a couple of weeks later I see him in the mailbag shop and asked him quietly if he wanted any more. He said he didn't, but I did hear his brothers might be waiting outside for me. It could have been quite an enjoyable release day for them, but not for me because they'd have been mob-handed.

I came out from Liverpool Prison at the very end of 1946. When it came to it there was no one there. I was just given my ticket back. It was the same when I'd come out of Chelmsford earlier; just the ticket, no clothes, no money. There was no reporting to an after-care officer either. They didn't exist then. It wasn't surprising people went straight back to work.

I was only out about a couple of months before I was arrested for suspicion, put under the Act, and given twelve months. I came out the end of 1947 and I was only out ten days. That was when I was arrested for the hilarious smash-and-grab in New Oxford Street at a middle-of-the-road jeweller's. Not bad, not top gear like your Cartiers but still reasonable.

Dodger Davies was the driver. We pulled up in New Oxford Street and he'd switched the engine off and we sat a bit reading a paper. There were no yellow lines in those days. It happened that as well as several other couples window-shopping, so was a Detective Sergeant with his wife. Dodger said, 'Don't do it yet, Frank. There's still too many people looking in the window.' Two and a half years after the War people were still happy just to look in windows. I said 'OK then' and waited until I saw there was only four or five people, then I put my paper down, opened the door said, 'Right, Dodge,' and I was out. I can remember hearing him say 'Frank'. I didn't hear the rest, what with the traffic, but apparently he'd shouted out, 'Not yet – I can't get the car going'. When I heard 'Frank' it sounded like encouragement, like, 'Go on, Frank, good boy.' I just went to the window, said, 'Excuse me please,' pushed people aside and done it. I got a couple of trays of rings back across the pavement, into the car and said, 'Straight on, Dodge'. He said, 'It won't go, Frank.' I said, 'Stop joking, straight on.' But he wasn't joking; he said, 'That's what I tried to tell you.' I soon found I couldn't lock the back door of the car he'd stolen and so I held it closed. People were now pounding on the windows and Dodge said, 'I'll go out this way.' I said, 'I'll try and join you.' He went out the road side but he was caught a hundred yards down the road. I was just surrounded. It got headlines in the papers. It was good in a way because it made us look hilarious and incompetent. We went to court the next day and were immediately committed for trial. Six days later we were up at the Sessions and pleaded guilty. He got twenty-one months and I got two years. Didn't do too bad really.

3

It was whilst I was in Pentonville during the smash-and-grab sentence that I really fell foul of the screw who became a Governor, Lawton, a man who to me was the epitome of vindictiveness. He literally lived and slept in the prison. He was a cruel, inhuman man who adhered strictly to the rules, which were unbelievably severe as it was but he added a few more of his own. It was in 1948 when he was Governor of Pentonville that he had a really good attempt to kill me. He really did. I'll never forget it. I have to say though that I had attacked him more than once. One time I'd thrown a pot of excrement all over him – it was a bit of each, I didn't like to leave one out – and the second time I'd given him a good punch. Remember this: to him, he considered himself untouchable. Even though he was strict with them the screws worshipped him. They loved him because they knew that whenever they put a prisoner on report they were gloried by him. The more prisoners they put on report the more certain they were of promotion. He must have put more prisoners on report than anyone in the Prison

Service. He used to walk round the cells at ten to 8 at night, and as he looked through the spyhole if anyone had their bed down he used to put them on report.[1] He must also have been the most assaulted man in prison history. I'm told that in the 1920s as a screw he would accept money to fetch in tobacco, but by the time I met him he was a very different kettle of fish.

I'd gone to Pentonville from Wandsworth where I'd got in a lot of trouble, and no sooner was I there than I was put straight back in the punishment cells. My trouble at Wandsworth had come about when a prisoner called Jimmy Rosen, a nice little fellow, done a screw in the pouch shop with what you'd call a clamp. You held it between your knees to do the making of the pouch. This particular screw had asked for it because he was an animal. Jimmy was only a little man and he'd been forced into it. A couple of prisoners went to help the screw, and this was an absolutely unforgivable thing in the eyes of us fellow prisoners, absolutely. So I did the prisoner who'd taken the leading part. It was the usual punishment – fifteen days No. 1 diet and so on. I had more trouble down the block and then when I'd finished it I was transferred to Pentonville. Lawton was there and he put me straight down into A2, the punishment landing. I didn't think he'd any

[1] Fraser is not alone in his recorded dislike of Lawton. 'Near the end of his service, his sadism had mellowed to a contemptuous indifference to his charges. Always he believed what he called "my officers". "If one of my officers told me you were riding round the gallery on a bicycle," he'd snarl with Cockney venom, "I'd believe him."' Donald Mackenzie, *Fugitives*, 1955, pp. 198–9.

right to do this, I hadn't committed any offence. It was from there I did him the twice.

For a start, when I was in Wandsworth and Pentonville as a young prisoner it was fashionable to mutilate yourself, make cuts in your arms. It was trendy at the time; now it seems daft – but it was anything to have a go at them. Silly, because they couldn't care less. Their only regret was you didn't die of it. It meant that the authorities were wary of me because they knew pain and punishment didn't mean anything to me. I never did anything by halves and I cut myself so I had to have seventy-eight stitches in one arm. When I was put in a strait jacket I burst open the stitches, and when I hit Lawton he got covered in blood. In those days, in particular, it was a black mark against a Governor if he was assaulted by a prisoner. The only way round this was if the prisoner turned out to be mental, and so to get himself out of difficulties Lawton said I should be under the observation of a doctor.

The hospital at Pentonville had been bombed and it hadn't yet been repaired. The hospital, such as it was, was just a few cells on, I think, B2 landing. There was another row when I threw muck over him, and this time Lawton had me put into a straitjacket. Then they came in three sizes, small, medium and large. Now I obviously would fit in the small category, but I was put in a large one and down the back of it were put heavy blankets soaked in water to make them heavier. Now I was like Humpty-Dumpty. I had a great big hump. There was no padded cell. It was just like a hospital cell deputizing for a prison cell.

Mattresses were slung on the floor. And they were all new – they were only prison coir, but they were still soft – and until they were worn they were softish and you sank into them. They looked good but after a month or so they were like lumps of iron. I was still young, not yet twenty-five, and fit. When I was lying on my back in my straitjacket I could manage to jump up and move about a bit. My arms were in sleeves tied in front of my body. The stitches on my arms where I'd cut them had broken and were bleeding. I couldn't move them, and there was a chain which padlocked the end of the sleeves behind my back. So when I was on my back and it became very painful lying on this sort of hump, I would try and move over on to my stomach.

By the early morning I'd had enough. I'd been in it for twenty-four hours. When I'd been lying on my belly with all this weight on me back, my face was pressing into the soft mattress and I'd be lifting me head up to breathe. Then I'd have to give a supreme effort to get on me back. Now as I was rolling over I didn't have the strength to manage to get right over. How I cursed myself when I was pressed into the mattress. I was exhausted and I was suffocating. I'll never forget that in those early hours Lawton came with the screws and opened the flap in the cell door to look at me. They could see what was happening. He laughed, 'Won't be long now. He'll soon be gone.' In a way it most probably saved my life because it made me determined to survive. I knew I had to hang on until just after 7 a.m., when my door would be opened and an arm would be released so I could drink a cup

of tea or water. Eventually I'd have to be taken out
of the straitjacket for an hour or so. Lawton came
and watched me twice or three times, chuckling with
pleasure. Last time about 5 a.m. he said, 'He's still
surviving.'

If I'd have died they'd have taken the blankets
out from the back and said somehow or other I'd
accidentally suffocated. They'd have said I'd been put
in the large straitjacket as a kindness so I could have
more movement. You must remember in them days
in 1947 you could still get away with it. Who would
take your case up? Much as your loved ones would
protest, who would listen to them? You were just
another rascal who'd died in prison. Accidentally of
course. The doctors would have said you were easily
susceptible to something like that. Nobody would
have give a damn.

But I survived, so I was sent back to Wandsworth
for mental observation. That was considered the top
medical prison in the country. Lawton as a Number
One Governor would lose face if he was attacked, and
so I was put down as a mentally disturbed prisoner
which covered him. You couldn't account for what
mental prisoners would do. 'This man would attack
any Governor.' There was no discredit. When I was
in their hospital it was G wing and one landing on
K2; this was another prison hospital which had been
bombed and still hadn't been rebuilt.

It was whilst I was there that Charlie Walters
from over Notting Hill said, 'Why don't you get
yourself certified insane, Frank? It's terrific.' And
it put the idea in me head. I said, 'Yes, but I'll

go to Broadmoor.' He said, 'No, you won't. Only people with three years' penal servitude and over go to Broadmoor.' That was the rules then. Up to two years you go to the mental hospital allocated to the county in which you were born. And he painted such a rosy picture – you played football and all; he made it sound very tempting. He said, 'Look, you've lost all your remission, what have you got to lose?'

I knew that when you were certified insane in prison you had to be a hundred per cent raving lunatic. They could just lock you up if you weren't quite up to the mark. No one bothered then. There were no outside bodies to come to your aid. They would certify you sane on the day you went out, so you hadn't cheated prison at all. There was no question of getting out early. They'd had their pound of flesh. I pointed this out to Charlie and said, 'I don't think I could do it, Charlie, what'd I have to go through?' He said, 'You'd be a walk-over, Frank. The screws are frightened of you.' I said, 'You're joking, Charlie.' I was skinny as anything with all the bread and water I'd had. 'No,' he said, 'you're a certainty.' And he described to me the events and put the germ of the idea into my head.

A couple of days later on the Thursday at 10 at night, I smashed my hospital cell up. I knew what would happen. More officers would be called in, and sure enough half an hour later mobs of them came. In those days they didn't have riot shields; they'd have mattresses with pockets in so they could put their arms down and use them as shields, but I did manage to hit one of them over the head with the leg of the table so that wasn't too bad. They had no really proper padded cells in Wandsworth because it was still being rebuilt after the bombing, and so they took me down to one of the really strong cells on H1. You had to go through two cells to get there. I was just left there and the Senior Medical Officer, a man called Murdoch, no relation to the one who owns the Sun or to Richard, came in the next day. It was about 11 on the Friday morning, and he asked if I was going to stop misbehaving myself. I just didn't answer and out he went. The same thing happened on the Saturday. Same question; no reply.

When I was smashing me cell up on G2, I'd already got the idea what to do. There were always mice and rats running around the prison and I was singing as I was smashing up, 'Come on, my army of rats, Onward Christian Soldiers. You've been slinging these rats in my cells, now they're my friends.' Really anything that came into my head.

On the Saturday morning when Dr Murdoch said stop misbehaving, I asked where my rats were. 'All right,' he said and went out of my cell. And on the Sunday in the afternoon just before tea, about 3 or half-past, they took me out the straitjacket – oh, it was wonderful – brought me tea in and just left me. Well, with this story about the rats by the next morning I had bread all slung all over the cell floor, and in this strong cell there was a ventilator, and God stone me if in the night rats wasn't coming down and helping themselves. I couldn't help laughing. I'm not particularly keen on them, but there's a sight. I'm only kidding and there they are; this is what I had to put up with.

On the Monday I reckoned I'd have at least another fortnight of this before I'd be certified. I was wondering whether I could do it – remember I couldn't have a wash, couldn't brush me teeth, things you like to do to keep yourself clean and tidy – but I thought that now I'd started I had to go on. I'd made me mind up there was no way I could give in. Then right out the blue about 11 o'clock Monday morning, I heard the footsteps on the stone flags outside and the cell door opened. In those days three magistrates and the doctor in the prison certified you. Now it's two doctors; no magistrate at all. They had the hospital Principal Officer with them. One of the magistrates was a little weedy man with a bowler hat and wing collar, typical magistrate sort of style. I'm just there with me shirt on. All the food's on the floor because I've had to sling it there for the rats.

'Morning, Mr Fraser.' This was the P.O. Now this was really clever him saying this, because the way he said it so polite and matter-of-fact, on the spur of the moment, if you was acting you might say, 'What do you mean, Mr Fraser?' and so shop myself. Fortunately I bit me tongue and ignored it, looking at the wall and the fictitious rats. He said it again and I ignored him again. Then he asked, 'Where's your friends, the rats?' 'Oh,' I said – it was my cue to come on the stage and say my piece – 'my friends the rats, well, there's Louis, there's Winston, there's Churchill' and I'm pointing. I said, 'They're all here and they're my friends, but there are enemies and I'll get you with one of them.' I pretended to pick one up and the magistrates looked terrified. 'We've seen enough,' said the one in the wing collar. Instinct told me I'd been certified. What I didn't know then was that, like the Cat and the birch, you didn't get it there and then. They had a fortnight to send you to whatever mental hospital you were going to from the day you were certified to the day you actually went. In those days the Home Secretary had to sign the order. I thought that I'd be going the next day, or at the worst the day after. Thankfully in the course of the next few days the screws, when they brought in my food, would be talking normally as if I couldn't understand what they were saying. That's when I overheard one of them saying that I could be kept up to a fortnight. What I had done with Charlie Walters was tell him to get a message out to Eva so she would not be worried that I really had gone potty.

Somehow he did it, and after a week or so mobs of screws came down and took me to a bath on G2 to make me all clean and tidy. Then I was taken to a cell on K2 where there was just a cell, nothing else, and suddenly my brother and sister came. It had never been known before for anyone to come in like this. I was dead lucky; the screws opened the cell door and stood aside to let Eva go in first. As she did so, the screws behind couldn't see that I winked at her. Now she knew for a fact that I was all right. I ignored them and started to sing about my rats. That's when the screws said I'd have to go any day. But they had their pound of flesh; they kept me the full fourteen days although, in fairness, they didn't put me back in the straitjacket again. They didn't want to upset me and give me any room to make more trouble. But the

63

Principal Officer knew I was acting. The screws come in with me tea and he said, 'Going on a spot of leave tomorrow? Look after yourself, enjoy it. You've done well.' He knew I was acting, as good as I was even though I say so myself. He must have seen through it. Perhaps he was still trying to test me, because it really was a body blow to them if I got out through acting. The next morning I was handcuffed and with three screws I was put in an ambulance and I was on me way to Cane Hill Hospital, Coulsdon, on the outskirts of London. It wasn't far from Wandsworth and in no time we were there. The cuffs were taken off in the doctor's office in the reception ward at Cane Hill, and the screws told the doctor I had to be watched and that I would kill him at the drop of a hat.

I looked at him and said, 'Take no notice, I'm only acting. There's nothing wrong with me at all.' Fortunately, I'd been told by Charlie to tell them the truth the moment I got there. 'They won't send you back,' he said. 'All people who're mad will say they're acting; even though they'll eventually believe you're not mad. They won't send you back. That's no worry.' But when I said this the prison officers' mouths dropped. They looked aghast. They really could have collapsed in a fit. I said the reason I had done this was because they'd made me live in such inhuman conditions that this was the only way I could escape and survive. The doctor was very good; he listened attentively and I think he could tell immediately that what I was saying was true. From that moment onwards everything was really good for me there.

The conditions compared to prison were paradise. I sent postcards back to my mates and I got in the football team. You used to have two games a week, one in the hospital and the other game outside. I went to every mental hospital in the London area. After the game you always had tea with the team, and the captains give a speech. Our captain gave a speech saying in the ten years he'd been in the team this was the first time we had ever beaten the hospital we'd played one day. That sent a shudder down me spine. I thought, 'Get out of the football team. It looks as though if you're in that football team they don't want to release you.' So I got out of that. Then twice a week there were dances. It was strict in a way, but the conditions were nothing like they were in the prisons at that time. Your visitors could have a pot of tea and a nice room for a chat. But I didn't stay very long, a few months. Then, when you were certified insane you had to do every day of your sentence, ten years, two years or whatever to make sure you weren't cheating and as a deterrent to others. On my release day in 1949 when my sentence finished Eva's husband, Jimmy Brindle, picked me up and had to sign for me. It was wonderful.

4

After the War London was up for grabs, and just before I went away it had all been sorted out. Before the War the Sabini brothers from Saffron Hill, Clerkenwell, for whom I'd worked as a bucket boy, had been the bosses. Towards the end of the 1930s they'd reached an accommodation with Alf White and his family from King's Cross. The Sabinis kept Soho but the Whites had King's Cross. Then during the War the Sabinis had been interned and when Derby Sabini's boy, Johnny, was killed in the Battle of Britain, this knocked the stuffing out of them. The Whites effectively took over. Then they had a good team with men like Jock Wyatt and Billy Goller on the strength, but now Alf White was old and Harry, his son, was a lovely man but with no stomach for a fight. Harry was in Wandsworth in 1944; he'd hit a geezer with a walking-stick and got a few months. That was all the time he'd done, and he didn't like it. He was very big, impressive, full of bonhomie, hail-fellow-well-met. And Alf was as well. If you had a crooked copper they were the ideal men to handle it. If anyone was in trouble and could get a bit of help they were the ones to go to, but as for leaders they didn't really have the style. All in all they were a weak mob, and they were ripe for taking.

Billy Hill didn't really have time for racing people. He thought they were phonies, frauds who'd never really done any proper bird. He booked them as sort of bullies. So I don't think he thought of turning them out, but there again he didn't have any time for them either. Jack Spot was the one who wanted control. Now Spot wasn't a thief. He would run a million miles from nicking something himself, but what he'd do was he'd then nick it off the thief. He was what they call a thieves' ponce. What he was was an enforcer. His real name was either Comacho or Comer. He reckoned he'd got the name Spot because he was always in the right spot when there was trouble. He'd got great ideas about protection at the races and Bill was friendly with him. Spot could see Bill would be a great asset, and when Spot had the row with the Whites he pulled Bill in. Bill had a tremendous amount of respect and clout, and that was the overwhelming factor.

Spot had good hard people like Teddy Machin and Franny Daniels, who were on the Airport job, solidly behind him then. They were all getting plenty of money where the Whites never had that muscle. They had some good people but not enough. Harry White never fancied a mill, and when Spot did White's team at the end of 1946 in Al Burnett's The Nut-House off Regent Street, he hid under a table.[1] That's when Billy Goller got his throat cut. The one who would have been terrific and who would have defended the territory was Alf White's son, also called Alf, but he had died in 1943. The other brothers, Johnny and Billy White, were really racing people and not involved in clubs. The Whites were literally eliminated. I wasn't surprised at all, but they still kept the race meetings. Old Alf and Harry were clever there.

It didn't really concern me, firstly because I was primarily a thief then and secondly, because I went away. People with the Whites tried to involve me, but they never knew how thick I was with Bill. To me it was a totally different league. I was a thief. I didn't look on these people seriously. But before this happened I'd been hard at work.

At first, after the War people didn't do bank safes. I can't remember a bank being successfully robbed in those days. People were in awe of them, even the Billy Hills of this world. They honestly believed there'd be secret gadgets which would link them to the police station. It was about 1950 before anybody really took on banks. What you did was take the money away either before it got into the bank or when it came out. I was the originator of the Friday gang. That

[1] Al Burnett owned a number of clubs and night-spots over the years, all of them frequented by the Fancy. When Nipper Read investigated the Krays' hold on the West End, Burnett vehemently denied paying them protection money although it is apparent that he was doing just that. Burnett was a follower of greyhounds in which he had some success. His dog 'Pigalle Wonder' won the Greyhound Derby and on retirement was a prepotent force in breeding. Burnett also wrote his memoirs, *Ace of Clubs*.

was the day wages were paid, and that's the day I and a team went for the clerks who went to the banks to collect them. That way the prize was in your control because you could see it and now it was up to you. Very few did it – doubt there was thirty in London – because you could get the Cat and birch for robbery with violence, plus you would automatically get a very hefty sentence. Plus also, if anyone died, you'd automatically hang. There was no question of it. So, not everybody entertained it. In turn that made it easier for the police because they knew there'd only be a certain number of people capable and willing to do that type of robbery.

You would look for a big firm and then see which bank was nearest to them. Then on the Friday one of us would go into the bank, dressed up respectable, and change a £5 note into silver. Then, if you saw two or three people getting a chunk of dough you'd wait until they came out. They would normally walk back to the firm – it might only be a couple of hundred yards away – and then the next week, if you had any brains, you'd watch them again. Same thing the third week except you would have a cosh with you, give them a couple, pinch the bags and be away into your car. You could do it yourself, and the benefit of that was no one except you knew about it.

It was incredibly easy and, then again, not so easy. There was the 'have a go' hero and so I used to give the people employed by the firm a real thump to make onlookers think twice before they got involved. I liked a starting-handle with the crooked bit cut off and the rest covered with rubber so as not to make it so severe.

The head was the target. If you hit them on the arm, sometimes they wouldn't let go.

I remember there was a boy I did at New Cross outside a bank there. I hit him and hit him. He and his mate held on and me and my mates – I had some with me this time – dragged them all across the tramlines and we still never got it. There were some navvies doing up the road and they came running over with sledgehammers and pickaxes and there was a tremendous fight. Eventually we got away with the bag and there was £250 in it. Sometimes the money was good, sometimes it wasn't. You could get in the region of £2,500 up to about £7,000, which was a chunk of money. In them days if a man was a drinker he could get himself blind drunk for a pound, whereas today he'd be lucky to get into a toilet with it. On the other hand I did a bank clerk in the New Kent Road one time. He hung on to his bag like grim death and I gave him a terrible pasting. Eventually I got it from him, got in the car and opened it up. All there was was cheese sandwiches.

I was the first man to put a stocking mask on my face, and with a stocking mask and a cap you were completely distorted. But almost at the beginning someone must have shopped me. It was also my own stupidity – spending too much money, which may have tipped off a grass. At the end the police knew who to go to when a robbery went off. In the evening after the robbery I would get put on an ID for it, but I was never picked out. Really the police weren't very intelligent. They couldn't have been watching me, but I did alter the *modus operandi* and I would go somewhere other than home on a Thursday evening, so that if they were watching my address on a Friday morning they wouldn't see me anyway. Even so they could have easily nicked me if they had put tabs on me. I was arrested for every single one, and I was never picked out on the IDs. It was ended by the Bedford case in 1951. I did every day of the three years for that. It was nearly three years eight months when I came out, because I lost time on appeal and time spent on remand didn't count. Men who'd been nicked after me and got five years came out before me.

It wasn't all robberies. John Parry, and a man called Henry Cohen who was with Parry and Tommy Brindle when they were nicked over thefts of Post Office parcels in 1953, hit on the ingenious idea of doing Post Office books, all forgeries. At the time there was an idea you bought them and to cash them you had to go through a big rigmarole, get the special form, fill it in, and when it was sent back with approval you could draw out so much. You always left something in so you got the book back. Post Offices were open all day Monday to Saturday, with plenty of extra staff in over the run-up to Christmas, so we had one week before Christmas when we could work. And we really went to town.

You could draw up to £30 per book, and we'd gone and got hundreds of them. They were all blanks and we passed them to Parry. At Christmas it was all ready. On my side there must have been twenty of us working, maybe there were up to fifty or sixty all told. We went out in little teams, two three-and four-handed. The night before, you checked the books. The stamps and the forms were the fakes. You passed the form over with the book. I would say £1million could have gone; I wouldn't be surprised, but there was nothing in the evening papers. I put the first one down at a little sub-Post Office at the back of the Old Kent Road; Billy Blythe was there with me as the back-up. A woman asked for my identification card in the name on the book. Of course I never had it. Luckily for me it was about noon, getting on for dinner-time. I said 'Oh blimey, I've left it in my jacket at work.' This was a try-out. When I came back everyone said, 'Oh no', because it meant we'd have to forge ID cards. We thought now we knew we'd have another try Monday. That Friday was the first and only time anyone asked for an ID. We realized that it was because the woman wasn't busy and was being nosey. In the main offices, as it was so near Christmas they were so busy they couldn't be bothered. The staff were so much more polite. In some offices I'd go in one queue in the name of Brown, and further down the counter I'd it in the name of Jones. We never stopped. We had sandwiches and a flask of tea with us and you could park anywhere. We just had those six days and had to make the most of it. We kept half, and the other half went to Parry; plus we could keep the silver. Jimmy Brindle, Bill Blythe, Jimmy Ford, Freddie Adams – who had a baby with the daughter of a screw and who committed suicide in a Cardiff hotel in the 1970s – were with us.

Billy Blythe was dead keen on gambling and on

the final Saturday about 12 noon he said, 'I've got to go to the dogs.' We said, 'Don't be daft, Bill, they don't shut for hours.' This was the Post Offices, not the dogs. 'No,' he said. 'I'm off.' We give him his share, and the rest of us carried on until the last Post Office closed.

Of course, all this time I was friendly with Billy Hill, both when I was outside and when I was in. In fact, during the sentence I had for the smash-and-grab when the car wouldn't start, I helped do him a favour in Wandsworth. Jack Rosa, one of the brothers from the Elephant, was waiting for the Cat in 1948. For a short time there was a rule came out that if you got the Cat you couldn't have no more punishment, no loss of remission, no No. 1 diet, bread and water, so everyone was queueing up for it. Billy got the idea that Jack should knock out a screw. He offered him £5,000 to do one, but before he got to him Billy was to block Jack from getting the screw. 'I want a black eye', he says to Jack, and he tells me that he didn't want any of the young men in the shop to get into trouble. There was Alfie Gerard, George Wallington and Lennie Garrett amongst them. He told me he'd got the Governor straightened as well.

Now in those days when you got the Cat you could be back working in a few hours, so Jack got it and was back in pouch shop No. 2 the next morning. He picks up a knife and goes for the screw and Billy goes after him. We all chorus, 'You bastard, you've saved the screw's life.' Jack was never charged with anything. He told the Governor he was very sorry, it was because he'd had a brainstorm because of the effect of the Cat the day before. The screw came up to Billy and said, 'Thanks, Hill. You saved my life.' Bill became a red-band in the bath house and had six months taken off his sentence. Jack got his £5,000 and everyone was happy.[2]

When he came out Billy Hill ran a spieler[3] in Ham Yard financed by Freddie Ford. Freddie was a very wealthy man who had a one billion-mark note framed on the wall of his flat. He'd invented the idea of having hotels round King's Cross for prostitutes. Provided the girls who were working in the area come in with suitcases, that covered them – there didn't have to be anything in them; they were then guests of the hotel. That sort of didn't make it a brothel, and he got a fortune from it and went from strength to strength. He died in a car crash in about 1959.

At that time Billy lived in Camden Town in an old house converted to flats with his wife Aggie. She had been a Scots brass who was very astute indeed with money. Eventually she owned the Modernaires Club

---

[2] The put-up fight was not an original idea of Hill's. In 1936 whilst in Brixton Prison waiting trial for the murder of Massimino, one of the Montecolumbo brothers, in a fight over a betting pitch at Wandsworth Greyhound Stadium, Bert Marsh and Bert Wilkins had 'saved' a prison warder in similar circumstances to the Hill-Rosa fight. This stood them in great stead not only during their trial, in which they were convicted only of manslaughter, but also in their sentences which, at twelve and nine months respectively, were extremely lenient. A former boxer, Marsh, whose real name was Pasqualino Papa, was a hard man for the Sabinis and had been involved in the pre-War Croydon Airport bullion raid. Later he was a close friend of Billy Hill and Albert Dimes, and was thought by some to be the real 'Guv'nor' of Soho.

[3] A gambling club, usually illegal.

which had once belonged to Jack Spot, and also the New Cabinet Club which she'd bought off a woman who got two years for swindling the coach of the Cambridge rowing crew. If you went in there, she'd call you over and expect you to buy her a drink. She never drank it, just rang it up. On the other hand, if you were skint you could always go to her for a few quid loan.

It was after I came out from the two years that I became a really close friend of Bill – at the time I was working as an independent snatch or thief. I'd work with people from a pool of up to say twenty people, so I always had something going for me, but Bill always had money behind him. That was the difference between us. I've never known him skint. I think he'd always got dough and sometimes big dough. He had a nest-egg somewhere along the line. He'd learned his lesson in drink. In drink he was foolish, and that's the only time I've ever known him to be like that. He couldn't hold his drink and he realized it and rarely drank seriously.

That's how he cut two people – Johnny Dove, who was a navvy, and Mikey Harris – in a club in Old Compton Street in 1942 after he finished his two years and before he got the four. Billy's sister was called Maggie. She used to like singing opera, and she hadn't a bad voice but not a particularly good one. She burst out in song 'Oo-oohooo-wooh' in the club one day, and these two guys were taking the rise out her. 'Turn it in,' 'Shut up' and so on. When they went to the toilet old 'Dodger' Mullins went and remonstrated with them and they started knocking him about.[4] They really steamed into him. Billy Hill came in, see them, and cut them to pieces. They nicked him and he was put on an ID parade, but by then people had got into Dove and Harris and they never picked him out. So that was the end of the matter. Then years later in the 1950s Billy did Mikey Harris again; cut him on the hand in the Cabinet Club – painful but not too serious.

Part of the reason he did him this time was just jealousy. One of the things Mikey Harris was telling Bill was that he had done a couple of robberies with me and in which Bill hadn't been included. He wasn't with us in another of the robberies in which we were unsuccessful. If we had succeeded, it would have come to a million. The successful one was a bank in Manchester. The money would go from Oldham or Stockport to the main bank. We were successful, but an innocent man named Huggy Craft got five years. He knew we'd done it but he wasn't involved. His wife's father had stuck it up for us. After the robbery we went round his house and cut the money. From the information we thought there'd be £7,000 to £9,000, but we only got £2,000. It was the most they'd had in one delivery. The information was complete rubbish. After we'd shared the money we headed back home.

The one which wasn't successful came from Huggy's

[4] 'Dodger' Mullins was an old-time villain, given the nickname because of his ability to avoid trouble. He was one of the men who ambushed the Sabini brothers on Derby Day 1921 in a fight for control of the race-tracks. Later he took part in the Dartmoor mutiny.

father-in-law as well. He told us there was a woman, a Mrs Post, who had made a substantial amount of money during the War. She lived in a big detached house on the outskirts of Manchester with a couple of maids. In the basement she was said to have big safes, and the house was burglar-alarmed up to the police station.

Normally her son-in-law would pick her up, take her to the firm and bring her back in the evening. On this occasion she wasn't very well; she had a cold and stayed home. Our information was that up to half-nine in the morning the burglar alarm was disconnected because of the milkman, the butcher and other delivery men calling. The man with us, Jock Robinson, who was known as 'Jock the Fitter', was the best key man in Britain. Personally I think he was better than Eddie Chapman, Johnny Ramesky and all the other Scots. I'd met him in Liverpool and he was Paddy O'Nione's step-father.[5] During the War he'd had a copper straightened in London who had put in a report that he'd been blown to pieces by a bomb. But when he was nicked in Liverpool they took his prints. 'Ain't it marvellous,' he said one day on the yard. 'I'm dead and I've been brought back to life to get some bird.' He was quite philosophical about it. Anyone who was anyone had worked with him. There can't have been a decent villain in England who hadn't asked him to do a lock or make keys for them.

Jock would know when he saw Mrs Post's keys which fitted what. We got a van, painted 'Florist' on

[5] See Chapter 7.

it and the driver dressed up in a smock and a peaked cap. He had a big bouquet of flowers and went and rang the bell. One of the maids answered the door. The rest of us were in the van looking through a little hole in the side. The driver said, 'Flowers for Mrs Post', and when she took them we got out and rushed in the house. We'd been told she'd be in the bedroom at the top of the stairs. Me and another man ran upstairs, but he was slow and the information was wrong. The bed was made but the room was empty. When Mrs Post heard the scuffling – the maid had given a yell as we bundled past her – she came on to the landing and bumped into the man. She too gave a tremendous scream. In the detached house next to us the chauffeur was looking through the privet hedge and saw the doors at the back of the van and three masked men, and then he heard the ferocious scream from Mrs Post. In a second we'd tied her up, taped her, but by now the chauffeur had gone in the house. Jock, who'd been left outside, had seen the chauffeur looking at us and now he came to the house, rang the bell, and said, 'Get out quick', without explaining. They shouted to me as I was running to find the keys. I came down the bannister convinced there would be a fight with the police. There was no one there at all. We all jumped in the van and drove off. We never saw anything. We were saying to Jock, 'Are you crazy?' But he was right. As we were driving away the police cars were coming towards us.

The headlines in the papers were 'FLOWERS FOR MRS POST'. Looking back I think we made a big mistake not putting Bill in the robbery. He'd have thought things through and perhaps had another man to have helped 'Jock the Fitter'. The others didn't want Bill because he would have wanted more, but it would have been worth it because he'd have laid things out.

Billy Hill was a great influence on me. He would say, 'Look after your money', and tell me wisely how to do it, something I never did, but he meant very well by it. He then introduced me to some very big people businesswise; people who were straight but who would turn a blind eye to whatever they bought, such as jewellery. This was very, very handy.

Even if he wanted something done, he wouldn't just stay away and let others do it for him. He'd be there. I remember doing a couple of guys with Bill in 1962. There was a casino on the Embankment – it's not there now – and Bill had seen a couple of guys were cheating him there. They were Italians, connected to the Mafia. Bill called me one day, got in the car and away we went to wait for them. We left them for dead more or less. Both of us did them; he was a good man, was Bill. I said, 'I'll do them', but he said, 'No, I'll be with you'. We did them in the square between there and the Houses of Parliament just by Dolphin Square. But mostly he drove. I was already on a pension from Bill, so it was part of what the pension was for. I was getting £100 a week. As soon as I came home from the seven years for Jack Spot I was put on it.

In October 1949, the same month Billy Hill came out of prison, I did really well. It was at the back of New Cross Docks and it was the first job we did with a print van. That came to about £3,000. Then shortly after that we had the Eldorado Ice Cream place and took a great deal of money from them. Their head office was near the Oxo building. They had a factory in Stanford Street and they used to collect money for the workers. Everything was cash, you weren't paid by cheque. The evening newspaper vans had roll-back shutters and I had a van driver straightened. He was to say his van was stolen, but he wouldn't scream until after the robbery had gone off. If for some reason the blag didn't take place, we'd put the van back and borrow it again the next week. We only had it half an hour if that. We'd give him £200 at the most, depending on what it came to. If we did well, so did he. If we didn't, he didn't.

By now Jack Rosa was running the spieler in Dean Street which Bill had given him as part of his reward over the fight. Someone had to stand up to be the owner when the police raided the joint. Of course they'd told us they were coming and it was Jack's turn to be arrested. There were no problems – it was a formality. He'd appear, plead guilty, be fined immediately and be out by about a quarter to eleven. Pay it and out. His problem was we had a job going, and it was just his luck that he was arrested on the Thursday and it was his turn to be at court the next day, so we recruited my brother-in-law, Jimmy Brindle, to do the driving. He was going to pick us up in the motor after we'd done the job, but since he was completely inexperienced he didn't wear any gloves. We made him take his socks off and use them. Suddenly there was Jack. He's made it. He'd got a taxi straight from the court and hadn't time to get gloves, so he took his socks off as well. It all sounds a joke, but it went all right and we got the money and away.

At the end of 1949 I had a short sentence for stealing a torch, and that was a total fit-up. In 1949 Patsy Lyons, who'd just come out from the five years for the jeweller's shop, a man named Burns and me just came to see the Christmas lights. Burns had won £25,000 on the pools which was the most you could win in those days, and he bought a car with the money. We parked it in King Charles Street between Haymarket and Lower Regent Street, and when we came back after seeing the lights there were people rushing at us from all angles. They'd been hiding in a charabanc, but we hadn't done anything to be worried about. We were taken down the police station. The police questioned Burns and found out the car was straight, so there was no way we could be arrested. What they did, however, was they'd taken a torch out of a car near us and had made out they'd found it in our car. They had to wait for the owner to identify it as his torch. He hadn't reported it as missing and he'd drove off home where they contacted him. Patsy got twelve months, I got six and Burns got probation. He wasn't a thief really; he'd got three years' penal servitude in an Army court-martial in the Middle East – he stole a gun. He did about eighteen months and there was a review and he was released. That was all he ever had. He died shortly afterwards.

We'd done what we could to help ourselves. Eva had been in the ABC café near the court, sitting with my kids and saying, 'Don't you worry, your Dad'll be home soon, he's innocent.' The jury who'd come in for their lunch could hear this, of course. We thought it might get into their subconscious, but they wouldn't be able to say what they'd heard. It worked the first time and we got a re-trial, but the second time the jurors didn't come near the ABC. In those days trials could be over in a couple of hours and there wasn't a chance, but I tried the same thing with Eva a couple of years later. Twelve months after the torch case, quite by chance I saw the man who owned it. I recognized him near the Bricklayers' Arms in the Old Kent Road and dragged him out of his car. He admitted he more or less knew I was innocent, and I was quite happy with that. At least I knew.

One particular robbery, the one at the United Dairies in Water Lane, I did get arrested for. I was put on an ID parade with Mikey Harris, the one who Billy cut in 1942. Anyway, this time Mikey was completely innocent of the robbery and when it came to it neither of us were picked out. A DI Clarke was in charge. He was a man who ended up Chief of the rubber-heeled squad, and Billy had him squared from his early days. A crooked copper then never dreamed he could ever be nicked. Normally they never even arrested them; they just retired them. I recall a couple of crooked coppers in around 1945 getting nicked. They got nine and twelve months, and were let out on appeal. No one was surprised; they were only surprised they ever got nicked. A bent policeman was supreme. He thought he was un-nickable in that period.

Bill had another copper, a very senior one, Peter

something – it was a very unusual name. He rose to be a very top copper. I was there when Nat, the stocking king, poured beer over him in the Cabinet Club. I think someone told Nat he was a copper and that was enough. No one told Nat he might be doing business and to leave him alone. Aggie was there, and when Bill came in and was told about it he just shrugged his shoulders.

Bill had the knack of getting into people. He used to have the head of the Flying Squad, Ernie Millen, round his flat and he had a very useful M.P., Mark Hewitson, on the books as well. Captain Mark Hewitson was the M.P. for Hull. Aggie had him on the notepaper for the Modernaires Club and he was useful in getting the licence through. I had many a drink with him after doing the seven years. I should think he was a very good M.P. because he was a caring man. He'd been a captain in the First World War, rose up from a private which was a very big thing to do in those days. He used to tell us of all the peculiarities and little mannerisms of members of the Conservative government in the Home Office part.

I remember him telling me about one M.P., and how crooked he was sexually, and I didn't believe him. I thought you can't be right, but lo and behold this particular M.P. was nicked in St James's Park performing with a guardsman. So from that moment onwards I knew whatever he was telling me was right. The M.P. was fined, and that was the end of him; he resigned and took the Chiltern Hundreds. The Captain had everything he wanted – a pension from Aggie, free drinks and women. When Eddie

Richardson and I had Atlantic Machines we had our equivalent, Sir Noel Dryden, and he had exactly the same from us. They were happy with it. They got a few bob on top of their pensions if they needed it. The M.P. Tom Driberg was the same sort of coup for the Krays, although there were no little boys or girls or filthy things with Captain Mark Hewitson.

In about 1963 the Captain was on the board of the Modernaires or the Cabinet, I forget which now, but the licence was in his name. Whilst he was still an M.P., when the licence came up for its yearly renewal the police objected – to a Member of Parliament, of all people. What had happened was that he'd met two young girls down Aggie's club and took them back to his flat in Phoenix Court which was round the corner from Old Compton Street. A couple of days later one of them went and burgled him. Instead of doing the sensible thing and having a word with Bill or Aggie, he went to the police and got the girl arrested. That was the worst thing he could ever have done. They said they'd been there before and he had given them permission to go back to his flat. They came back with stories of three in a bed and he was finished. He didn't stand the next election. He told us that Harold Wilson had promised him a peerage if he didn't stand, but he never got it. He'd been kidded. He died whilst I was doing the twenty. To me he was a smashing fellow. He was a man of his word, but his indiscretion was his undoing. Why didn't he go to Bill? I think when he came home and saw the damage he phoned the police immediately without giving it the serious thought he should have done. I think too that's why Harold Wilson didn't want him as an M.P. for acting so impulsively. When me and Albert had the Bonsoir he used to come in regularly, and he'd come to Atlantic Machines for a drink as well. He still kept around, but he was not the same man.[6] All these people we had around us were all looking for an extra pound note. It was parallel with what happened in 1960 with Robert Boothby. He'd befriended a boy in the Strand; the lad later burgled his flat and that all came out in court, but he got away with it.

Personally I never met Reggie Maudling, but Bill told me – and I didn't disbelieve him – that he was OK with him and could get help. He would have got in to Maudling through Hewitson. Bill was always a man who took out policies ever since he got the three years' penal servitude over a raid on a furrier's in Oxford Street in 1947, when they tunnelled through the bricks into next door. He was innocent and just happened to be in the basement flat of a guy who was on it, Stuttery Robinson, who lived over Camden Town. Bill was visiting him when the police raided Robinson, and swore blind they found brick-dust. Bail was granted and Bill then skipped to South Africa. He came back and now the Law went crooked. Bill paid the money, and the brick-dust which should have appeared in the envelope never did but he still went down. However, he never forgot the lesson and was always on the look-out for help.

[6] Hewitson, who fought in both World Wars and who was the National Industrial Officer for the General and Municipal Workers Union, was the M.P. for Hull Central in 1945–1955 and Hull West in 1955–1964. He died on 27 February 1973.

In February 1950 we did a wages snatch. The wages clerks came out of Stanford Street across the road, and we did them on the way to their car the other side of the road. One of them wouldn't let go and I remember I dragged him all over the tramlines. I was nicked and put on an ID. Now I had a bit of luck. Eva, my sister, was a shoplifter in the War; then she got married and turned it in. She married Jimmy Brindle who'd been in Borstal with me. He and his brothers had been doing the cellar in a pub over in South East London when the Law had come across them and got knocked about a bit with some hurricane lamps. His brother Tommy, 'Tom Thumb', who was in the Black Market, got two years and Whippo, another brother, eighteen months. Jimmy had brains. I got out and knocked me dough out. He got out and put his away. He only ever done another six months and that was a liberty. He'd nicked a car wheel; complete rubbish. It was the only bit of bird he did over the forty years he was married. Tommy got another eighteen months in early 1944 over some stolen petrol coupons, and then after the War became a respectable bookmaker.

Anyway, the previous year in 1949 Eva had been on a reunion with an old shoplifting pal, took a cab home to South London and had a row with the driver. She was arrested for not paying her fare, fined and given time to pay. She gave her address at our brother James's house and she forgot to pay. One day the police sergeant turned up to arrest Eva for non-payment. James paid it, and told Eva she'd have to pay him back.

My bit of luck was that I asked James if he'd come

with me on the ID for the wages snatch, and at the last minute I changed my overcoat with him. It was a very distinctive one. Instinct told me it was a crooked ID and the witnesses picked out James. They arrested him and he had the complete alibi. At the time and day of the robbery he was paying Eva's fine for her.

In the early part of 1950 I was on the run for about six weeks – it was the only year I didn't do a single day's bird in that particular period. In January or February, I forget which, I was going up the stairs of the Cabinet Club in Gerrard Street with Jackie Rosa and Dickie 'Dido' Frett when a row developed with a man coming down the stairs. He was with the girl who'd been done over the Cambridge rowing coach, and a tremendous fight occurred. The three of us got away and Dickie, who'd had the row, said it was over something that had happened whilst he was in prison. I'd never seen the people before. One of the other side went to the police and nicked us. I didn't know this then and I never dreamed anything would come of it. Most people were like me; they wouldn't go screaming to the police if they were hurt. Dickie and Jack stayed over my place in Mason Street, and the police came to arrest me around 8 the next morning. One of the police was a Detective Sergeant, who was later nicked and found not guilty at the Old Bailey. I knew he was crooked and he brought down two from West End Central. I said, 'My mother's very ill. I give you my word I'll come to West End Central later.' He talked the West End Central coppers into grudgingly accepting it. I winked; he winked. He knew there was no way I'd be there, but there'd be a drink in it for him. He told me that 'Dido' was also wanted, but they didn't search the premises. I went straight over to Notting Hill and camped out there for a while until I heard Billy Hill had got into the witnesses. Then I went to Notting Hill nick, went on an ID parade and wasn't picked out. Meanwhile I'd seen Bert and give him the few quid to which he was entitled. In fairness, the man in the club shouldn't have nicked us at all. He'd done a five himself.

The next time I saw the Detective Sergeant was in 1964 when I was flying to Jersey with my wife Doreen and our boy, and I bumped into him at Gatwick. He'd retired because he'd just been acquitted at the Old Bailey, and we had a little chat. We went on to Jersey, and who was in the hotel where we were staying but the Rolling Stones. They were on the same floor and I was introduced to them. They gave my son their autographs. The nicest was Brian Jones, the one who died in the swimming pool. I told them I was a travelling salesman.

Shortly after I got out of the one with 'Dido' we had a big score near Ridley Road market in Hackney. I was told how they came out with all the money on a Friday night, the week's tåkings, and we got it – £2,500, a reasonable chunk of money in them days. And after that I never stopped getting money that year.

A job which didn't go quite right was one Bert Marsh stuck up at Porthcawl.[7] It was a fairground owner who kept readies in a caravan on the site.

[7] See footnote 2.

There was to be no need for real villainy. All we had to do is watch until the man left the van and then we'd do it. Me and Billy Blythe drove to Porthcawl and when we got there the place was deserted. We drove back to London and Bert apologized, saying he was sorry he'd wasted our time. I didn't really think about it for another fourteen years; when I was telling this story to George James, a Welshman with whom I was doing business, he said, 'Wasn't it lucky I'd moved on?' And he burst out laughing.

I was with Billy Hill and Franny Daniels in Shaftesbury Avenue in 1950 when I saw Lawton, the prison Governor. There was a conference on capital punishment and whether to abolish it, and the offices where this was taking place must have been somewhere in the vicinity because I saw him in Shaftesbury Avenue.[8] He was on the other side of the road and I shouted out at him and tried to chase him, but by the time I crossed the road he'd popped in a cab and was off. This was the man who, to me, had tried to kill me without laying a glove on me. I thought he'd taken great delight looking through the flap of the door. That's what put the idea into my head to have him, and in autumn of 1951 I done him on Wandsworth Common between 8 and 9 in the evening just as it was getting dark. Then every Governor's house adjoined the prison and I just waited, caught up with him, knocked him about and strung him up with his dog – it was a sort of terrier.

[8] A Royal Commission on Capital Punishment was established in 1949. It sat in Spring Gardens near Trafalgar Square, not that far from Shaftesbury Avenue.

I had a stocking mask on but he must have known who it was because I was saying, 'You tried to kill me, now it's my turn', and things like that. I know it seems daft now, but then I had to do it.

I just left him. I didn't make a very good job of it unfortunately because of being on me own. But I made a good attempt. What saved him I think was the branch; it was supple and it bent. I don't know what happened to the dog. It was a bit timid, barked a bit and tried to get away, but I caught it. I should think it died. To be honest I like dogs, but with Lawton anything went as far as I was concerned. I don't know if this was the reason, but afterwards Lawton always walked with his head on one side. I wasn't the first to try to do him. Three men had tried to do him when he was an officer at Wandsworth, but they got the wrong screw. The one they got was called Jackson. They were convicted and got three years, but they were released on appeal.

The next day after stringing up Lawton I went and got the evening papers, all three of them, *Star*, *News* and *Standard*, but there was nothing in them. A year later when I went back to Wandsworth from Pentonville after finishing my punishment for assaulting a screw, Lawton came down to the reception cubicles. Now that was unheard of. He had the Chief Officer with him and I fancy he thought 'My turn now' when he looked me over. And that was the start of it all over again.

Before that, at the beginning of January 1951, I got another twelve months. Again I was a bit unlucky. Jimmy Brindle and me had taken a girl from the

Cabinet Club home to Edgware, and on the way back
I got a bit lost somewhere around Golders Green. We
pulled up to ask the way back to the West End and
a man who was cleaning his taxi got right saucy. He
shaped up to me and I knocked him down. I asked
if he'd had enough and when he nodded I told him
it needn't have happened if he'd just been civil. I
thought that was the end of it. But instead he'd taken
the number of the car and nicked us. He picked me
out on an ID. That was how I met the ex-Detective
Sergeant who ran a pub in Carnaby Street. He was a
sort of ponce and went with a woman who ran a club
in Romilly Street; he was the man who did all the
deals for West End Central. I knew about him and
went to him. I've always fought shy of bent coppers.
With all the bird I've done I can't trust them. They
all have their price and they'd still swear your life
away. But sometimes it's a gamble you have to take.
His fee came to £100 but the damage had already
been done. He did his best but the taxi-driver was
adamant. Then I got three months' concurrent for
hitting a barrister over the head with a bottle in a row
in a late-night restaurant in Mayfair called Bolsom's.
I got away in a cab, but I realized Jimmy Brindle
hadn't come with me. I went back to find him and got
nicked. In fairness, this time the barrister didn't want
to prosecute, but again the damage had been done.

There's a lot of talk about nobbling the jury, but
what the public don't know is there's a fair bit of
it done by the police themselves – subtle, outright
boldness in approaching, clever and cunning. I had
a bit of luck in 1951 and it came about because the

police tried to be too clever with a jury. Usually they did it much more successfully twenty years ago when they had more scope for it. In the jury room an old newspaper cutting could be seen with details of a previous conviction when the jury isn't meant to know of your conviction. The police could give it to the usher to leave for the jury to see. Or the police will be talking two or three together where there's a juror near, so they can hear that you're a rascal. There's no way the juror could report this, because the detectives would be talking amongst themselves and it would mean they'd been eavesdropping. They'd also know about the jurors and what they were like. They'd take advantage of everything.

I came out from the six months in April and Jimmy Brindle, Jimmy Humphries (the porn king) and I were all brought up at the County of London Sessions accused of trying to break into what is now the Howard Hotel just off the Embankment near Temple tube station. We'd been trying to get a few quid together for Jack Rosa who was up for hitting a screw at Pentonville. The police had said they saw us climbing a drainpipe. After the judge had summed up we went down the cells and Jimmy Humphries said, 'We won't be found guilty.' When we asked him how he knew, he said a Jewish juror had winked and given him the thumbs-up sign. Both Jim and I said, 'You're mad, we've never seen it.' When the jury came back, Humphries was completely vindicated. Outside the Sessions House in Newington Causeway I saw the juror and went up to him and thanked him for reaching a true verdict. He burst out laughing. I said, 'What are you laughing for?' and he said, 'Look, between the three of you you have records stretching from here to the Marble Arch.' As we hadn't challenged the police and called them liars, the jury shouldn't have known that. I said, 'Tell me a couple of my convictions,' and he gave them to me. He said the police had told him. I asked him to come with us to see my solicitor so we could take this further and make an official complaint. He said let sleeping dogs lie. He said he came from the East End and didn't like the way the police had let them know our convictions. That was why we'd been found not guilty.

You can't be lucky all the time. Take poor Wally Challis. He picked up 'Dodger' Mullins from Dartmoor after 'Dodger' finished a nine-year sentence and drove him back to London. On the way he knocked a man down and got five years. My luck wasn't as bad as that. At least I was working and not just doing a favour when I was done at Bedford Quarter Sessions in early 1952 for stealing cigarettes.

I was nicked in Edgware over a warehouse we'd had in Bedford. As soon as they turned the bell off at 5 o'clock, in we went. It was in a street with little terraced houses on either side. There was a guy in one of the houses we were frightened of. He'd seen us drive up and had come out and started looking. There we were three-quarters of an hour after it should have been shut. Very sensibly we loaded up; we'd already got the safe. There were two of us with smocks on. The man with me was older and acted as the manager. 'All right, all right, driver,' he said, signed things and away he went. I went back in the warehouse and five or ten minutes later came out with my smock on. But the man next door was dead shrewd. He rang up the police and said he might be wrong but he thought there'd been a robbery. The van had been requisitioned over Christmas for delivering the mail, and it still had 'Post Office' on it; he could only remember that. We got to our car to discuss whether to unload the cigarettes, take the van and dump it and come back with another van, but we decided he hadn't got anything on us. We were wrong. I was sitting with the driver in the van and the other two were in the car following behind about eighteen miles from London when suddenly the chase was on. They never tumbled the car behind, but there was nothing those people could do to help us. Then we went down a cul-de-sac. The driver was lucky, he went out his side and fortunately he managed to get away. I got caught.

At the first trial I had Joe Yahuda defend me, and the jury disagreed. Eva brought my kids along again and sat in a café near the court at lunchtime, telling them how I was innocent so the jury could overhear. It worked this first time, but on the re-trial we were out of luck. In those days trials only lasted a day or so. Eva never got a chance to do her bit.

For the re-trial I brought in G.L. Hardy, who'd been a top man in his time but now he was getting on. This time Yahuda was his junior. After I'd got the disagreement on the first trial, that's when they produced some additional evidence. They brought out the old chestnut, the verbal, by having a police officer saying I'd made an admission to him. No one would believe it today. They did then. I got three years.

5

When I was sentenced I went first to Bedford Prison, then to Pentonville, and on to Wandsworth which is where I met Albert Pierrepoint, the hangman, at the time of Derek Bentley's execution. It came about because of my quarrel with the Carter family. I hit Johnny, one of the brothers, and was put in the strong cell after I had a fight with the prison officers who were dragging me off him. The cells on E1, the punishment landing, had little windows – one end was the main centre, the other end was near the entrance to the hospital.

I got bread and water as usual, and I used to make a habit of always going sick whenever possible because then you were allowed your bed in your cell. Normally, on punishment in those days your bed had to be outside your cell from 7 a.m., but as the doctor didn't see you until 10 or so you kept your bed for the extra three hours. On this morning when Bentley was going to be hanged they didn't want me to report sick, because the doctor would be busy. I persisted. Shortly after 8 o'clock the door opened and here was a prison officer on his own – normally there's two, more likely three or four. He told me to go and wait at the centre of the wing rather than the hospital end. The landing was deserted; it was very eerie and you could sense the foreboding over the prison. I made my way to the centre. In 1953 all the prisoners had to be out at work, and it stayed that way until 1959. If people were on the punishment, which was the wing where the execution chamber was, on a hanging day they had to be out on exercise until about 11.30. I was there on my own for a time until two prisoners came round: Patsy Lyons, who was now doing four years for GBH, and Spiro, who I'd been at approved school with. We were the only three to report sick that day. As we stood in a line facing the door leading to the condemned cell, round the corner from F wing came Pierrepoint, a dapper little man with Brylcreemed hair, and two big prison officers. As they got near, on the spur of the moment I sprung at Pierrepoint. Patsy Lyons and Spiro didn't take part but they were encouraging me. I was shouting 'Good luck, son' at the condemned cell and was spitting at Pierrepoint. The prison officers jumped on me and I was rushed down the cell. Ten minutes later I was taken to see the doctor and then put out on exercise. The next day I was charged with assaulting a servant of the prison. Pierrepoint didn't give evidence and his name wasn't mentioned, but that was par for the course if you assaulted a civilian who worked in the prison, and I got more punishment. Shortly after that I was charged with assaulting another prison officer. Everyone said he was a Dutchman. He wasn't born in Britain. I was charged with assaulting him three times. He really put me through it and so I used to chase after him. After that he was called the Flying Dutchman. If I was due for a visit the other officers would give him my visiting order, but in the end he would refuse to bring it to me. He should have been the last man allowed near me.

Then I was transferred to Leeds. That was as a result of Billy Benstead, who'd been with Billy Hill on the Eastcastle Street job, writing the letter to the Governor saying I was going to stab him. One day the prison officers pounced on me, searched me, put me in a car and transferred me. Then it was Wormwood Scrubs and back to Wandsworth where there was more trouble.

I was already in one of the strong cells in E1 at Wandsworth at the time there was a riot, so I didn't know what had happened until one of the men who'd taken part, and had been placed in the next cell, managed to tell me part of the story. Lawton was the Governor then, and when I was exercised it was on my own.

I was being exercised in a great big yard when who came round but Lawton and Duncan Fairns. He had been the Governor at Rochester Borstal when I got the birch for putting the screw in the bath. Now he was the Commissioner of Prisons. I picked up some pebbles which were in the yard and started throwing them at Lawton and Fairns. 'Bosh, that's for beating prisoners up.' It was only seconds before the screws were on me, sticked me and dragged me off the exercise. The very next morning, a Saturday which in itself was an odd day for moving prisoners, I was transferred. I was taken to King's Cross with three screws and put in a special reserved compartment. On the journey I asked the prison officer in charge, Lingfield I think his name was, if I could go to the toilet. Now he was a man who'd put his stick across me plenty of times, but I think in his way he respected me. He took me down the corridor and on the way said, 'Watch it at Durham, Frank, they're after you. You'll have a tough time, be careful.' What he meant was that Durham was the last outpost and its reputation was fearsome. Remember that no one then was interested in prisoners. It was a long way for people to visit you, and it really was the end of the prison world. The boast was that Durham was the last prison to put any reforms into effect. For example, when corporal punishment was abolished as of 1 June 1962 most of the prisons had begun fading it out in anticipation, but not Durham, nor Wandsworth for that matter. They kept it right up to the time it was abolished.

By the time we arrived at Durham it was late afternoon and the prisoners, including the red-bands, had all been locked up and the prison visitors had gone. The prisoners who worked in reception, they'd been locked up as well. There was just me and the screws and an eerily brooding silence. I knew there was something wrong. The biggest screws you could wish to see were there including one called Delap, a giant of a man who'd joined before the War. The handcuffs were taken off and the Wandsworth screws were sent over to find their quarters. There was a Charles Dickens desk with a sloping top. Delap stood behind it and the others surrounded me.

'Naaame?'

'Francis Davidson Fraser.'

'Naaaaame?'

'Francis Davidson Fraser.'

Of course I knew what they wanted. They wanted me to say 'Sir' and I wasn't going to. And I knew what was going to happen. I got one punch in first and then the sticks just rained over my head. I was dragged off to the punishment strong cell and after about an hour I was taken, covered in blood, to the hospital where I saw the Principal Medical Officer – he later became head of the Prison Medical Service. He looked just a young boy. He was stitching me head with screws sitting on either side. He went over to the sink to put more catgut in. Whilst he was doing this and not looking a hospital screw, who three years later got nicked for murder, got hold of a wet towel and started hitting me around the head with it.[1] The doctor then came back and carried on stitching me.

I was taken back to the strong cell and on the Monday I went before the Governor whose name was Richards. He was the image of Gordon Richards, the jockey. Years later when he was Governor of

[1] In 1958 a Durham Prison Officer, William Ernest Moodie, killed his 12-year-old daughter to whom he was 'passionately devoted' with an overdose of drugs. The girl, who had been an imbecile since birth and who could neither walk nor talk, was also subject to terrible epileptic fits. The jury found Moodie guilty of manslaughter and added a recommendation of mercy. He was sentenced to 3 years' imprisonment, reduced to 12 months on appeal. Moodie was the first prison officer to be indicted for murder. In a note on the case in A *Calendar of Murder*, Terence Morris and Louis Blom-Cooper add that Moodie's colleagues collected a very substantial sum of money to ensure his financial security on his release.

Birmingham I asked him, but he said he wasn't related. Whilst I was standing there a screw called Appleton hit me over the head about three times with his stick, right in front of the Governor. I hadn't done anything. It was so blatant. Out I was dragged again and off to the hospital for more stitches. But what they didn't know was me and how I would react. Quite apart from writing a petition and complaint, when I eventually finished my bread and water weeks and weeks later and I was up in the prison proper, every prison officer who I see who was present during the beatings I attacked them one by one. Eventually one day when I was in the punishment cells during my dinner hour and a number of prison officers came in, I thought I was in for another beating, but one said I was being taken to the prison hospital. I asked why since I hadn't reported sick, and I was told it was Governor's orders and I'd be told when I got there.

I was put in a special cell with a mattress which was better than the punishment cell. There was an iron ladder attached to the wall outside so a screw could look through a spy-hole in the roof. I saw the doctor the next day and I asked him why I was in the hospital. He said, 'I think you need a rest; keep you out of trouble.' When I saw the Governor I told him I'd made an application to see a full Board of Visiting Magistrates with a number of complaints, and I asked what the position was now I was in the hospital? He said I would either be taken over to see them in the Board room or they would come over to see me. Whichever way, they would see me.

About two days later about dinner-time I saw three

or four magistrates along with discipline officers. I told them of my complaints but as I was trying to emphasize a point, forcibly trying to get it over, I could see the fear in their faces. Even though I was surrounded by prison officers they were drawing back. Instinct told me that there was something wrong. That afternoon I was due for a visit from Eva and sure enough she came. She'd travelled all on her own from London for the half-hour visit, but in that time I managed to tell her my fears that, although no one had said anything, I'd been certified.

She told me she wouldn't leave until she'd found out, and she would send me a registered letter so there was no way it could get lost. After the visit she got to the gate and demanded to see the Governor. They refused to let her but she said she would wait. The screws called the police and she still refused to go. The police weren't prepared to drag her out at this stage. She was quite sensible and said why she wanted to see the Governor or the doctor, and eventually that's what happened. An official came to the gate and told her I'd been certified. She wrote the letter telling me what had occurred and I had it the next day from the doctor when he made his regular visit. He told me he'd see me again that afternoon.

He had me brought over to his room, sent the screws out, and offered me a cup of tea. I said I didn't want it nor a cigarette. When he said I'd been certified I asked if this meant Broadmoor, and he told me it would depend on the Home Secretary which secure hospital I was sent to. It could have been back to Cane Hill or to Rampton or anywhere.

I asked why he'd done it – 'You know there's nothing wrong with me' – and he said he'd done me a favour. 'Look at the prisons you've been to. In every one you've assaulted an officer.' I said, 'Don't you think they haven't assaulted me?'

'I'm not denying that, but it's reached a stage where you'll be taken outside, charged with assaulting an officer, and be given a further sentence. Then you'll get into more trouble and you'll never get out. This way, if you keep your nose clean you will be released one day. I think I'm doing you a good turn.'

I said, 'I don't think you have. If what you're telling me proves right then you have, but I don't think so.'

Sure enough a few days later, the night before I went to Broadmoor, a screw climbed the ladder, looked down and told me where I was going, adding, 'That's where your sins'll find you out. You'll be lucky to come out alive.' It was really spiteful, vindictive behaviour.

The next day we all set off in a taxi, about five of us crushed in, and we got to Broadmoor, but luckily I knew what it was going to be like. Before I got my sentence I had been to see Jackie Rosa – after he'd been sent there during the five year he had for hitting the Pentonville screw – in the visiting room, which was then by the gate, and he had marked my card. By way of making conversation really I'd asked him the routine. It was just I never dreamed it would happen to me.

'Well,' he said, 'when you arrive you come in this room and you have twelve of the biggest screws you've ever seen in your life, and they strip you naked. Ignore them, because they're waiting for you to take umbrage and that's the excuse to really pay you. And in here they can do it with a licence because you're officially mad. They then walk you naked across the courtyards to the refractory block, Block 6, and as you go along all the really insane guys will have been gee'd up and will be pounding at the doors and singing and going 'Arrrgh'. They put you in a cell with a canvas sheet, and your shirt's like canvas – it can stand up by itself in the corner. It's freezing cold. They have two punishments here which they put in your food. One's called the Sleeper. The other's called the Shitter if they're being really spiteful and you wind up like having dysentery. In no time you'll die. But the Sleeper, all it does is you're like a baby. You couldn't defend yourself against anybody. You're an imbecile like. The Chief'll come in the first morning you're there and you'll be in the Sleeper, the milder one. And he'll ask you where you are and when you tell him he'll say, "This is letting you know this is what we can do if you don't keep out of trouble." But if you do keep out of trouble it's terrific. It's very easy; so remember that. Everything after that you just cruise through.'

And Jack was dead right. Everything he said was correct.

When I got there I was stripped, marched across and given my supper. It tasted better than prison stuff, but next day I woke up feeling bad. The Chief came in and asked me where I was.

'Broadmoor.'

'Well, at Broadmoor we can do things they can't do in prison. When's your time up?'

I told him.

'Well, behave yourself and you'll go out. We won't make life bad unless you upset us.'

He was right to a T. I didn't have any serious trouble there.

That's where I saw the guy who told me he was innocent. He'd been convicted of a murder in Blackburn. He was sentenced to hang, but then reprieved and sent to Broadmoor, and he'd been there twenty years. He seemed very sensible but he was withdrawn. He insisted he was innocent. When I came out I went to see the *Sunday Pictorial*, which was a very campaigning paper, but they didn't want to know about him. Then in one of the Sunday papers Fabian wrote his life story. He'd been one of the coppers who'd been sent to Blackburn on the case. Outside police forces used to call in Scotland Yard. He said he'd always thought this man was innocent. This was 1955, and the case would have been about 1927. In 1967–8 this man was being transferred to an ordinary mental hospital, and I saw the headlines in the *Mirror* that he'd absconded and all roads to Blackburn were being watched. It said he had an obsession with the town. I never heard what happened.

Another man there used to stand pretending to be an electric light bulb. He did this all day long. I would creep up and say, 'I've pulled your plug out' and he would squeal, 'Put it back in', jumping up and down.

Everyone arrested at airports would have their

cigarettes confiscated and these were handed out at the special hospitals, so you would get packets of twenty twice a week. I used to hand out mine because I didn't smoke. There were a couple of guys with great big heads – I remember one of them was called Bogey Knight, in for murder. If I gave Bogey cigarettes, the other would nick them and Bogey would start crying. It was unbelievable to see him cry. The screws would say, don't give them cigarettes; I said it's not fair, how can I refuse? If I didn't hand mine out the screws would only have kept them for themselves. They would have more than the patients. There was one man, a Welshman who'd been a boxer, Cyril something. He was a pathetic case – he didn't know where he was. He'd killed his wife and children. Your family could leave money to buy food and things for you, and every now and again the Boxing Board of Control would leave a sum of money for him. All the screws would do was give him eggs and bacon. He'd put his porridge on it, add salt and pepper and scoff it. There was no way you could complain he wasn't getting proper stuff for the money he'd been left because you'd get nowhere. After all, you were mad, weren't you?

One guy aged nineteen had been done for a murder up in Yorkshire. Whilst at Broadmoor he got into the band, and once a week he'd go and play at the dances. The wall on the women's side of the hospital was much lower and one day he ran to get to it to escape. When they tried to stop him he stabbed one of the screws. They didn't touch him. They simply brought him back to the refractory block and then eventually let him up into the main part. A guy who worked in the scullery who had killed three or four people told Jack Rosa the boy wouldn't live long. All the food comes up from the kitchen to the scullery and it's dished out. 'When they're dishing his food all the screws gather round so I can't see'. Six weeks later he died.

I was still in the refractory block when I was released. Normally, before you would be released you had to get into an ordinary block, but I was one of the few who got straight out of a refractory block. At that time if you'd been sentenced to death and reprieved you never came out of Broadmoor – the only one was John Allen, 'the Mad Parson'.[2]

They let me out a day early. I was due out on a Sunday and I came out on the Saturday in, I think, the oldest suit they'd ever give out. It must have been a hundred years old. Jimmy Brindle, 'Battles Rossi' and Billy Blythe, God rest his soul – he got three years for cutting that copper, Vibart, years ago – came to collect me.

They drove me back to Aggie Hill's Cabinet Club in Gerrard Street and then we went on to the Italian Club – its real name was the Central Club – Clerkenwell. It's gone now, but it was a marvellous place. No strangers, coppers or nothing could get in.

Those years may not have been that good for me, but they were the great years for Billy Hill. He was now the 'Guv'nor'. Jack Spot was being eased out and

[2] Allen, who in June 1937 murdered a young girl, the daughter of a workmate, escaped from Broadmoor wearing a parson's collar he had used in a concert party performance. He worked in a baker's shop for several months before being captured. He was returned to Broadmoor and released after a short period.

it was during this time that Billy organized the great coup of the mailbag robbery from Eastcastle Street on the morning of 21 May 1952, and later the bullion robbery in Jockeys' Fields. After that he never needed to work again.[3]

What was amazing was no one was ever charged for the robberies themselves. After the Eastcastle Street job two were done for receiving: Eddie Noble and Bobbie King. Bobby was taken off the *Queen Mary* with his wife and four children, but Billy Hill got in to the jury and both were found not guilty. They got back the £2,500 taken from them on their arrest, and their costs.

Billy was arrested himself over the Eastcastle Street mail van, and he was taken to the Yard to see a very senior officer. Later Bill told me he'd found out about him and his connection with a man called Brixton Jock who did the crooked business. When they took Bill in, he tells me the first thing he says is, 'By the way, I see Brixton Jock yesterday. He told me to give you his regards.' And in no time at all he was out.

[3] In a raid on a Post Office van £287,000 was stolen. The van was hi-jacked after the driver and guards were pulled from it. It was later found in Augustus Street, Camden Town, with only thirteen of its thirty-one sacks remaining. On 21 September 1954 some £45,000 of gold bullion was stolen from outside the KLM Dutch Airlines offices off Theobalds Road, Holborn. There is a full if not totally dispassionate description of the raids in Billy Hill's *Boss of the Underworld*, pp. 162–167 and pp. 217–219.

6

I was just out of Broadmoor when the Albert Dimes –
Jack Spot 'fight that never was' took place in August
1955, but I'd missed the build-up. Part of the trouble, I
think, was with the women. Billy Hill had left Aggie and
taken up with Gipsy Riley by now, and they would go
with Jack and Rita to the South of France. From what I
heard the women didn't get on. They were always trying
to outdo each other. So were Bill and Jack, but the truth
is Jack was on the slide. On the other hand Bill had
pulled off Eastcastle and the Jockeys' Field coups. Jack
had written his memoirs and Bill had his done in the
People by Duncan Webb, the writer from the *People*
with whom Billy was very pally, and both him and Jack
claimed they were King of the Underworld. They were
both jealous of each other. Something had to happen
and so Jack simply went after Albert, who was Bill's
best man, to teach him a lesson.[1]

[1] Both men were arrested and charged with an affray. There is little
doubt now that Spot was the attacker but he called both Christopher
Glinski (see Chapter 12) for his defence and an elderly retired
clergyman, the Rev. Basil Andrews, who gave perjured evidence
to say that Dimes was the aggressor. Both were acquitted and the
incident was dubbed 'the fight that never was'. Later Rita Comer
and two others were convicted of conspiracy to pervert the course
of justice.

Funnily enough I'd seen Jack at Brighton Races just a few days before the fight. I'd gone down with Billy Bythe, and Georgie Wood – who'd just come out from eight years in the London Airport robbery – was there with Spot on the free course. He'd asked if I would go in as partner in a drinking club with him if Spot put up the money, and I'd said no. When I heard about the fight I was in Billy Howard's spieler in South East London with Billy Blythe, and we went straight over to see what it was all about. I was already on the run when the Spot slashing, which really broke up what was left of Jack's hold on Soho, took place nearly a year later.

My problems in 1956 came about as a result of a long family feud really. In fact it went back almost fifteen years on and off. Despite what books and the papers have said, there never was a quarrel between the Brindles and the Frasers. What there had been was a feud between two Elephant and Castle families, the Carters and the Brindles – 'Tom Thumb,' who was the eldest, Georgie, Jimmy, Whippo and Bobby. The Carters first of all nicked Whippo and Tommy in 1943 over a fight somewhere. They were found not guilty. In 1941 Whippo got two years for a fight in a club with the Carters' half-brother; Hughie was his name, but he was called Buey. Whilst Whippo was away Buey never give Whippo's wife any money which was the traditional thing to do, so when Whippo came home he went looking for him. Then 'Tom Thumb' and John Parry did Buey, but this time he never nicked them. Then Johnny Carter cut Johnny Parry round the throat outside the World Upside Down, the pub in the Old Kent Road. He was nicked for that and he got twenty-one months. He came out of doing that and then went and cut Bobby Brindle. He was nicked for that but was found not guilty. He then stabbed Whippo Brindle and got five years for that.

In the meantime my sister Eva had married Jimmy Brindle, who hadn't been involved at this stage and I bumped into Johnny Carter in January or February 1948 in Wandsworth when he was doing five years. He was about a month older than me. He was a Young Prisoner when I got three months in Feltham, and I'd met him in Chelmsford in 1942 when he was doing two months for cutting Hoppy Smith, a geezer with a club foot: put a V on his forehead. Two months seems ridiculously short, but in those days you could cut a man to pieces and only get half a stretch.[2] Whippo was in Chelmsford at the time so I heard both sides of the quarrel. I'd known Johnny on and off and I'd been friendly with him.

When I met Johnny Carter in 1948 he asked, 'Where do you stand?' and I said I was neutral provided he didn't interfere with Jimmy, Eva's husband. He must have took umbrage at what I said and have nursed this. He finished a five-year sentence in Parkhurst in the autumn of 1951, and as I had gone out thieving just before he came home – a furrier's in Marble Arch – I give him a good drink to help him on his way. I'd also

---

[2] A *stretch* is twelve months' imprisonment and therefore *half a stretch*, six months. A *carpet* is three months, from the time it took to make one on the prison's loom, and a *lay down* one month. Two months or two years is a *bottle* from pickpocket's slang and twenty-one months, a *pontoon*, after the card game. To be *JR'd* is to be remanded in custody (Judge's Remand) pending sentence.

been up to Scotland with Tony Mella, Eddie Anthony and Jimmy Ford to do a big tie-up. Mella was then still a professional boxer in those days and we'd got him as a late substitute for a bout in Glasgow. That was to be our reason for going to Scotland if we was nicked. The fellow who put up the job must have been living in a dream world. The job simply didn't exist, and so on the way back we stopped off in Manchester to do a jeweller's. Our luck seemed to be out because by the time we got there it was closed. Then Eddie Anthony remembered there was a silk stocking factory he done once, and we thought of doing it again. When we got there it was closed as well, but there was a note on the door to say it had been moved to new premises, with a telephone number. We rang to make sure no one was there and then we did it. We had two cars and we filled the boots up and stopped the night in the Midland Hotel which had a private car park. Every so often one of us would nip down and have a look and make sure things were still there. Next day was Armistice Sunday and we thought it would be better to travel south then rather than late at night. I gave Johnny Carter some of the takings from this as well.

Unfortunately he took this for weakness and not out of friendship. A week or so later I was in a near beer club in Rupert Street when he started a row. I said to the people, 'Turn it in, he's just finished five years.' Next I knew he'd jumped on me back and stabbed me three times in the face. Then he ran off down the stairs. I and Albert went back and smashed the club to pieces. I still don't understand it. Despite the family row I thought I was friendly with the man.

I sent a message to him that that was it. It was war. I also sent a message to Buey and he said he was siding with his brother. I also met up with Tony Mella, who was one of Johnny Carter's close friends as well as mine, outside the Spread Eagle in the City Road, Shoreditch. I had a gun with me and I let him know it. I told him if he tried to make one with Johnny Carter then he'd get what he deserved. I said if he bumped into him, well, that couldn't be helped, but he wasn't to be going round keeping company with him. But he did and so I smashed my way into his flat in the back of Shoreditch and I did him – boxer or not.

So on Christmas Eve 1951 when the pubs stayed open late, I went with Albert and another man and caught Buey and Harry Carter as they came out of the Lord Nelson in the Old Kent Road. We really done Buey, but Harry managed to get away. On the morning of Christmas Day Albert and I went to the hospital where Buey was and waited to see if Johnny – who was the one I was really after – and the family came along, but they never showed up, so Albert went off to his family and I went back to mine.

Later that day it turned out it was just as well I had a gun. I was sensible enough to give the Carters the credit that they would make a comeback. Kath, the girl I was with at the time, and I was living in very old flats in Mason Street in the Old Kent Road. Wooden stairways; if there'd ever been a fire, God knows. The toilet was on the landing shared between two flats. There were some Irish people in the flat opposite. After Christmas dinner I'd gone in their bedroom to have a sleep for an hour. Instinct told me if the Carters were coming round that would be the time. I'd got the gun under me pillow. It wasn't a case of being frightened, it was a case of being sensible. I expected they'd go and see their brother, have a few drinks and then come looking and I was dead right. The Irish guy woke me up saying, 'They're here.' I just had me pants and vest on and I hurriedly put my trousers on for propriety like, no shoes or socks. Kath had our youngest son, who wasn't twelve months old, in her arms and another by the hand. She gone and opened the door on to the landing to see who it was knocking, and Carter had smacked her round the face when she'd done so. When I opened the door there was Carter right in front of me. I put the gun right to his head, put the safety-catch out and it never went. I tried three times. Carter had a tool in his hand and he was staring at me. I put one up the bolt and put it to his head and again it never went off. There were about five of them in the flat and they all screamed and were fighting with each other to get down the stairs. I was hitting at them with the butt. The reason it hadn't gone off was that one of my friends who used to drop round had been in the Army at Dunkirk and he had done something to it in case my kids, who were all small, found it and tampered with it.

The Irishman had been in the British Army and knew about guns. In a flash he had it going. I leaned out of the window and shot at them as they chased to their car. Then I ran down the stairs and shot at them in the street. The Law heard about it and they came round and arrested me, but they couldn't do anything about it because no one would say anything. It was a few days after this I was nicked over the cigarettes at Bedford.

Whilst doing that three years I'd been moved to Pentonville from Bedford and I was in the mailbag shop there. They had a strict rule of 'no talking' in the workshop and I never used to talk – ever. One, because you couldn't talk properly anyway and if you did the best was a whisper. Secondly, the screws had to put on report a certain number of prisoners every week and it was your bad luck if your number came up. Horricks was now the Governor. A screw called Rice, a fit young guy who was the PT officer, put me on report for talking. Anyone under thirty doing corrective training had to do PT in the yard. When I went in front of the Governor and I was asked what I wanted to say I should have said nothing because you had no chance, but the sheer injustice of it – I could have been on bread and water for nothing – made me open my mouth. I said I never spoke. I never speak in workshops. 'And the first chance I get I'm going to knock the screw spark out.' Really foolish of me to say it. The Governor gave the usual, 'My officers can look after themselves, three days' Number 1, seven days' Number 2 and ten days' loss of remission.' He never even looked up.

When I came out of the workshop the first day after I came out of punishment there were mobs of screws, always were, but this day there was more. You had to go single file past them. Who was standing watching? The Governor and the Chief Officer; most unusual to see him at this time of day. Instinct told me that somewhere along this line of officers would be Rice. It really was a challenge, like, 'Come on, let's see what you can do. You said you'd chin him.' Instinct was right. There he was bold as brass standing there grinning. I just ignored him and walked by, then in a flash turned round and flung a lovely punch. His knees buckled and I was on to him and they was on to me. The usual clubs, sticks and whistles. I was knocked unconscious and taken to the punishment wing, where I got the usual bread and water and I think 180 days' loss of remission. I had a bit more trouble down the block, but eventually I came out and I was transferred to Wandsworth.

Who was the Governor but Lawton, the man I'd hung along with his dog on Wandsworth Common? Everyone knew I'd done it and so did he. 'Back,' he said. So I knew it was going to be a very unpleasant time for me. A month or so after I was there, in came Johnny Carter. He'd hit Charlie Hawkins over the head with a starting handle and had got two years at the Old Bailey. As soon as I see him in prison I went for him; straight at him. I had a big lump of lead which I'd smuggled out of a workshop and attacked him. I just went for him. I hit him quite a few times over the head and the next thing I was in the strong cell and I lost another two months' remission. I could see Johnny being taken away to Pentonville. I knew I was going to get plenty of punishment for it but I didn't mind. I'd already lost about nine months' remission then.

When I came out of that sentence in 1955 I was still

looking for Carter. Then in April the next year two fellows, Benny Harris and a kid called Harvey, had a fight with Harry Carter and, I think, Johnny in Billy Howard's Sunset Club in Brockley. Whilst they were having a fair fight Buey and others hit them over the head with bottles. Of course, that revived my interest even more because the Harrises were friends of mine. This Sunday I went looking for Johnny Carter. The pubs then closed at 10 o'clock at night. The very last pub round the back off Lambeth Walk we looked in, we were told the man he'd been drinking with had an Austin Westminster car. We drove round looking for it, saw it parked and, as we got out of our car, someone came out of the pub, see us and ran back in to tell Carter. He jumped over the counter into the public bar and over the counter there as well. When we came in we couldn't see him, and then we spotted him running out of the public bar. He had a good start and ran to a garage with double doors and a little gate in one of them; you don't often see them nowadays. He got through and shut the door. There was a man outside in his shirtsleeves and we thought he was Carter's friend. We smashed our way in, knocked everyone out of the way and found Carter hiding in the bathroom where we cut him to pieces. As we left, an Alsatian dog went for me and I cut its throat. Now I like dogs, but I had to do it.

Later we heard the people who owned the house were innocent and Carter had just got through the door to get away. So, of course I went round, apologized and paid compensation. Later still I heard that Harry and Johnny Carter had broken a man's arm.

Harry had been weighed off but Johnny was still on his toes. He was arrested as he was discharged from the hospital where I'd put him. And so I arranged that the man with the broken arm wouldn't recognize Carter at the magistrates' court. Patrick Marrinan, the brief, was sent round to defend Carter and to tell him that when he was found not guilty he'd get £750, but that he wasn't to put any blame on me for his cutting in Lambeth. True enough, the man went along with it and Johnny was found not guilty. I couldn't do anything else. I didn't want to be responsible for Johnny going away simply because I'd put him in hospital. But in turn Johnny went wrong on me. That was how I came to be on the run at the time Spotty was slashed.

Spot took a right liberty with Albert. His prestige was going down before the fight and he'd fallen out with Hilly who was very clever. In 1936 Spot had three people put away for grievous bodily harm on him. One of them was Jimmy Wooder and there were two others. One got fifteen months, one twelve and the third nine at the Old Bailey. Hill must somehow have known this. In 1943 Spot met Wooder in a club in the East End and gave him the most ferocious scar you've ever seen – getting on for a finger wide. Jimmy Wooder never nicked him – it wouldn't have entered his head. He told everyone what a dog Spot was, but no one would believe him.

Spot had watched Albert Dimes at Ascot Races and thought he was just happy-go-lucky. He was a generous, good-hearted man. He'd lend you money, and all he'd do when you couldn't pay him back would be to say 'God blind me'. He'd killed a man in a street fight in 1939 off the City Road, but no one had ever found out about it. He went to Nottingham for a time and worked for a man called Cucan or something like that at the races. That and the 'Babe' Mancini killing gave him a reputation in the underworld which was a big plus.[3] He'd also broken a police sergeant's jaw, and got six months after he was absent without leave a bit after the Mancini case. Albert was not an aggressive man at all, but he was 6'2" and very powerful. You'd really have to provoke him before he'd lay a finger on you. But Spot wasn't intelligent. If he'd done any proper bird he'd have realized there was more to Albert than meets the eye. He put Albert to the top of his list and thought he was an easy fellow to have over.

When Albert Dimes was working he'd go to Frith Street every morning around 10 a.m. Albert always used to buy fruit from the people on the corner shop. They were Jewish people, I think, and so Spot knew his routine. Albert didn't have a clue that Spot was thinking of slashing him. If he did he'd have tried to talk to the man.

At the time Jack Spot was very thick with a fellow, Sammy Bellson, who was the Guv'nor' of Brighton. He was worth at least £80,000, which was real money in those days. Once the Spot–Dimes fight had taken

[3] In 1941 Dimes was arrested and charged over the murder of Hubby Distleman in a fight in the Palm Beach Club in Wardour Street, Soho. He was found not guilty but Antonio 'Babe' Mancini was convicted and hanged in October 1941. Dimes, then a deserter from the R.A.F., was bound over to 'come up for sentence' and returned to the service.

place I went to Brighton with Billy Hill, who was now collecting money for Albert's defence. Bill could easily have paid for it himself, but he deliberately did this to let Spot see how popular Albert was in contrast with what Spot would get. We went to all the people who Spot had been very thick with so they would elbow him and only contribute to Albert. Sammy Bellson was one of them and yes, he knew Albert very well and he put up quite a good sum, around £500. Billy suggested that I stay there in Brighton with him to keep Spot's men away from him. Sam agreed and a few days later he had a very nice flat for me which normally Spot would have had in Marine Parade going up towards Rottingdean. That's how I come to be at Brighton where I met Doreen, my wife. Her uncle was Georgie Shillingford, a friend of Darbo Sabini, who had died down in Brighton a few years earlier. George was about the best judge of jewellery I ever met. Doreen's mother had a dry-cleaning business there and she worked behind the counter. When I took me suits in to be pressed I met her and fell in love and the rest is history. I stayed down in Brighton commuting every day until I went to Ireland. I met Max Miller there, as well as that Chief Constable Charlie Ridge. It was an absolutely bent town. In 1957 Sammy did three years in Pentonville for his part in the corruption trial in which two detectives were convicted and Ridge was acquitted. Once he'd finished his time Sam foolishly then went and wrote his story in, I think, the *People* saying, 'I was the Al Capone of Brighton but I used bribes not machine guns' – that sort of thing – and he went on to say how he had the coppers straightened. Well, after that he couldn't go back to Brighton where he'd been since the end of the War. He went back to the East End.

Billy Hill was living in a flat in Barnes at the time. I'm pretty sure Bill owned the block. Patrick Marrinan, the brief, lived in the flats as well. I suppose I could be called Bill's minder and anyway he knew he could rely on me. Sometimes he'd say there was no need to come up and sometimes I'd stay a couple of days. It was a loose sort of thing. He had three full-size poodles and we'd walk them on the common together. Then we'd drive up to London to organize Albert's defence. Bill was writing his book with Duncan Webb, so he was busy. In an evening he'd go out for a meal with Gypsy and I'd get the train back to Sammy in Brighton.

Within a few days Bill had got all Spot's henchmen on Albert's side. He'd put ten grand into some showrooms over at Chiswick and Teddy Machin, Jackie Reynolds and others went to a meeting there. They all dropped Spot out. No, they said, he took a liberty, and Bill said, 'Fair enough.' It really was an ultimatum. He said they should go to the hospital and tell Jack they were through with him, and they did. Eva's husband Jimmy drove me over to the meeting and waited outside. He wasn't big enough to get involved.

When I was in Brighton I was at the August Bank Holiday race meeting there, giving the change at Albert's pitch. By now he was on remand in Brixton. We were on the free course and it was packed. I was looking right over the heads – they were twenty feet

deep. I remember seeing a guy called John Sambridge
who was always called 'Happy'. I saw him looking at
me with two or three burly men who looked like
plain-clothes policemen. It was an instinct. I forgot
about it, but half an hour later a bookmaker came
up to say the Racing Squad was down to arrest me.
What did I want to do? Did I want to make a run? I
said, 'No, what could I have got up to?' I'd been away
nearly four years and hadn't been in trouble since I got
out not much above a week earlier, and so I stayed
where I was. Sure enough I was taken to the cells
under the stands. There was Ted Greeno who was
now in charge of racing, Herbert Sparks, head of the
Flying Squad who had nicked Alfie Hinds, and Charlie
Ridge. Greeno said, 'We've heard you're down here
to shoot a man – one of Spot's supporters.' He told
me I was going to be searched and I said, 'You'll put
something on me.' He said, 'No, this'll be a straight
search. Next time we may make out we've found
something.' I was stripped and searched and they
found nothing. 'What you going to do now?' asked
Greeno. 'I'll have a drink in town and go back to
London,' I said and so they left me. That was in 1955.
In about 1959 whilst I was in Birmingham Prison, a
former top copper of Scotland Yard had been arrested
and charged with helping to get a false passport for a
South African woman. He was fined and then wrote
his story in the *News of the World*. He told how no
one knew what I looked like, and that's why they got
'Happy' Sambridge to finger me.

After I finished me seven I got later for slashing
Spot, Sambridge had his leg blown off in London

and everyone thought it was me and they was quite right.

He deserved it for fingering me. I'd never done him any harm. I'd been in prison with him. Even if I'd done him harm, that's the sort of thing that shouldn't happen. They'd taken him down there, given him a tenner or something. I sent word and he knew what to expect. Even if he'd come and said he was sorry the punishment would have been the same. He knew exactly the crime he was committing when he was helping the police. He knew exactly the perils that went with it.[4] I only knew about it because that policeman had the hump.

After Spot was acquitted, a few days later Albert Dimes was released when no evidence was offered against him. That evening I went after Spot and stabbed Bobby Ramsey, the boxer who was very pally with him and later with the Twins, just as he was going into a club in Crawford Street in Marylebone. He was with a brass who used to hang out in Gerrard Street. I slung the knife and straight away bumped into some coppers. I cut my hand as I was stabbing him. Bobby was brought into the station house and me with him. Chaps in Soho used to take the piss out of this ex-brass, but I didn't and it paid off. I said to

---

[4] Before the loss of his leg John Sambridge claimed that in July 1956 he had fitted up Dennis Stafford by planting a Luger pistol in Stafford's car parked outside the Molton Club in Panton Street. This had been done, so he said, at the request of a police officer who had given Sambridge £5. Stafford, who was later convicted of the murder of Angus Sibbett in Newcastle, received a two-year sentence for the gun to run concurrently with a seven-year sentence for housebreaking. *Daily Mail*, 9 August 1960.

Bobby, 'Didn't I come to your aid? Didn't I help?' She was standing by and confirmed that I had.

I was taken to hospital to have a couple of stitches in my hand, and was then brought back and locked up at Paddington. I had a few quid with me, reasonable money. The Detective Sergeant come in to see me and asked if I wanted anything. I said I'd like a sandwich, and I gave him four fivers or something like that – anyway much more than any sandwich could ever cost. He didn't say it won't come to that, and he went off and came back with the sandwich but he did bring back the change. I said, 'You can keep it,' and he did. Then he said, 'You're lucky that I'm on tonight. The Divisional Detective Inspector's on holiday, the D.I. is sick and that's how I'm in charge. I'll have to hold you for a while but I'll let you out.' A few hours later I was let out and met him down the road. He wanted a couple of hundred quid, so I gave him a drink and arranged a meet later. I went straight to Billy Hill to get the dough.

It was after the acquittals that Spot made a bad decision. If he'd done nothing the whole affair would have all died down, but he did do something and it was then Bill took umbrage. The Joe Cannon story in his book *Tough Guys Don't Cry* about taking a pop at Albert and Billy is mostly complete rubbish. It's right though that him and three other kids were given guns by Spot to shoot Bill and Albert. Every Sunday Bill used to have Sunday dinner in Kentish Town with Aggie, and the kids were supposed to do him then but they had no intention of trying. Instead of doing the sensible thing and forgetting it, they boasted about it. Bill got to hear and so him and Albert and I got hold of them, gave them a slap, and explained the facts of life to them over in Bayswater where they came from. Joe and the other kids went and gave the guns back to Spot.

But so far as Spot and Billy was concerned, now things were different. If he hadn't got hold of the kids, the slashing would never have occurred. In fact, if it hadn't been for the kids' foolish talk we wouldn't have known anything about it. But talk they did, and so it was decided in a meeting at Bill's flat over Barnes High Street that Spot must be punished. He knew it was coming because he kept on going round to Paddington police station pleading for protection from them, but they wouldn't help him.

All this didn't happen until the May of the next year, and in the meantime Bill and I tried to help out Alfie Hinds who'd been convicted on pretty dodgy evidence of a safe-breaking at Maples, the department store in Tottenham Court Road, and who was still protesting his innocence.[5]

The real reason Alfie Hinds was nicked for Maples was his meanness. He had parked his Landrover in a side street off Tottenham Court Road and unbeknown

---

[5] In 1953 Alfie Hinds was convicted of a robbery of £35,000 at the department store Maples in Tottenham Court Road. He continually pleaded his innocence and twice escaped from prison and once from the Law Courts. Fraser is talking about the first escape in 1955, when he managed to stay out 245 days. After his third escape in 1958 he was not re-arrested for over two years. Hinds eventually sued Bert Sparks, the officer whose evidence had convicted him and who had published his memoirs in the *People*. He was successful and was awarded £1,300. The Court of Appeal was not impressed by the result and refused to quash Hinds' conviction.

to him Freddie Sewell, who was later done for shooting the copper in Blackpool,[6] was employed by Warren Street car dealers who worked nearby. He used to get £100 whatever sort of motor he nicked. They would then sell it on. This night he was asked to nick a Landrover. He hadn't walked two turnings and there's a lovely Landrover. As I said, Alf was very mean and engine-wise it needed work done, which he wouldn't pay for. Freddie only drove two or three turnings and he knows it's useless and he just abandons it. Alf comes out of the pub and it isn't there. What he thought was that if he didn't report it some kid would do a grab with it and he'd be in even more trouble. He never dreamed if he walked two or three turnings it would be found. So he reports it to the police station and that's what put him in the vicinity of Maples. Then there was a bit of verbals and some fibres found on his clothing against him. He wasn't innocent, of course, but he never knew till the day he died how he really came to be in the frame. In fact apart from the bad luck with the car he'd been really clever. He'd had the keys from an employee, but he blew the safes rather than use them. If he had it would have been clear it was an inside job.

Now he'd escaped from Nottingham Prison along with Patsy Fleming and there was a hue and cry after him. It was tremendous news. All sorts of people wrote to the papers about the case and how Alfie

---

[6] On 23 August 1971 Sewell shot and killed Superintendent Gerald Richardson, head of the Blackpool Borough Police, in an armed robbery in the Strand, Blackpool. He received life imprisonment, with a recommendation that he serve a minimum of thirty years.

could survive on the run. John Allen, 'the Mad Parson', had his say in one of the papers, and so did a wartime escaper from Colditz, and Geoffrey Household who wrote that book *Rogue Male*.

It was Bill and me who set up the interview with Duncan Webb about Alfie for the *People*. Webb was keen on hanging around Billy and he asked me if Patsy would like to earn a few quid whilst he was on the run. He would get a story in the *Sunday People*, and it would help Alfie Hinds who was still protesting his innocence. Patsy Fleming would get a grand for his troubles. I asked Patsy, who in turn asked Alf who said of course. We, that's me and Billy, arranged for Patsy to meet Webb outside a phone box in Penton Street near the Angel between 6 and 7 in the evening. Webb and Fleming had never met and there had to be a password: 'Where can I get a cup of coffee?' Patsy would then give him the letter and there would be a photographer 10–12 feet away to get a flash. Billy Hill and I were to be around the corner in a car to take Patsy away with us.

As we were walking up a turning, what is there but a police car coming. We honestly thought Webb had shopped us. Patsy wants to get on his toes but Billy took hold of his arm and said, 'I've faith in Webb. Keep walking.' The police car came straight by us. We went back to the car and toured the area. Webb is there by the phone box. It's pissing down with rain and he's been walking around asking everybody where he can get a cup of coffee. So then Patsy gives him the envelope and in the paper that Sunday, Duncan Webb says he's had a mystery telephone call. He's thought it might be a trap to give him a hiding, and that's why he had a photographer. The letter was from Patsy saying he was sleeping in hedges, and that it was he who had opened the doors at Nottingham and Alf had just followed him. Webb got his story; Patsy got a grand and everyone was happy.

After that I took Patsy down to Brighton with me for a bit, but he would go out drinking. I tried to tell him that Brighton was like a little village, and when fresh faces came down from London it didn't take long for them to be recognized. So after a couple of weeks I pushed him gently back in the direction of London. He was recaptured when he did another bit of villainy, and this time he got eight years' preventive detention.

Billy could do what he wanted with Webb. I think Duncan was frightened he'd get a hiding because of Donald Hume's wife. Hume had been convicted after a re-trial for the murder of Stanley Setty. On the second go round the prosecution were in a mess, because it wasn't popular to hang someone when the jury had disagreed; so Hume was offered a plea to being accessory. He thought he'd get 2–3 years; he never dreamed he'd get twelve, and he wasn't pleased. That's when his wife divorced him – she was a night-club hostess – and married Webb. He'd gone to interview her and wound up marrying her. By now Webb was shit scared. Hume's time was getting on and he was up for remission. Duncan wanted protection and Hilly was intelligent enough to know that he could feed Webb with information and Webb could be useful to him.

Bill used to wind Webb up something rotten. We'd be sitting in Peter Mario's restaurant in Gerrard Street and Billy would say about Hume, 'What's he like, Frank? You've done bird with him.' And I would nod and say, 'He never forgets, Bill, he never forgets.' And you'd see Duncan literally cringe and shrivel.

I saw Donald Hume late last year. He'd been out some time and I recognized him right away. The last time I'd seen him had been in Dartmoor years ago. He'd been playing table tennis with 'Yocker' Robinson, a good-time thief, who was in for robbery with violence. Hume was losing fairly badly and he fell on the ball and crushed it so the game had to be called a draw. We only got a ball every six months, and we could have killed him.

Fred 'Yocker' Robinson came from Notting Hill and had been a professional boxer. He'd had about nineteen fights and won every one of them, but he then went into thieving instead. He got eighteen strokes of the birch and nine months for robbery with violence in about 1941. He was arrested again in 1942 and then he got Borstal. He had an elder brother, Wally, who was also known as 'Yocker'.[7] Wally was serving a sentence of three years in 1953 and was also waiting to go up for the second big mail van robbery. The Billy Hill one twelve months before in Eastcastle Street had been successful but Wally, another man called Bill and the Josephs brothers failed in theirs. The older 'Yocker' died of cancer in prison before he come

---

[7] 'Yocker' was turn-of-the-century fairground slang for a fool or a chump. It was probably a corruption of yokel.

to trial. The others wound up with fourteen years'
preventive detention. Some people who got convicted
of another mail van robbery did very well out of Wally
'Yocker's' arrest. A policeman had been badly injured
and three men were convicted – Lennie Emery who
got ten, Arthur Thompson who got seven and Eddie
Power who received four.[8] As it happens they were
all innocent, and when Wally Robinson and the others
were caught they admitted they'd done it. Emery and
the others were released, granted a free pardon and
given compensation. I think Emery got £750 and the
others a bit less. Inside of weeks of getting released,
Emery did another job and got eight years' PD.

Bill was a great fixer. For example, when the
cat-burglar Raymond Jones' brother Taffy nicked
Slip Sullivan over a stabbing Billy Hill got into Ray
who, in turn, sorted it out with his brother. When
his Polish girlfriend stabbed Slip Sullivan, Billy got
hold of Slip's brother Sonny. He went to see Slip,
who was dying. Sonny made a statement saying his
brother had told him it was an accident. He was never
charged.

That autumn, Bill's book with Duncan Webb came
out and there was a great party at Gennaro's which
was a big restaurant with a complete warren of rooms
on the upper floors in Dean Street, where the Groucho
Club is now: Lord and Lady Docker came along, and
when Albert and I were wandering about looking for
Bill we opened a door and there was Hilly giving her
ladyship one. Albert gave her a slap; he thought it was

---

[8] This Arthur Thompson is not the legendary Glasgow gang leader.

My mother.

Below: On holiday in Southend after my father
eceived compensation for his injuries. From left: me, my sister
Kathleen, my mother, my sister Eva, and Jimmy my brother.

All unacknowledged pictures are courtesy of the author

My sister Eva on an outing of the Bingo Club in the early 1950s. Eva is third from the left in the front row.

Above: At the publication party at Gennaro's for Billy Hill's book, *Boss of Britain's Underworld*. From extreme left to right: Bobby Warren, Tommy Falco, Battles Rossi (smoking), Billy Hill (in bow tie), Ruby Sparks, me. I can't remember who is next to me but on his left is Franey Daniels. On his left is Cherry Titmuss. At the back wearing glasses is Johnny Rice. The girl is Albert Dimes's sister and on her left is her husband Russian Bill. I don't know the policeman playing the piano.

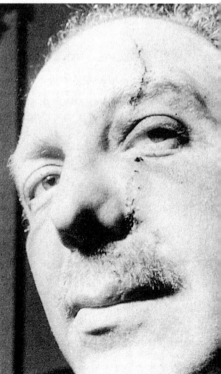

Jack Spot and his injuries.
© Topham

Billy Hill in 1956
at the time of the
Spot-Dimes fight.
© Mail Newspapers

Below: Albert Dimes
celebrates his
acquittal after the
Spot-Dimes trial.
©Topham

Jack Spot at the races
in about 1957.
© Topham

The barrister
Patrick Marrinan.

Above: Errol Garner, the pianist, and me at the Astor Club.

Robert Warren in 1965.

1960. Master escaper Alfie Hinds on his way to
Parkhurst Prison on the Isle of Wight.

© Topham.

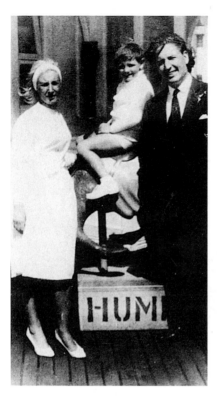

Me, Doreen and Francis
in the early 1960s.
© S&G Press Agency

Me on holiday in Jersey
© S&G Press Agency

disrespectful because her husband was at the party. I just burst out laughing.[9]

In March 1956 Duncan Webb was awarded over £700 against Spot who'd broken his arm. He had already nicked him, and Spot had been fined in the police court. Spot was fed up with Webb writing Billy's memoirs and it all being 'Billy this and Billy that' and none of Spotty.

At the trial Spot made poor Harry White, who was terrified of him, give evidence. The story was when he came home from the races Spot came with him because White had a lot of money on him. That's why Spot had a cosh with him when he hit Duncan Webb. The problem for him was he couldn't ever give a proper explanation why. Hill didn't give Spot any help over the Webb case, but he could have squared it up if he'd wanted to. In fact he was probably geeing Webb up to go on with the action. Archie Hill, Bill's brother, once said to me, 'If Bill ever gets nicked, his downfall could be Duncan Webb. If the law ever gets into Duncan he won't stand up.' Fortunately for everyone it never happened. What happened was, he went on an assignment to Burma, got bitten, got a virus and died.

About that time Bert Marsh put up a winner for us. It involved a man called Fearless Fred who never did a day's bird in his life. You'd never look at him twice. He was an unassuming little man with glasses and was

---

[9] According to Edward Hart in *True Detective* (September 1993), Lady Docker had asked for police protection when she went to the party. Instead she was provided with a minder, Ted Bushell. After the party Lady Docker was quoted in the *Daily Mirror* as saying, 'I didn't know Mr Hill before, but now I think he's a charming person.'

a very, very good thief. He had a second-hand car
business and a parking lot somewhere over in Ealing.
Bert stuck up this wholesale snouter[10] from Southend.
The man used to go to the dogs three times a week
– Harringay, White City and Hackney. You never
knew for sure which one he was going to. When he'd
get there he would bet incredible sums on a dog at
odds-on. He couldn't lose, but he'd win nothing in
comparison with what he'd laid out. He'd win £500
or so, and all he would give Bert Marsh was a fiver
for the work he'd done placing the bets which had to
be put on at the track. So, after a bit, Bert was fed
up with this and stuck him up. Lots of people had
a look at it but decided against the job. It was on
offer for twelve months or more. The problem was
the man had a big Austin Princess, and if he went to
White City he would drive to Hainault tube station
on the outskirts of London and leave it. He wouldn't
get out of his car or go down the tube unless there was
other people about. On the other hand, if he went
to Harringay he would drive all the way there. Bert
would get a last-minute phone call from him telling
him at which track to meet him.

I came into the job late and Fearless and I, along
with Cherry Titmuss and Alfie Allpress, were near the
tube at Hainault watching in case he went to White
City. He went straight by so that meant Harringay,
and we'd no chance to follow him. He made it really
difficult. When he got in the car park at the track he
still wouldn't get out until there were people about.

[10] Tobacconist.

Bert then gave us the tip he was leaving before they went into the traps for the last race. We still couldn't do him, but at least we were behind him in two cars and when he got on what was called the Seven Mile Lane – dual-carriageway then which was considered a very fast bit of road – that was the first time he realized we were after him. Our driver was really good; he overtook and forced him to stop. Fearless was in a second motor and we backed on so we got the man before he could lock his doors. We slung him in the back of his car and Alfie Allpress drove it away with me in the back with him. We took him down a country lane and we took the money from him. He had it all over him – overcoat, jacket, socks, money belt, it was unbelievable; the old white fivers, bundles of them. It came to a lot of money.

We left him in his car, took the ignition key and drove off. We took out what we had to give to Bert, a full whack, and shared it out. Then, a week or so later I had a pleasant surprise. The motor that had stopped him was a rung motor which Fearless had had for years. He was convinced the guy wouldn't have the numbers, but to be on the safe side he put it on his car park prominently so if the police had of got the numbers they would have come to Fred first and tell him they were keeping an eye on the motor. After a few days when nothing happened Fred was giving it a good clean, and in one of the pockets he found another £2,000 which we must have put down in the excitement. I got a call from Alfie Allpress to meet him in the Star which was on the corner of Old Street. I came up from Brighton and he gave me another £500. Bert had said he didn't want any more. What a good man Fearless was; dead honest. He could have kept it himself. All the wholesale snouter screamed for was £900. He daren't scream for more because of the income tax.

Two months later when it was arranged that Spot should be done I was given a shillelagh, the same one Spot had given Billy when they were getting on together. Bill and Albert thought if I had a knife I might get carried away and kill him. And I might have done because I think he deserved it, getting hold of those four boys and giving them guns. But Bill and Albert didn't want him dead. Don't get me wrong; they wasn't bothered if he died. Who cared? But the thing was to teach him a lesson. He wasn't important enough to kill. The death penalty was about, but you couldn't care about that because you could easy have killed him by mistake anyway. That's a chance you take. But the purpose was to let him see what a loud-mouthed chump he was.

It didn't work out. We never realized he actually would nick us, otherwise we'd have done it different. He should either have been killed, I should have masked myself up, or no one he knew should have taken part. But I didn't think he would do that. It honestly didn't enter my head. What Spot did was break the most important code of all by going to the police. Here he is, he's cut men for many many years, dished out beatings, cut people just to give his prestige a boost, had Jimmy Wooder chopped by Teddy Machin at Ascot Races, and no one ever went to the police about him. Then he gets hurt and screams his head off to the police. That is the worst thing of all. You couldn't do a worser crime. You can't have it both ways and he did. There was no excuse.

Those who weren't going to be present were going about getting their alibis, just in case. Quite right too because Spot was a very wicked, evil man. Whilst in hospital, when he was interviewed by the police he said twenty-seven people attacked him and gave names. Bill and Albert were clever and they had arranged their alibis because they must have realized he could nick them. But that was also to make sure the police couldn't fit them up, not necessarily Spot. As I was already on the run over Johnny Carter and his slashing it made no difference to me.

A man from Manchester gave us the tip where Spot was going to be. The man had realized what a bad man Spot was and give us the information which was required so we knew what time he would be about and what restaurant he would be in. We waited outside his flat and did him outside 56 Capel Street off the Edgware Road as he and Rita, his wife, came home. Spot had a couple of guys with him, including an Irishman who did the right thing and never picked anyone out on the ID parade.

There was no fee as such for doing Spot. I knew it would stand you in good stead financially in the long run but even if it hadn't I'd still have done him.

After the stabbing I quietly went to Brighton. There was already the Carter warrant out because he'd nicked me and there was no point in staying in town. Once I was back in Brighton I got in contact with Billy Hill, and he arranged for me to go to Ireland. Billy and

I went in one car and Dicky 'Dido' Frett, Ray Rosa and Patsy Lyons followed in another. They were going to stay with Bobby McDermott in Manchester whilst I was going to get the boat for Ireland. Somewhere on the way we lost them. We went on to Manchester to wait for them, but they didn't show and then Bill took me across to Liverpool where I caught the ferry to Dun Laoghaire. Unbeknown to us was the reason – they'd been nicked and put on an ID for a snatch from a jeweller's boot. Apparently the number of the car had been taken and there was a warrant out for them in Leicestershire. This was where Patsy pulled a great stroke. It had been his own car in which he'd been seen but when he got out on bail he nicked a car, rung the plates to the same as his, parked it in Birmingham and called the police. It was enough to create a doubt and he was chucked.

Bill had rented a doctor's house on the outskirts of Dublin and there I stayed leading an orderly existence for about ten days. Then I flew back to London as Dicky 'Dido' Frett and Ray Rosa had been arrested over the Johnny Carter affair and I came back to help them out. They hadn't been picked out on the ID in Leicester and had been brought down to London where Rosa had been ID'd. I felt it was my responsibility to try and see some people to help them. I was nicked at London Airport. I had telephoned England to get someone to meet me and the phone had been tapped so the police knew that I was to be met at the airport. I didn't have a clue. I came off the plane like any ordinary traveller and half a minute later I was surrounded.

Among the twenty-seven people Spot named first time around were Albert, Bill, Tommy Falco and me. They'd been having a meal in a genuine restaurant, one where they were sure they'd be remembered. Then Spot cut it down to about sixteen and once more the police went to work. They went back to Spot again and he made a third statement. He stuck to me, Bobby Warren, 'Battles' Rossi, Billy Blythe and Ginger Dennis. Bobby and 'Battles' were innocent. 'Battles' was miles away at the dog racing – he was a gambling fanatic. And Bobby arrived after it was all over. That's why he walked in the nick and made a statement saying he was innocent. I couldn't do that because of the Carter trouble.

Just before this Billy had been to see Jimmy Wooder to ask what the story was that he had been prosecuted by Spot for cutting him before the War. When Jimmy told him, I don't think at first Hill believed him. He sent him to Bow Street to get the depositions and had copies made and posted up in clubs over London.

When Bobby Warren and I were at Bow Street in May 1956 Billy arranged that all the people whom Spot had cut, including Jimmy Wooder, should be in the public gallery. There was at least ten men in the gallery at the committal proceedings – all men whom Spot had cut, and none of them had ever nicked him or even ever thought about such a thing. They were there to let him know. He went white when he saw them. All Spot had to do was say, 'They're not the men' – meaning me and Billy Blythe – and we'd have been slung then and there.

Instead, at the committal when Spot was asked if

he recognized us he said, 'I don't know who was there.' This was cunning. When Bobby Warren and me went for trial Mr Justice Donovan allowed Spot to be made a hostile witness and his three statements were produced. It was bad luck that Patrick Marrinan asked a police officer whether Rita hadn't made a statement naming other people as well as Bobby and me. The copper replied, 'No, it was Mr Comer.' And as a result all his statements came out.[11]

Patrick Marrinan defended Bobby Warren; he was a brief who seemed to come from out of nowhere. When I got the three years for the cigarettes no one had even heard of him. But from 1952 onwards his name came into focus. I heard his name time and again whilst I was away, and when I came out from Broadmoor in 1955 he was the predominant figure. I had had many drinks with him at Bill's flat over at Barnes. He was a good drinker; he'd start with Guinness and go on to Irish whiskey. Then he lost his brief when his phone was tapped and he was slung out of the Bar. It led to the Denning Report on phone taps. I think Marrinan was a rebel. It was the unfairness and corruptness of the legal profession he fought against. Also he got better money from fighting hard for a case. Bill was intelligent enough to recognize this.

Billy Blythe and 'Battles' Rossi had gone over to

[11] Dismissing Fraser's application for leave to appeal, the Court of Appeal said, 'Where a Crown witness gives evidence on oath in direct contradiction of a previous statement made by him which is in the possession of the prosecution, it is the duty of counsel for the prosecution at once to show the statement to the judge and ask the judge's leave to cross-examine the witness as hostile.' [40 Cr App R 160]

Ireland after me and they stayed in the same doctor's house. Tommy Butler, the main copper in the Train Robbery, just about kidnapped them over the border into Northern Ireland. They were on the court steps after they were released by the magistrate when he did it. Marrinan flew to Ireland to defend them over the extradition without being instructed, and that caused his downfall. Later in the early 1960s he was accused of obtaining false passports along with Brown, the man who'd had the Bucket of Blood Club in Brighton, and who'd gone to the police about Charlie Ridge and the Brighton detectives. Patrick got some bird I think.[12]

The other lawyer you could get into was Ellis Lincoln. He was bent, but not in the way Patrick was. With the likes of Lincoln, he would take your

---

[12] Marrinan's downfall came in June 1957. In October 1956 he had made a complaint against the police alleging perjury in the case of Blythe, Rossi and Dennis. Now the Establishment hit back with a vengeance. As a result of the telephone tap on Billy Hill's line, conversations between him and Marrinan were recorded. Disciplinary charges were preferred by the Bar counsel that (1) he associated on terms of personal friendship and familiarity with Billy Hill and Albert Dimes and with Robert or Albert Rossi, persons who to his knowledge were of bad and disreputable character . . . (3) without being instructed by a solicitor on 29 June he went to Dublin in order to give legal aid and advice to William Patrick Blythe and Robert or Albert Rossi in connection with a charge against them of wounding Jack Comer . . . (3)(d) gave advice and assistance to Blythe and Rossi with a view to avoiding their identification at an identification parade; (4) at the Bridewell Prison in Dublin attempted to obstruct an officer in the execution of his duties; (5) [attempted to obstruct officers] by saying to Blythe 'They are all outside and are going to nick you again. If I were you I should make a dive for it.' Marrinan wrote to the sub-committee inquiring into his conduct, saying he had erred in allowing himself to be imposed upon by worthless people, and asked that he be suspended rather than be expelled. His plea was to no avail. He returned to Ireland and became a successful solicitor there.

money and still shop your defence. It was a chance people took. He played it both ways. Patrick did not. If he defended you, he defended you. But he hadn't a good appearance. He had the brain but not the talk. Marrinan had it up there but a very poor speaking voice. In his enthusiasm to do his best he stuttered. A barrister has to have a lot of the actor in him which helps to carry the day. If he gets overheated he loses a lot of the punch, and that's what was wrong with him.

On the other hand Marrinan had a razor-sharp mind. My alibi for the slashing of Spot was that I was in the office of a bookmaker who was taking bets over the phone for an evening at a dog meeting. They were called SP offices in those days. Sammy Bellson was to be a witness, along with another man who worked in the office. When Reginald Seaton, who was leading counsel for the Crown, was cross-examining me, he asked how many phones there were and what colours they were. I'd been to the office but I'd never worked there and I was in a bit of a quandary. I hadn't squared this with my witnesses at all, and whatever I said they was stuck with; they would have to answer correctly and it could be fatal. I see Patrick Marrinan who was representing Bobby Warren looking at me very intently and instinct told me that I could say whatever I wanted and somehow he would see it was conveyed to my witnesses. It was proved correct. I said there were three phones, one green, one red and one black or whatever. Marrinan stood up, bowed to the judge rather indicating he wished to go to the lavatory. Out he went – security was not the same in those days –

and he saw my two witnesses and told them what I said. He came back and looked at me again; it told me he'd done it. Both witnesses gave exactly the same evidence as I had done. Not that it did me any good. Those three statements of Spot did for me, plus the fact that I said I was a great friend of Billy and Albert. They said I should have said I just knew them, but I couldn't bring myself to deny that they were my friends. Bobby and me both got seven years.

Marrinan came to see me in prison and wrote out the appeal forms the next day. He told me that Quintin Hogg, who later became Lord Hailsham, would be representing us. He came a second time along with Mr Hogg to say as he was now in the Cabinet he had to withdraw. Marrinan brought two ounces of tobacco and slipped them over to me. I don't think Mr Hogg realized what he was doing. Even though I don't smoke, I didn't like to tell Pat that. How could I refuse when he'd smuggled the tobacco in? Eventually I had Bernard Gillis, who later became an Old Bailey judge, plus Patrick on the appeal, but it didn't do us any good at all although it was reported in the *Law Reports*.

Afterwards Spot opened the Highball club in Bayswater and had Johnny and Benny Harris nicked over breaking it up. They were also nicked for GBH on Harry Carter, Johnny's brother.

Benny Harris, I think it was, had a straight fight with the Carters in Benny Coulston's The Sunset Club in around 1955. Whilst Harris and one of his friends were beating Johnny and Harry Carter, their half-brother Buey and another man crept behind them with bottles.

It was a complete turn-round then. The Harrises never went to the police to make a complaint. I don't even think they went to hospital, but after that they went looking for the Carters who were now protecting Spot and did Harry. They found Harry Carter in a totter's yard in Trundley Road, Deptford, and did him properly. He immediately went to the police and they were arrested for it, Harry giving very damaging evidence. He'd taken the number of the van they'd used and their fingerprints were in it, but I'm happy to say they were found not guilty at the Old Bailey despite his evidence. They said they'd got a lift over Waterloo Bridge on their way home from Covent Garden, and that was how the prints must have got there, and the jury believed them.

Then in 1957, whilst looking for Johnny Carter, the Harris brothers went to the Highball and smashed it up. They were arrested for that and, with Rita's evidence being vindictive and Spot hiding behind her as usual, the Harrises were convicted along with another man and got twelve or fifteen months. It was the last thing that Spot and Rita should have done. This time the club had to go, and it was eventually set on fire. Spot and his wife had broken the code of conduct time and again by going to the police, and it was burned down completely. If you go to the police like Spot and his wife done, then you pay the consequences. No one was ever charged with that one. Nor was anyone charged when Johnny Carter was run over in Peckham and then beaten up three or four times. Some people called Dunne were said to have driven the car, but Carter had learned by this time and never went to the police. If I hadn't been away I expect I'd have been blamed. The Carters were finished then; they just faded away. Johnny's been dead years.

7

During that Spot sentence I was moved pretty regularly. I went straight to Wandsworth, then to Bristol and on to Pentonville, and just after I arrived there so did Alfie Hinds. He'd been recaptured in Dublin. He'd bought a tumbledown cottage and was renovating it and he was caught when he went to collect tools he needed at Dun Laoghaire. He was arrested and was brought back to Pentonville. The next few weeks he spent his time trying to force the authorities to charge him with escaping from custody. They didn't want the publicity but eventually he managed it; it was all part of a campaign to re-open his case. Now, in the meantime, Alfie had another idea for a great escape, and I think it might have worked.

In the 'Ville there was also another man, Ernie Gregory, who'd done about five years of twelve for a GBH on a publican at the Elephant. His brother, Alf, had got seven. In fact, the man who'd attacked the publican was Paddy O'Nione who was always known as 'Onions'. He's dead now – shot outside his son's wine bar near Tower Bridge by, so the police say, Jimmy Davey. We'll never know because Jimmy

Davey died in a chokehold at Coventry police station. The police say he attacked an officer as he was being taken from his cell for an interview.

Well, there's Lennie Emery, Ernie Gregory, Jimmy Essex and me in Pentonville, along with Alfie Hinds who was still protesting his innocence and wanted to smash his way out of the workshop. The idea was to use a great big long but slim table which was out in the yard, and make a run for the wall. There were legs on the table, and if we'd put it on its end they could have been used like rungs on a ladder and we could then have given each other a heave to the top. There were no security fences in those days. You didn't even need to get the keys off the screws. All it wanted was split-second timing. There'd have to have been transport, a couple of cars parked, the other side of the wall. There was no good getting the other side and then running round the streets in distinctive prison clothing without the transport waiting. It was a brilliant idea and it would have worked, because it was easy enough to do. But before it could be put into operation, Alfie was sent to Lincoln en route for Nottingham to be charged with his first escape in November 1955, and I was transferred to Wandsworth. So that was the end of that.

Actually I've never been lucky with escapes. I've always ended up at a prison which has just had one, or been moved before one came off. In fact, I think the nearest I ever came was that run for the wall at Feltham all those years earlier.

The reason for my transfer was the same old story. Lennie Emery had a ruck with a screw and I got

involved. Funnily enough the screw who Lennie Emery
whacked was one of the two that Hinds locked in the
toilets at the Law Courts in May the next year when
he got out with the help of Tony Maffia – I was
in Dartmoor, and we all cheered when we got that
news.[1] The screw pulled his stick out on the landing
at slopping-out time where he was having a few cross
words. He went to hit Lennie and Emery really done
him. The whistles were going and I and a few other
prisoners wouldn't let them get hold of Emery unless
we could be assured he wouldn't be beaten up.

It was now a confrontation with fifty prison officers
and ten or so prisoners with Lennie behind us. The
Chief Officer and the Deputy Governor came to the
landing and assured us there would be no violence,
but he'd have to be put on report. I asked Len if
he was satisfied with this and he said he was, so he
was then taken down the punishment block. Later
on we heard he had been knocked about down the
block. As we were all locked up there was no way we
could confirm this, so we started smashing our cells
up and shouting out the windows. Screws bashed in
the door and I was immediately taken straight to
Wandsworth. From there I went to Lincoln where
Alfie and Frank Mitchell, who the Krays later got
out of Dartmoor, already were. It was there I did
a grass and a screw and in an indirect way brought
a libel action because of it. Not that it did me
much good.

[1] Hinds only lasted a few hours on the outside on this occasion but
he later escaped once more, this time staying out for twenty months
before being arrested near Belfast where he was ringing cars.

Alfie Hinds, Frank Mitchell and me were on Governor's applications when the screws brought a man named Harry Cowans by us to get some socks from the part-worn store. Cowans had been the driver in an armed robbery where they'd cleared £37,000 in Nottingham in October, and had gone and grassed on his mates. It had been a really good snatch, with a car with the same plates as the getaway car deliberately left two miles up the road in the other direction. In return for his evidence he'd been given eighteen months. Cowans was a big hulking man, 6' 4" or so, and the screws had him working in the laundry to keep him away from the rest of the prisoners. I don't know why they brought him past the applications that day, not when there was plenty of us about who knew who he was, as well as the guys he'd grassed. It must have been some sort of a get-up, because working in the laundry he could have got socks at any time. He was brought right by us and I asked Frank and Alfie what they were going to do. Alfie didn't want to know, so Frank and I just flew at him and gave him a right beating. As the screws dragged us off I did one of them and so it was down into the strong cell. I got two months' loss of remission for the grass, five for the screw and fifteen days' No. 1 diet followed by twenty-eight days' No. 2. When I was finished I was transferred to Durham.

In May 1957 I was sent to Dartmoor. The train from London went down on the second Tuesday of the month and one good thing about the journey was that your friends could come and see you off at Waterloo Station – unofficially, of course – and give you food for the journey. The day I went down, Billy and Albert were going to bring me some when I was told there was going to be no grub allowed us from outside. What had happened was that they were very good, top men, the fellows at Dartmoor. If you had your visits you were brought to London so that your family didn't have to travel all the time. One man was going to his visits; a gun had been smuggled in and he was going to use it on an escape. The gun had been driven down and left in the quarry and he'd got it into the prison. It was a fantastic feat. The night before you left Dartmoor you always went down the block for thorough searching, but somehow or other the gun was smuggled on to the train. One of the prisoners was going to shoot the screws. He asked to go to the lavatory and had his cuff taken off to do so. Then, at the last minute, his nerve went and he hid the gun and the bullets in the toilet. It would have been a topping offence if a screw had been killed. The cleaners found the gun the next day and so it was headlines in the papers what with me being on the train. Was it a plot to release me? In fact it was nothing to do with me at all. That's why they didn't want us to have the grub. I kicked up murders and in the end they let us.[2]

The food on the Moor was truly disgusting and it reached a stage where I decided to test the prisoners' reaction for a hunger strike in protest. I knew that if you had a strike for every meal it would crumble because it was asking too much; prisoners could not

[2] In fact another pistol and ammunition were found on the Moor a few days later and R.A. Butler, the Home Secretary, admitted in the House of Commons that there might have been more.

go on day in and out eating nothing at all. On a hunger strike your food was put in your cell, and the next meal-time it was taken away and another plate put in. I hit on the idea of refusing the lunchtime-dinner meal. Breakfast was tea, porridge, a little lump of goulash and a bit of bread and marge. Tea was bread and marge and tea and another lump of the stew. That was the end of your meals. Plus, you also got cocoa for supper. Prisoners could survive without the dinner. The whole prison took part, even the snides and people who might be grasses, even they took part. In about four days the prison was locked up and it got write-ups in the papers in December 1957. It was then the Army was called in to surround the prison.

In less than a fortnight they moved twenty of us who they thought were the ringleaders and put us down on E wing, the dreaded punishment block, where damp just dripped off the walls. Venables, the Prison Director, the same one I saw at Birmingham, was flown there by helicopter. I told him what the food was like. A prisoner called Lithgow had been badly beaten in the block and I had a go about that to Venables as well. I have a feeling in a way he respected me. On a Saturday morning a few days after that my door was opened about 5 a.m. I was handcuffed to screws and I was taken to Pentonville where I was put in a reception cell until the Sunday. I was asked if I wanted to go to chapel; I said no because I'd have missed my exercise. About 10.30, suddenly there's all the Dartmoor screws. I asked what they were doing and they said I was being transferred again, this time it was to Lincoln. I should have gone to Durham, but

at the last minute they wouldn't have me because
Ray Rosa was still there. There I stayed almost three
months before I was moved to Stafford.

Bainton was the Governor at Stafford and he was
a good man. He'd been a housemaster at Borstal with
me and then Deputy Governor of Liverpool and he,
too, rose to be Director of Prisons. Somewhere along
the line he saw through the prison officers and had
turned right around in his attitude.

Bainton moved about April, and I was almost
immediately locked up by the new Governor because
a prisoner had said I'd given him a right-hander. In
the July I was moved. Again it was done just like
that. Albert and Tommy Falco came to see me that
afternoon, found I had gone to Liverpool and drove
straight on there. When they arrived they were told
they couldn't see me; the excuse given was that Albert
had been a convict and as such wasn't allowed to visit
me. An old screw was wheeled out to say he'd known
Albert in Portland Borstal before the War. For a time
after that they didn't even let Albert write to me.

It was about this time the police were looking into a
conspiracy to pervert the course of justice against Billy
and Albert. After my trial in 1956 Jack Spot had been
done for slashing Tommy Falco, but his defence was
that it was a put-up job by Albert and Bill. In fact, a
Scot called Victor 'Scarface' Russo turned up in court
to say he'd been propositioned to let himself be slashed
and to finger Spot. Anyway Jack was acquitted and
the police were making themselves busy. The *Empire
News* printed a bit to say that I was being interviewed
and helping the police. This was rubbish, because I was

in the strong cell at Lincoln after doing Harry Cowans and the screws and they'd never been near me. It made me look as though I was grassing Bill and Albert and so I sued for libel. Ginger Dennis, who'd got four years for our attack on Spot, smuggled a letter out for me, and I also petitioned the Home Office for permission to sue. The *Empire News* sent a letter offering to print an apology and offering a sum of money, something like £50, but I turned it down. I had the solicitor's clerk, Brian Field – who later went down in the Great Train Robbery – to act for me and he got John Platts Mills, who later defended Charlie Richardson, as my brief. Helenus Milmo, who later became a High Court judge, was for the paper. I didn't do any good. I could show the article was wrong but what damages would anyone award me? The judge said I had no reputation to libel.

I had been brought to Pentonville for the action – it was the day Henry Cooper knocked out Brian London to win the British heavyweight title – and I stayed there until May 1959. It was then I had what was one of my greatest coups in prison – I had buttons put in the locks on the cell doors the evening before Ronnie Marwood was hanged.[3] It brought Pentonville to a standstill that night.

---

[3] Ronald Marwood was convicted of the murder of a police officer who was stabbed to death in December 1959 when he tried to break up a fight outside a dance-hall in Islington. He went into hiding and gave himself up early in 1960. Many thought he would be reprieved and his execution was accompanied by a demonstration outside Pentonville. The police were booed when cinema newsreels were shown. Marwood's execution was one of the planks on which abolitionists founded their campaign in the 1960s.

In prison there were little tin buttons for your shirts with 'Made in HM Prison' stamped on them. At that time they'd just had new modern locks put on every cell door. Instinct told me that so many of these buttons in a lock would jam it. During the day these cell doors were left open, and the hard thing would be to shut the doors whilst we were all at work without the screws noticing. I got six of the buttons and slipped up to a geezer's cell – I was on A2 and he was on A3 – and tried it on a guy who we thought was half a grass to the screws. I shut his door, made a little paper funnel and slipped the buttons into the lock. Then I watched the screw open it quite easily. So the next night I picked another prisoner who was also a bit iffy, and this time put in more buttons. This time it worked. I could watch from my little spy-hole and it took a good three hours to get engineers in to take off the lock and put it on again.

I then got hold of Johnny Isaacs, who is mentioned in Ronnie Knight's book,[4] and 'Little Legs' Johnny Garrett. They were doing three months each in Pentonville and working as cleaners. 'If I get the buttons, can you recruit the other cleaners? You think you can handle it?' I asked, and they said they thought they could. The afternoon before Marwood was due to

[4] *Black Knight*. Johnny Isaacs was with Knight's brother David when a quarrel broke out in an Islington club. David received a bad beating and when Ronnie went with him to the Latin Quarter night-club to remonstrate, David was stabbed to death by Tony Zomparelli who received four years for manslaughter. After his release Zomparelli was shot dead in the Golden Goose pinball arcade in Old Compton Street by Alfie Bradshaw, who maintained he and Nicky Gerard (son of Alf) had been hired by Ronnie Knight. Knight was acquitted of conspiracy to murder and Gerard of the murder.

hang, Jimmy Andrews and I and another guy nicked the buttons from the shop, thousands of them, and made little pouches with string for the buttons and funnels, to be put round the distributors' necks. It was an attempt to try and delay the hanging or to help Marwood in some way.

The cleaners went round closing the doors and putting the buttons in. I'd said to those prisoners I could trust, 'Do your own to save the cleaners' time.' When it came to it they'd managed to do about 300, near enough half the prison, and it caused havoc. But just their luck, a guy went sick in one of the shops about 3 in the afternoon. What would normally happen is the screws would take him to a little cell converted to a sort of pharmacy, and a hospital screw would give him a dose of white mixture and bring him back to the shop. When this guy went sick there was no hospital screw about, so he was taken to his cell on C3 or C4. When he gets there his door was locked. The key wouldn't open it. So the screw tried to put him in the next cell and this too was locked. Then he looked round the landing and the one below and it was the same there. The screw now realizes that there's hundreds more cells been done. Emergency! Fortunately Johnny Isaacs has seen him and now the cleaners were doing as many as they could in the time.

People had to be put in other people's cells and I refused. I said I had me own mug and I wanted to drink from that and no one else's. That night there was a smash-up in the cells and screws were rushed in. The next day we were all locked up. I was nearly opposite where Marwood was hung. Up till then, for an execution all the inmates had to be out of their cells and in the workshops or on exercise by half-past eight. After what I did in May 1959 we were always kept locked up.

The screws never actually found out who did the buttons, but I was the first one moved out after the incident. I went to Wandsworth where Podola[5] was waiting to be hung, and after a fortnight in June 1959 I went to Birmingham. Whilst I was there a prisoner told me a screw who took the mailbags to people on punishment was crooked, and if there was anything I wanted he could get it. I got in touch with Billy Hill, and he sent money to the prisoner's family for onward transmission. The screw used to fetch in little delicacies, chocolate and so on. Sending the money via the prisoner was a safety in the case of emergency, but when it came to it the screw turned out to be a real good fellow. After four months at Birmingham the Prison Director, Venables, interviewed me and said I was being sent back to Dartmoor where I'd been moved from after the hunger strike. First, I was to go to Exeter for a month, but if I was in any trouble I'd go back on the circuit trailing from

[5] In early July 1959 Gunther Podola, born in Berlin and now living in Soho under the name Mike Colato, broke into the flat of a model and tried to blackmail her over some letters he stole. He was traced by the police when he made a call to her from South Kensington station, and whilst under arrest managed to shoot and kill D.S. Ray Purdy and escape. Several days later he was traced to a hotel in Notting Hill and in the course of his rearrest was knocked unconscious. He claimed he had amnesia and so could not give a defence. A jury empanelled to hear this special issue decided he was faking. After a second trial, at which he was found guilty of Purdy's murder, he was hanged.

local prison to local prison every few weeks. Now, although it was an evil place, the Moor had certain advantages. In a way it was a privilege to get there. You weren't allowed radios in local prisons. In fact you had to have done four years in Dartmoor before you got your radio there. By now I would be allowed a radio and also I could have meals in association, perhaps watch a bit of television even. In local prisons like Exeter and Birmingham you had nothing.

A visit to Dartmoor would also be a bit longer than your local prison. Sometimes it would take Doreen five days to visit me. First, she'd have to travel from Brighton to London, stay overnight with my mother, then catch a very early train to Exeter, then get a bus to Dartmoor. By the time she got there it would be too late to see me and she'd stay in the Prince of Wales, a pub which did bed and breakfast in Princetown. She'd visit me the next day and then do the journey in reverse. Billy and Albert offered to bring her down, but she preferred to do things on her own.

So I went to Exeter and there at the end of October I got into really serious trouble. It was all over Jack 'The Hat' McVitie and a screw he decided to have a fight with. You had to walk round the exercise yard in twos, and the screws liked to see a gap of three feet between each couple to prevent people talking to the people behind. Everyone did talk, but now and then a screw would put his arm out, halt the pair behind and, when there was a gap, let that pair go on. You could sometimes tell that certain prison officers would have it in for certain persons and they would deliberately stop a particular person or couple.

McVitie eventually got annoyed being stopped continually and said, 'Why don't you leave me alone? Why do you keep doing this?' The screw pushed him and told him to get on with his exercise. With that McVitie couldn't stand it any more and squared up to him, saying, 'Come on, me and you.' The screw said, 'All right', and they started fighting. The prisoners made a circle so the other prison officers couldn't interfere. It was a fair fight, and McVitie knocked him out inside no time. The other prison officers on the exercise yard had rang the alarm bells, but by the time the heavy mob came out the fight was over and the screw was getting up off the ground. No one else had interfered with the fight; it was perfectly fair. Of course, McVitie's in real trouble and we asked what he wanted to happen next. He said he didn't want anyone to be in trouble for him; he would just go in, but would we see they didn't give him a belting, meaning let the authorities know that it was a fair fight and he's gone in quietly. The Chief Officer and about a dozen officers had come running out and Jimmy Andrews, who was a bit impulsive but very genuine, said to the Chief, 'It was a fair fight and he's going in without causing trouble. Don't lay a finger on him or you'll get it.' The beaten screw didn't confirm it but he didn't deny it, which is an indication it had been a fair fight. That was about all you could expect him to do. By tradition he didn't have to admit it, but his silence was acquiescence.

But what Jim said to the Chief was unfortunate. To say that in those days was like a red rag to the bull. It was a challenge that if they laid a glove on McVitie there'd be a retaliation. Once you said anything like that, they would beat McVitie up just to see what you would do. Sure enough after the exercise finished and we were in the workshop, prisoners in the shop who'd gone in to get their pay and go to the canteen told everyone how the heavy mob had gone to McVitie's cell in full view, opened it up, brutally beaten him with sticks and kicks and slung him down the stairs to the punishment cells.

Jimmy Andrews and me discussed it and he said, 'Shall we smash the shop up, Frank?' I said no. It was old-fashioned and had been done too often. We should do something different, much better. He said, 'What?' and I said, 'Let me think about it.' After a few minutes I suggested that the next day when the Governor and Chief came into the workshop, as they had to on a daily basis, we would knock them both out. Jim thought that was a terrific idea and was all for it. But, I said, first we should make an official complaint on Jack's behalf. In those days you worked on a Saturday morning and although you could still make a complaint and see the Governor, the authorities would do their best to stop you making an application that day. I said to Jimmy that we should insist.

I knew from experience that the Governor himself would try to kid us and get us out of his office without registering our complaints. So I told Jimmy to make sure it was written down. Then if we were charged and taken to court, at least it was all written down and we'd got some sort of defence going for us. And that's what we did the next morning.

They tried to pooh-pooh us but we did make our

complaint officially. However, the Governor at the time – Rundle-Harris, a big arrogant man – was dismissive of our complaint and told us in turn to, 'Get out the office'. In a way the Governor had done us a favour. It was a big thing to attack the Governor and Chief. After sleeping on it your nerve might be failing, but now we were fuming. He didn't have to be so arrogant and he could have said he'd investigate it as a governor should do. Screws loved a governor like Rundle-Harris. Any governor who was hard was adored by the prison officers. Screws hated a governor with reforming instincts, and did what they could to thwart him by not co-operating until he got the message. Lawton, for example, would come in a workshop, look at a group of prisoners and say, 'There's some noise coming from that direction.' Next day there'd be five or six on report. There hadn't been talking; it was to keep prison officers on their toes. The prisoners would lose remission and have a bread and water diet. He ran the prison on sheer fear.

When we got back into the shop, which was in a Nissen hut, there was a surprise. We had a little job tucked away at the back. The Governor would stride through it, the officers would stand up, salute and give the tally of men. My worry was I might not be able to get to them in the time. Now we found we'd been moved to sew mailbags in the front row. The prison authorities and officers had done this over Jim's remarks about warning the Chief Officer. By putting us sewing mailbags they were looking to see what we would do. They looked surprised that we accepted this meekly and didn't complain. Now the Governor would have to walk directly in front of us with the Chief. By now we'd alerted those fellow prisoners we could trust to tell them not to get into trouble. It would be just the two of us. Everything went lovely, couldn't have planned it better.

'All correct,' like a hawker round a market. With that Andrews and I were off our mailbag stools and knocked them out. As the Governor was going down he shouted out, 'What's that for?' And I said, 'It's for you doing for McVitie.' We just walked over to the door, the pair of us, and stood there waiting for the heavy mob to come.

We went out with them – no trouble or anything – and were locked up in our respective cells. Not a blow was struck, but we knew from experience what would happen next. I could have delayed things and barricaded, but eventually they'd have smashed their way in. I'd have only been postponing the inevitable. There were no tools to use in the cell to keep them out with. Sure enough, inside five or ten minutes in they come and I got the usual treatment, only this time double. We were both really paid. We were put in the strong cells in the punishment block, and in fact our punishments were so severe both of us were taken to the Royal Devon and Exeter Hospital. For this to happen in 1959 you had to really, really be hurt. I had untold stitches, broken ribs, cuts, bruises. I was black and blue all over and urinating blood, but that would be par for the course after a beating. I was then brought back and put down the punishment cells again and remanded to see the Visiting Magistrates. We went in separately. If you got corporal punishment you didn't lose remission or any other punishment. I was awarded eighteen strokes of the birch, which was the maximum. Jimmy Andrews got fifteen and McVitie twelve strokes.

It was now Billy Hill and Eva started to go to work. Bill's tame M.P., Captain Mark Hewitson, travelled down with Albert Dimes and my sister. Albert and Eva came in first to see me, and then when they went I had a proper visit from Hewitson. Eva told me the attack on the Governor had made the headlines of the *Daily Mail*; it caused an unbelievable amount of publicity. Hewitson made me take my shirt off so he could see the bruises all over my back for himself. The screws didn't like it, but they couldn't stop him because he'd come down for that very purpose with the Home Office's sanction. So when he raised the matter in the House of Commons he knew what he was talking about. He raised a motion, something which was very rare, suggesting that the 'hoodlum warders had a Belsen mentality'. The House had to stop and debate it. Of course it was all denied. The Home Secretary said I had only minor injuries, and had been taken out of the prison not for treatment but to have an X-ray on an old shoulder injury. He said there had been no trouble since Rundle-Harris had taken over as Governor four years earlier. Unfortunately Hewitson's help rebounded on us. The Home Secretary who had to authorize the corporal punishment went into the matter, and to our great disappointment we were informed he had not approved the birching. As a result I lost 400 days' remission, Andrews 300 and McVitie 200, plus we were all put on bread and water in solitary confinement. The screws weren't pleased either. As I've said, they'd have loved it because the birch was worse than the Cat.

I was sent back to Birmingham where I was on bread and water again, and when I finished that the Governor, Richards, who'd been at Durham with me, told me the Home Office had said I was to remain in solitary confinement. I was right at the end of the landing, with the instructions that three prison officers had to be with me. But the officer who Billy had straightened came to see me on his own and produced a box of tags to hook on mailbags. This was to be my work in my cell. Underneath were a lot already done, and underneath that were toothpaste, soap and a bar of chocolate. This went on for seven months. Every so often the screw would bring me something, and all the time the money would go to the prisoner's home where he would collect it.

The Chief Officer there was called Garrett; I thought he was an animal of a man. All the food was brought by an officer, complete solitary confinement. Another officer asked if I would like a bit of onion with the cheese. I said, 'Yes, of course,' and next time he pulled out half a dozen spring onions from his pocket. I said 'Thanks' and marged me bread and cut up the little bit of cheese and the onions. Right out of the blue, about five or seven minutes later, the door opened and there was Garrett and three screws. He'd brought the result of a petition I'd written about my treatment and he saw the onions. He went to grab them, but I got to them first and ate them. I was laughing but it put a seed in Garrett's head: 'How could I have got the onions?'

They knew it would be a waste of time asking me, but they knew no prisoner could have given them to me.

In the June of 1960 I went back to Dartmoor. About five months later I was on a barrow party and we were allowed to finish a little bit early to wash up. It was about 4.30 and dark already. A screw came and said I'd got a visit. I didn't bother to ask, thinking it might be a friend who'd been at a race meeting in Devon as we had some pitches at the Haldon Hill track.

There were two or three burly men, and one said he was a Detective Superintendent from Birmingham CID. What do you know about the prison officer? I said, 'You're mad.' 'Then we'll see your sister,' he said. Again I said 'You're mad,' and spat at them. What had happened was the prisoner to who Billy sent the money had finished his sentence, been re-arrested, and whilst on remand Garrett had approached him. He had told him that if the man had any information he was well in with the Birmingham police and it would help him. So now this prisoner cracked up and told him about the officer.

After seeing me they asked the local police to see Eva, as by now Bill had been giving Eva the money and she'd been registering it to the prisoner's home. Luckily her husband, Jimmy, was now a local bookmaker and well in with the Carter Street police. He got to see a copper who blocked the Birmingham CID off, reporting back that there was no truth in the allegation whatsoever. This got the screw off the hook totally. He'd been suspended, but with the police getting no help from Eva and me he had to be reinstated. He sent a message back to thank the pair of us. The last I heard of him, he was promoted and went on with his career.

I never did any fixing of the tabs, and although I was on solitary I was paid and could buy things from the canteen. It gave me the chance to get messages in and out. I could have a visit but my visits were terrible; I'd go in an old visiting box and there'd be three screws behind me and three behind my visitors. I'd only have about twenty minutes.

I stayed where I was down the punishment block even when I'd officially finished my time. Reggie Kray brought Eva to see me, along with the great fixer, Red-Faced Tommy Plumley,[6] and they managed to get a bit in the papers. In April 1960, the man who'd taken over from Duncan Webb in the *People* wrote about how unfair it was, and the local newspapers picked it up. Venables, along with the Governor, saw me in May in Birmingham and said he was considering sending me back to Dartmoor. I could tell he was seriously thinking about it because otherwise he wouldn't have even bothered to see me, and I waited for the Home Office to consider his report. It must have been favourable because I was told in the June I'd be going to Dartmoor the next day. It was quite an experience because the M1 had only been opened a few months and I remember going along it. Bill and Archie Hill and Albert had been to visit me in Birmingham and Bill had arranged for a man known as the Italian Major, who lived in Brighton and whose

---

[6] Red-Faced Tommy Plumley was one of the people who acted as go-betweens when you wanted bail or some evidence dropped out and you had to have someone negotiate with a police officer for you.

brother had a restaurant next to Albert's betting shop in Soho, to see Doreen got her money every week. All in all things were a bit better.

In 1961 I nearly took Joe Cannon's eye out in Pentonville. I was back there for visits and now Joey was doing his seven for armed robbery – he was about twenty when he got it – and he had a name as a grass in prison. At the time Pentonville was reasonably lax – he was on the same landing but in the reception part in A wing. The four landings to the top were cut off, and during the day a door on each side of the landing was open so I could nip in there quick. The reception was usually empty. I think he'd been on home leave and not come back, but then he'd got caught and was in Pentonville before being shipped back to Bristol. He'd only been there a day or two. He knew there'd be people who'd be really after him.

When the prisoners were out of their cells, doors were still left unlocked in the local prisons. I'd gone round, knocked out the spy-hole whilst he was out on exercise and swept up all the glass. I'd got a great big, long needle which was used for sewing mailbags. When he came in and was locked up, I crept up to his cell. He said, 'Who is it?' I said, 'It's me. Look through the spy-hole,' and as he did I stabbed it through. He screamed out and immediately rung his cell bell. I just drifted away. He told the authorities that it was me, but there was nothing they could do because by the time they got to me the needle was long gone and I was back in my cell. It was his word or mine, and the screws weren't going to act just on his word. He was immediately taken to the hospital and then transferred out of the prison.

I went back to Dartmoor, where Reggie and Ronnie Kray came to visit me and told me about Dennis Stafford giving evidence against them. They showed me the cuttings and asked that I put it round to everyone. I saw Stafford about this, and he said he'd been only sixteen when this happened and he didn't realize. Be that as it may, he should have known better. I did put it round the prison and very soon he was transferred out.

That summer the food was so bad I organized another hunger strike at Dartmoor. This was in the August and it was exactly the same performance, almost a repeat of 1957. After a few days they locked the prison up and sure enough the screws came down my cell, took me out and we drove straight to Bristol to catch the train to Durham, which is where I stayed.

Towards the end of my sentence Bill sent a letter to the prison Governor asking him to give me another letter which he enclosed. It authorized the manager of a bank in Cambridge Circus, near the Charing Cross Road, to pay me £5,000. Billy had already sent in cheques for me, 'Dido' and Ray whilst we were in Dartmoor. After my sentence, when I took the letter in the manager couldn't do enough for me. It was obvious Bill was a valued customer.

8

When I'd finished my seven years for the Spot case in Durham, I was collected at the gate by a friend of Billy Hill's who had a petrol station in Holland Park. He was a pilot and had written a letter to the Governor saying he was picking me up and flying me home. He asked what luggage did I have, and what time I was being released so he could check the weather. The Governor called me in to see him and told me this himself. The day before I left, Eva and Ginger Dennis had come and collected most of my stuff and taken it down to London.

When the man picked me up from the gate we drove to Newcastle where the plane was at the airport. I said, 'When we fly back can we go past Durham? Can you get as near as possible?' He said that he thought he could get quite near. 'I'm going to throw a parcel into the prison. It'll be a present for the screws,' I said. He said, 'Yes, of course.'I told him what time the exercise would be, and sure enough I did it. Just before we took off I went to the lavatory and put the mess in a bag. He flew over the prison and I slung it into the yard.

The message from people in the prison confirmed it landed safely.

We flew on down south and landed at Elstree where Billy, Albert, and Bobby Warren were there to meet us. It was great. The bad news was that a fortnight after my release the pilot took two girls who worked at the petrol pumps for a spin on a Sunday afternoon. He must have had a drink or two, and he crashed and killed both the girls and himself.

To celebrate my release there was a party thrown for me at the Pigalle in Piccadilly. It was paid for by Albert and Billy and came to £600 odd, which wasn't a bad sum in those days. The pianist Winifred Atwell was on our table and Shirley Bassey, who used to sing at Al Burnett's clubs, came over. Harry White's daughter, Sandra, was there. She was killed in a road accident in California a few weeks later; she'd been over there making a film, *Ocean's Eleven*. She was a lovely-looking, big girl, only about twenty when she died.

I also went to the Krays' club down the East End which featured in *Sparrows Can't Sing*. There was a whip for me and it came to between £300 and £400, nothing like the £30,000 that's been written about. The Krays hadn't exactly been courting me whilst I was in prison. They'd been to see me in Dartmoor, Pentonville and Birmingham, and they'd brought Eva with them. They got in all right. I'd met Ronnie at a point-to-point when he was with Teddy Machin, but I didn't really know them well. It would be par for the course for them to come and see me in prison and to give me a party when I got out. Everyone rallies round if you're away if you've met them even once or twice. And if someone else is in prison you'll offer to go and see them; it doesn't mean to say they're courting you to get them on your side. Albert, Bill and I must have put £600 into the Kray defence on the Hideaway Club case where they were acquitted, but it doesn't mean to say we were looking for an alliance or anything like that.

After the parties I went to the South of France with Bill and Ray Rosa, Jack's brother, and we stayed in the Carlton in Nice where Bill had an in. We went to the island where the 'Man in the Iron Mask' had been held, and me and Ray Rosa locked Bill up in the cell. We thought that was great even if Billy didn't. But Bill really did the holiday in style. There was champagne when we arrived, and the best rooms. Eventually I had to fly home to be best man at my nephew Jimmy's wedding, and Bill gave me a cheque for him as a wedding present.

At this time I was running the machines with Albert, but I had to go to see the Richardsons to thank them for helping Jimmy Brindle over the beating he'd got from Jack Rosa, Bill Noyes and Eric Mason. Jack had wanted Jimmy to drive him around because he was disqualified, and when Jimmy refused he got a beating. Charlie and Eddie went in search of Jack and the others and really did them in the Reform Club, Lambeth. A short time later it became the Crown and was run by Bobby Welch from the Train Robbery. Later Jack Rosa apologized. It was incredible after all we'd been through together he should do such a thing. He said he must have been completely drunk because, quite apart from him and me going back over the years, Eva and Jimmy had put him up when he came out of the nick.

There was also another problem. Jimmy Essex had been arrested at Leysdown for shopbreaking for which he eventually got eight years' preventive detention. He sent a message for me to get down to Canterbury to see him. I was running one of Albert's betting shops in Mount Pleasant for him although, of course, they weren't in his name: he bet as A. Barnett. During Saturday's racing I went to Canterbury Prison to see Essex, along with Albert. In those days you could take prisoners food on remand. By the time Albert and I got there we were late, and anyway we hadn't anything with us. When we saw Jim and told him how late we were, we said we'd go and buy something and leave it at the gate. Could we help him to get his defence money together? We said, 'Of course.' We said to the screws on the gate we were going to get him some food, and we asked if we could hand stuff in. They said that was all right, but when we came back with sandwiches, chocolates and stuff they wouldn't let us hand it in. We couldn't believe it.

At the time all Governors lived adjacent to the prison (it's the screws' mess now), and so we went and rang the bell of this one's house. His wife answered. We explained our problem and she invited us in and rang her husband up. The Chief Officer was Simmonds; he was called 'Milkbottle' because that was how he was built. He put her through to her husband, the Governor, and he was telling her off over the phone. You could see her face change. 'My husband will be at the gate in five minutes,' she told us, and when we got there he was in a fury. 'How dare you go to my home?' he asked us. We said she'd showed us their bedroom and how nice it was. She hadn't of course, but we were winding him up. 'Now you're seeing us at the gate when before we couldn't get any help.' There was murders; they called the police and we had to explain things to them. Later we sent a parcel in for Jimmy marked, 'Only to be opened in the Governor's presence'. Apparently there was a bucket nearby and the screws were going to put it in it as if there was a bomb in it. Essex protested and it was opened. Of course, it only contained food, cigarettes and money. Another day I went back and we had a good laugh together about it. It was good at the time, but really all this was storing up trouble for me in years to come.

I went to see Eddie and Charlie Richardson and they put in quite a nice sum and immediately I posted it to Essex. That was the first time I ever saw them. Jimmy Wooder also pitched in with some money.

In about the September of 1962 Alfie Fraser, who had done ten years for a robbery on a branch of Martin's Bank, got arrested for a top-quality burglary. I busied myself and got various people who were prepared to give evidence on his behalf, but he was found guilty and got five years. For a time it looked possible I might be arrested for conspiracy to pervert. Albert suggested I get out of the way. He didn't think it was really serious, but if the police got hold of you right away in those days they'd charge you. He said Dick, an American I'd met in Rome with Bert Marsh, would be happy to have me, but it was decided I should be sent to Paris where I was put up by the French Mafia in the Latin Quarter. It was arranged through a man called French Lou who had an off-licence in Soho. I had the time of my life there and was introduced to Edith Piaf. After about a fortnight I was told I could come back. The men bought a present for Doreen and for my boy, and when later they came to London I did the same for them.

Around this time also a man from Brighton, Harry Rogers, got in touch. I remembered him from my days with Sammy Bellson, so I wasn't surprised when he asked to see me. He asked me to join with him; I said I couldn't, I was with Bill, but I'd pop in to him and see if I could help. His wife was having an affair with the manager of his bingo hall in Lewes. He asked me to do him and I did. The guy complained but I got out of it – he couldn't recognize me, and although he'd given a description of the motor to the police I couldn't be linked to it.

Then Rogers wanted me to do the bingo hall in Eastbourne which the man was opening. Bingo was taking off like wildfire, and it would have damaged Rogers if he'd had a rival bingo hall almost next door. I went there about 4 a.m. and put in the petrol bombs. All the prizes were there for the first night's opening. By 6 or 7 in the morning it blew up and destroyed the building. I did several other things for Rogers. He wanted me to go to America and do a guy who'd also been having an affair with his wife, but nothing came of it. I didn't get paid for these things. It was more or less like friendship. He'd give me a drink and that would be that. I'd also introduced another guy who Rogers would give a job to – Jack the Rat.

When Jack the Rat was in Lewes Prison he asked a friend, Joe Lowery, if I could get him a job. This was the sort of thing which would look well in his mitigation: 'My Lord, he has a job to go to and his employer is here in court' – that sort of rubbish. Joe said he was all right. On the other hand Georgie Shillingsford and Billy told me what a rotten man he was, that he'd given evidence against others in London, but I didn't listen. Rogers got one of his men to speak for Jack and he ended up with probation. He was to work in one of the bingo halls, but then later when Rogers turned against me Jack forgot the help I'd given him and he became a prosecution witness. He said I'd hit him with a gun.

Joe Wilkins, who was the nephew of Bert,[1] knew about the work I'd been doing for Rogers and said I was entitled to more money than just the drinks I was getting, but when I asked, Harry Rogers wouldn't pay me. So this particular night I bashed Jack the Rat up outside Harry's house as a sort of warning. I went round to Harry one night and there were the police; he'd called them. Faced with this, Harry said he didn't know who'd been threatening him. He never told the coppers who it was at the time, but he did tell them it was me the next day or so. He nicked me and Joe for demanding with menaces.

---

[1] In 1936 Bert Wilkins was charged with Bert Marsh over the murder of Massimo Montecolumbo at the Wandsworth dog-track. He was convicted of manslaughter and sentenced to nine months' imprisonment.

At that time Joe Wilkins and I were trying to buy the Starlight Club in Stratford Place off Oxford Street. It was a good club and Wilkins had arranged to meet the guy in the Grand Hotel in Brighton to complete the finances. When betting shops became legal, for a short while Bert Wilkins went in partnership with Albert Dimes in his shop in Frith Street. I met him there in about 1963 and that was the first time I'd ever met Joe and I teamed up with him. He was in the one-armed bandits then as well. At the time he was very friendly with Jimmy Evans, who turned out no good and who shot Georgie Foreman.[2] Joe Wilkins was then about twenty-seven, and was a very impressive-looking man with an extremely astute mind. At that stage he'd never been in any trouble, and he was one of the last men I thought would ever get in any. Like all businessmen he was sharp and would cut corners, but he wasn't doing anything illegal at that stage.

Before we completed the deal, every Friday night we would be at the Starlight watching how it was managed, and so I didn't go home until about 2 p.m. Saturday afternoons. Wilkins had a clothing factory in Stoke Newington. He now had better premises and was getting out of the old ones, but he had a

[2] In a quarrel relating to Jimmy Evans' wife, George Foreman was shot on 17 December 1964. Evans was acquitted six months later but on 2 January 1965, whilst he was out on a burglary expedition with 'Ginger' Marks, a car pulled up and a voice called out 'Jimmy'. Marks mistook it for his nickname 'Ginger', went over to speak to the men in the car and was shot. His body was never found. Evans escaped by hiding under a lorry. On 30 October 1975 Alf Gerard, Jeremiah Callaghan and George Foreman's brother, Frederick, were acquitted of his murder on the direction of the trial judge, Mr Justice Donaldson. Ronald Everett had been acquitted earlier in the trial.

flat attached which still had a bit of furniture and that's where we'd sleep. About 6 a.m. one morning in July 1963, the police crashed into the flat in Brighton where I lived with Doreen and they found a gun in her handbag in the wardrobe. They asked her where I was, and she told them she had no idea and so they left. She now had the awful task of trying to locate me. She rang Eva but she didn't know, then fortunately Doreen found this card which said 'Joe's Clothing Factory' with a number on it. She rang and Joe answered. She said, 'Don't come home,' and we left the factory straight away. I was never charged with the gun when it came to it; they were holding it for some reason of their own.

We had no time to do anything because there was a big write-up in one of the evening papers. Although it didn't mention my name it was one of those 'This man is dangerous' stories. Joe Wilkins had a copper straightened and he said, 'You're red-hot, both of you.' Joe picked up his then wife, and baby daughter, and the four of us drove straight to North Wales where we checked into a hotel in a place where Lloyd-George was born. Who owned it? The man and the girl who'd nicked us in the Cabinet fight. Talk about coincidence! To their credit, they never indicated they recognized me or anything. I told Joe this and he said we'd better move on. I said I was sure they'd be all right, after all it had been fourteen years earlier and they hadn't picked us out at the identification parade then.

They had a baby-sitter in the hotel and Joe, his wife and I went to the local pub. We were over in one corner and when I came back with the drinks

I said, 'You'll never believe it, the man at the bar is Dr Lloyd who was at Dartmoor.' Joe said, 'Does he recognize you?' I saw Lloyd looking at me and I thought he might have done. We didn't want to run out, so we had our drinks, said good-night and left. But next day, 31 July, we checked out and moved further on into North Wales.

We had about a week there letting the initial fire die down. For a few days that's when they really look, and then other cases come up and you go further and further down. Joe went to Moisher Cohen and I went to Billy Hill. We stayed in Marble Arch a few days and then Joe got into a copper. He again told us to keep out of the way: 'You're red hot. The longer you can stay out the quicker it'll cool.' As it was a case in Brighton, the Met would soon begin to lose interest. Billy put me up in Chelsea Cloisters for a bit, and after that I went down to Clacton. Now I was on the run and would stay that way for nearly six months.

I knew Joe Wilkins' Uncle Bert first. He's still alive, living on the South Coast. He was always a good businessman. His mother and father had dining rooms in Clerkenwell before the war and they were considered well off. So he had a good background businesswise. Bert then got very well in with George Dawson just before the War ended. Dawson was going from strength to strength, buying surplus Army trucks from the Americans and the British in Germany. He was doing fantastic business with thousands and thousands of trucks, and Bert was involved with him. Bert was one of the very first making trouser zips in a factory somewhere off the

Tottenham Court Road when it was still a novelty, and went on from there. By now he'd dropped anything illegal long ago; he was a very successful businessman. He owned The Nightingale in Berkeley Square which was a well-known club and casino. He didn't need protection; he was friendly with everyone. I heard the Kray twins had once tried to take an interest and he'd told them to piss off and they did. He could call on a lot of old friends if he needed. For instance, when George Dawson was burgled and his wife's mink was stolen, Bert went to Billy Hill to see if he could get it back for George. It was Billy Benstead, who Billy put in the Eastcastle Street robbery, who returned it. By giving the things back he would clinch his position with Billy Hill. Benstead's wife was the daughter of Alice Diamond, the famous shoplifter from the First World War and up to the 1930s. Her team were known as the '40 Thieves', and Billy Hill's sister Maggie was one of them.

Billy Benstead was a fantastic man; he came from an impeccable criminal background. He suffered from asthma and even climbing up drainpipes he used the inhaler. He had very long arms and could go up a drainpipe in seconds. But he had a weakness; he was a fantastic gambler, so he had to keep climbing round Belgravia and all the country houses.

In September 1962, a bit before Rogers went bent on me, I'd also been chucking petrol bombs through the windows of screws' houses. I'd drive up to them, throw a petrol bomb made out of a milk bottle with a rag in the top, and off. I put one through the Deputy Governor's window at Pentonville and those of a couple of Principal Officers at Pentonville, then some at Brixton and another at Wandsworth. Then in the *News of the World* one Sunday it said it was me in all but name. Georgie Cornell came with me on one of them, but he wouldn't do it a second time. 'Once is enough, Frank,' he said. In those days the police looked down on the screws and didn't push themselves to talk to me about the bombings, but I'd have been nicked if it had happened now – they work more closely together now because of security. It couldn't have been difficult to work out who was doing it. There weren't too many capable in the first place. With the write-up I'd had, I knew the police would have had no option but to fit me up if I did it again and so I stopped. There'd have been a bent ID or petrol stains found somewhere. It wouldn't have been hard.

So to let things die down a bit I took Doreen and my son and we went to Torquay. Whilst I was there I sent a letter to Jimmy Andrews – who was in for doing a bank with Eddie Power and Patsy Bloggs – asking him to leave a visiting order for me on the gate. I drove to the prison and they wouldn't let me in because of the hunger strike which I had led, but Doreen and my son were allowed in. Jimmy asked if we would send in a photo of my boy, and he got a picture drawn and sent it out. It was lovely. Whilst they were in there visiting I was walking round Princetown pretending I was noting down numbers. Someone saw me and the police were called; in fact I was writing down nothing – just worrying them like they worry people in prison. If you think I shouldn't have done it, remember they'd done cruel things to me and terrorized other people's wives and mothers and children. They'd certainly made my family suffer. Every prison officer knew I'd done it, and later when they said time and again, 'It's our turn,' I accepted it. After about three weeks in Torquay and the fire bomb trouble had all died down, I came back to London.

It was the petrol bombs which got me invited to go on the Great Train Robbery. I had already done the Deputy Governor's drum[3] at Pentonville and I was in the Bon Soir in Gerrard Street one afternoon with Georgie Cornell and several others. Gilbert France, Billy and George Walker and Tommy McCarthy all had shares in it before it became the Hideaway and then, after the Twins' acquittal, the El Morocco. Tom Wisbey was there with two or three others and I was leaving to do some other screws' houses. They half asked if they could come and I said 'No', it would be too many. Everyone hated screws and that's why, a bit later, I was asked to join the Train.

I was on the run for the Brighton thing and had been for a month or more living on a caravan site in Clacton, owned by friends of relations. Doreen and my youngest son were in Brighton at first, and then they joined me in the caravan. Only Eva knew roughly where I was. Every so often I would phone in. Was there any news? Had they managed to find Rogers and talk to him?

Eva didn't know where to find the guy whose caravan it was. Everyone had to wait until I phoned

---

[3] A flat or house.

in and then Eva told me I had to speak to Tom Wisbey. He'd left a message and Eva rang and gave him a train time. I was met at Liverpool Street. It was then he told me about the Great Train Robbery. I was driven straight to the Farm just like that; I was there two nights.

I knew Jimmy Hussey from before when he was doing a five. I'd worked a bit with Bobby Welch and I'd bumped into Charlie Wilson and Roy James in prison. I didn't know White or Goody except casually in prison. I never had met Buster Edwards. I was going to be pulled in for my sheer violence. At that time I didn't realize it, but they thought this guy'll stop at nothing if it had to come to it. It wasn't needed because it didn't. The train driver's injuries were greatly exaggerated. They made a terrific fuss of it. By today's standards it was laughable. People of all ages on the street are being beaten up now, but then the authorities went hammer and tongs about the driver to defuse the cowboy heroes for stopping the train. They played that up for all they were worth. If they'd have told the full truth about his injuries it would have made a great deal of difference to the jury and to the public.

I think it's a fallacy that anyone was really in charge at the Farm. Everybody had their say. There were certain personalities who were more dominant, but everyone had their part to play. In modern times in a major crime like that everybody has to be equal. No one was paid extra; everyone has exactly the same. But if a man lays out serious expenses then obviously he is reimbursed on top.

The Farm was to be strictly run. I think they'd been there only a couple of days before I arrived. I hadn't a clue what I was wanted for but I was ripe for anything. I was more than grateful to be chosen, but their judgement of me was very good. They knew I wouldn't start questioning things – I wouldn't start saying, 'I'll think about it, I'll let you know tomorrow.' If caught with the screws' houses I'd have got life and been lucky to get out alive. In something like the Train I was happy to volunteer to play any role. But after we'd talked it over, with me on the run with the Rogers matter it was reckoned I could be a liability.

It stood me in good stead because no one knew I was attached. I just disappeared again, which again stood me in good stead. Everything is history. Buster says he clobbered the driver, but I don't believe him. When they found out exactly what they'd pulled they were ecstatic. It was mind-boggling with happiness. I think there were five others who were never arrested.

After the Train I did the shrewdest thing ever. I left the caravan and went back to my flat in Brighton. I would only come out in an evening, and once a week I came up to get me money from Bill. If I didn't, people might think I'd been in on the Train. I never told even him. I'd get off the train at Victoria, and walk all the way to Moscow Road where he had his flat and back. That was my exercise for the week. I'd always get off at Hove and walk home; I wouldn't come out again. No one ever see me. I kept a very, very low profile. If in robbery you're put in at the last moment it's almost invariably successful, especially one which has had quite a lot of work put into it. Little bits of information may have leaked out somehow or other, not enough for anyone to be arrested at the scene of the robbery but handy for the police afterwards. If you're the one who's lucky enough to be put in at the last minute you're in with a reasonable chance of great success. Everyone on the robbery may be all right, but in the build-up someone amongst you may have said something to someone they shouldn't have. It's always a possibility, and if you've come late at that stage your name won't be known.

I would have said in August 1963 any number from fifty to a hundred good thieves could have been or would have liked to have been involved in the robbery. What I'm getting at is that the police never nicked that particular fifty to a hundred, so therefore they must have had good information. If they'd had no information of any kind, they would have been picked up and quizzed. Nothing like that occurred. That's why I'm firmly of the opinion they must have had good information. That was standard police procedure in those days – if they hadn't got any leads at all, pull in everyone and question them.

The police did have a bit of luck when Roger Cordery was arrested in Bournemouth with the money in the boot of his car, along with Billy Boal who wasn't on the robbery at all. The police would know who was close to Roger. He was a South London man, and that would be a bit helpful. Given that, they wouldn't look at people from the Angel first. A lot of these people on the Train hadn't been heard of before, and no one would have had a clue that they were capable of doing this type of robbery. I know Charlie Wilson and Bruce Reynolds were faces, but Tommy Wisbey was a proper bookmaker who had two or three betting shops at the time. Buster Edwards had done nothing, fourteen days, something like that. Jimmy White was very good at making keys and suchlike, but he had no form. Bobby Welch had never been arrested. He was a Covent Garden porter; had been for years. You'd never have dreamed he was a train robber in a million years.

By a sheer coincidence Roger Cordery's wife apparently ran off with Jack the Rat just before the Train Robbery took place. That was Cordery's undoing because he had no anchor; that's how he got hold of the idiot Bill Boal. When a 'Roger from Brighton' came up in the enquiry, my name was linked with Harry Rogers. That's how the coppers came to be looking for me. Charlie and Eddie got into one of the coppers on Butler's team and that's how I got out. The London and Brighton police were looking into me, but then I was dropped out.

Billy Hill knew nothing about the Train Robbery. Although he now had a house in Spain he was living in England at the time, and I used to go every week to get my money from him. If he'd heard of it he would have asked me to make enquiries and he would have wanted the lion's share. Having said that, I also emphasize that if Bill had been in control I don't think anyone would ever have been nicked, and the authorities would have been very lucky to have got £100 back. His planning would have been superb. He'd have had plan A, plan B and plan C. He'd have looked at the possibility of the Farm, but I think he would have decided against that and found a place, say a garage or an old warehouse a few miles from Brigedo, but by cutting every telephone wire within a mile radius of the train he would have known you'd have a terrific start. As for the warehouse, he wouldn't have gone to the estate agent's to try to rent it. He'd have had the locks fitted and in an emergency he'd have put the money in there. And he'd have had a plan for how long that money would have been there. Otherwise the money would have gone straight through to London. He would have known it would have been too long in the area. In Bill's case he would have set off from London, but the gear and the motors would have been hidden up there all ready to go. He'd have had all these different plans for the night.

Bill would have insisted that whilst everyone had a few quid to live on, the bulk would have had to be hidden and changed up and this, of course, was the hard part. They'd have had to trust Bill implicitly. No one would have been cheated. They wouldn't have got as much as they actually did, but the difference was no one would have been nicked either. The only way they were nicked was through that Farm. No one was identified. It wouldn't have happened with Cordery because he wouldn't have had his money for about three months from the robbery. No one would have.

Bill would have had the intelligence to deal with that crime superbly. If we look at the comparisons, although the Eastcastle Street was much easier, the sum of money, around £280,000 – eleven years later in 1963 that was near enough the sum of money the Train was. Not one penny of the Eastcastle money was recovered. The £2,000 allegedly from that robbery over which them two men were arrested was returned to them. Bill wasn't greedy. That was why he left some money in the bags at Eastcastle Street. They had a certain amount of time and stuck rigidly to it. Bill was always careful with an alibi. For example, he was with Duncan Webb and Hannen Swaffer as well, at Odhams Press in Long Acre where the *People* were, when the KLM bullion raid went off.

If Bill had known about me and the Train he'd have been pleased, but if the Train had been Bill's thing there's no way he'd have had a solicitor involved, like they did with Wheater and Brian Field; he'd have known it wasn't fair to them. You couldn't expect them to stand up. No way. Bill's planning from the word go would be to get that money back to London straight from the robbery.

To change money would have been easy to Bill. He had contacts in Switzerland, it would have been child's play. He'd been heavily involved in legal and illegal gambling for some time, a great deal of money was passing through his hands. Money could go into banks then and the manager wouldn't blink an eyelid if you put £50,000 into your account. Nor would he be duty bound to inform the authorities. In fact that's the last thing he'd want to do. His clients' private affairs were his responsibility.

Back in 1956, Bill was in Paris when we tried to get the platinum. Alfie Allpress and I found this one; It was really a replica of the KLM robbery.

I'd read in the *South London Press* that there was a platinum firm in Kennington Lane near the Lambeth Magistrates' Court, and that someone had broken in through an office window and had helped themselves to platinum scrap. I went to see Bill, showed him this. He said watch it and I did so. That's when I saw the van which would take the load to a square at the back of Bloomsbury. Then in the evening they would go back and pick it up, put it on a trolley and take it into the van. Three would squeeze into the van front and the others would go to the offices. We tailed the van to where it was garaged, got into the garage and found the keys of the van in the ignition. We had duplicate keys made, and the plan was we were going to take the rotary arm out whilst they were in the office. Once they got in their van on the way home we would jam the doors – they couldn't get into the back. We would have a couple of cars parked – no yellow lines then. The cars would be moved and our van would back on to their lorry. We'd have a car on the pavement and in the road. But by sheer accident and good luck Patsy Fleming saw Flying Squad coppers in the Bloomsbury vicinity having a last-minute conference. We were just going to have a final watch, but it was a ready eye. The Law had found out about it. Bill wouldn't even think about it after that.

In the months after the Train, Joe Wilkins gave himself up and when he wasn't picked out on the ID by Rogers, I knew things were getting better and it was just a question of waiting. By this time people were into the man. Rogers' story was that I had introduced a man named Joe Wilkins to him, so all he had to do was say this wasn't the Joe Wilkins he'd met. I don't think Joe was even charged.

Then in January 1964 I was arrested. I was caught one of the few times I didn't go up to town by train. I was driving home to Brighton and there was a roadblock just about by Crawley; it was down the old A23. I got out of the car and ran away into a bit of a forest, but they had dogs and they knew I couldn't get very far. I don't know if they'd had a tip, or if it was nothing to do with me and I was just unlucky.

By then Joe wasn't really my cup of tea. The case against him had collapsed in the September, and I probably thought he could have done more to help me than he did. We never bought the Starlight. We were unlucky there, that deal fell through whilst we were on the run.

Meanwhile, I got a lot of help from everyone else over Rogers – Billy Hill and Albert, 'Harry Boy' Sabini, and Georgie Shillingford. I was with Doreen in town and met her Uncle George in Hoxton. When we left we bumped into 'Harry Boy' as we were walking down Chapel Street market, and I asked him if he would see Rogers for us. Rogers may have dropped Joe out, but that man wanted to make me suffer. It took ages to find him; he'd moved, and you had to get messages through people who worked for him and then you'd get messages back. At one time there was about six weeks or two months before people managed to get to him. When contact was made, I'd leave a phone number and he'd phone from a hotel. He'd be speaking for two hours, and as part of the deal I had to pay for the phone calls and hotel bill. It took months to get it settled. It was a double-edged sword. It got me out of the Train in a way.

Albert said I should go to the States and Dick, the American I'd met in Rome and who was supplying gaming machines, agreed to have me, but I said no. Whilst here I could at least track Rogers down. If you go away people tend to leave it and do nothing, and it was the right decision. It was different to the trouble with Alfie Fraser; then it was just a question of keeping out of sight. This time it was a case where action had to be taken.

Even as late as when Rogers was giving his evidence, we couldn't guarantee he wouldn't go bent on us. My solicitor, James Fellowes, found out Rogers was engaged in a long firm, some fraud thing. When Rogers was giving evidence at the committal he put that to him because he could see Rogers was turning nasty even though we thought we'd got him squared. 'Do you know a Mr Brown?' I can't remember the exact name, but it sounded the warning bells. Rogers then changed his evidence and told the truth. Fellowes was more or less saying if you don't tell the truth we'll go further into the scheme you were running with this man. The case was rightly slung and I got my costs. That completely took the Train off me when I was released in February 1964. By now the committal proceedings had started and Charlie and Eddie had done their bit for me on that one.

At Brighton, James Fellowes was at his peak. He was a fashionable man to have. I think he'd already defended Jimmy Tibbs Senior for the murder at the

Ranch House in 1958 in Essex.[4] There were three of them and they were all acquitted. Fellowes did so well that he was suspended because it was thought he was trying too hard. They said he had approached a witness. He eventually proved there was no foundation and he was reinstated. At this stage of his career he was very, very good.

Whilst I was on the run for that case, I saw him occasionally at his office in Walthamstow. He was advising me when it would be right to give myself up but I got caught first. At this stage I think he let the police know I'd been in touch with him. Most solicitors were frightened of upsetting the prosecution or fighting too hard for their client. A stern look over his glasses from the judge or magistrate was enough to make them quail to their toenails and quieted them down without even saying a word. So James was a bold and able and daring solicitor of that period.

It was whilst I was in Brighton I got to know Harvey Holford very well. He was a gun expert and the owner of the Blue Gardenia Club in Brighton. It was in Queen Square at the Clock Tower, up West Street towards the station. It was a very good pitch to have a club and it had Legalite tables, a sort of roulette.

---

[4] James Tibbs Snr, together with George Wood, Edward Robins and Donald Mooney, was accused of the murder of Ronald Coomber in a fight outside the Ranch House Club in Ilford. At the trial in March 1961 evidence was given that there had been offensive behaviour by Coomber and others and there was no evidence that any of the accused had hit him. Mr Justice Edmund Davies ordered the jury to find all men not guilty and awarded them costs. In 1972 James Tibbs Snr was alleged to have led a protection gang in the East End. Along with other members of his family he was convicted and received ten years.

They were my machines in there. Harvey was a very likeable man. His mother, who was Belgian, used to serve behind the bar. I'd met him before I did the seven, but I didn't know his wife, Christine. I don't think he'd even married her when I went away, but by the time I came out things were very bitter between them; he wanted to do away with her and asked me if I would do it for him. We never got to discussing a price because I turned it down and told him not to be so foolish. Sooner or later, I thought, they'd have made things up and got back together. But he really did mean it. On the night of 15 September 1962, he shot and killed her; she had five bullets in her body and one in her brain. Holford was found in his club cradling her in his arms, and he'd taken a quantity of drugs. Apparently Christine had been sleeping not only with John Bloom, the washing-machine tycoon, but, said the pros, also with 'a string of studs'.

I went to visit him in Brixton, because when you were nicked for murder with a gun you could still be hung then and the medical doctors who could say you were sane were superior to those at a local prison. Harvey asked if he could mention Bill and Albert's name, and that they'd terrorized him which was why he'd had the gun. I saw Bill and he said, 'By all means if it's going to help him.' Albert didn't want it because he'd just got his licence for betting shops and he thought it might harm him, although he wasn't too greatly against it. After all, he could well understand the circumstances of the man. It stood Harvey in good stead because the judge pointed out how dangerous Bill and Albert were. Harvey had already pulled a great stroke. He'd chucked himself off the landing at Lewes and severely injured himself. It was a chance he took, and it turned out to be the clincher. I think he was genuinely depressed because he loved his wife. He'd had the gun for a couple of years; he'd bought it off an American serviceman. He was a go-ahead[5] man but he wasn't in the same class as Sammy Bellson.

[5] In February 1974 under the name of Robert Keith Beaumont, but disclosing that he was indeed Holford, he stood as Independent candidate in the General Election for the constituency of Brighton Pavilion. He received 428 votes.

9

The officer Charlie and Eddie Richardson had squared over the Train was as bent as they come, and had been from the time he was a DC in south London. After I was acquitted of demanding the money from Rogers I was with them at a boxing tournament at Bermondsey Baths promoted by my old friend John Parry, now a respectable businessman, and I was introduced to the copper there. The idea was for me to thank him for dropping me out of the enquiries over the Train and letting the Brighton case take its natural course. That's the first and only time I ever met the man. They'd already paid him. I've no idea how much it was; they never told me and I never asked. They wouldn't take the money back they'd paid, and it would have been insulting to mention it. If it was a case where you had to pay they'd have been straight forward and said, 'Well, Frank, this will cost you so much because that's what it cost us. We've done the necessary thing and he has also.' But when nothing is said at all, then you know they're doing you that as a good turn for friendship. No mercenary consideration comes into it at all.

I'd really only got to know them in about March 1964, a month or so after I was acquitted. I'd met them before to thank them about Jimmy Brindle and, of course, when I was collecting for Jimmy Essex's defence. When I was on the run for the Rogers case Charlie had sent a message to me that the Train coppers wanted to see me. I went to see him and he told me about the particular copper. Billy Howard told me the same and all. He knew him even better. 'Do you want to leave it to us, Frank, we think we can handle it?' I said, 'Yes, definite.' So that's how it come about I joined up with Charlie and Eddie. When I was out of both the Train and the demanding [with menaces], I naturally felt a bond between us for what they'd done for me. So this is how Eddie and me came to set up Atlantic Machines.

In the 1950s Dick, the Jewish guy in the Mafia, had brought over the first one-armed bandits. In 1956 I'd been taken over to Rome by Bert Marsh and Albert to meet Angelo Bruno. I'd already met Angelo in Bianca's in Soho and now he introduced us to Dick. No one was quite sure if this Jewish guy was straight – I mean there weren't too many Jewish people working for them in the 1950s – so we got Harry Levine, the boxing promoter, to do a check and he came back OK. Whilst I was in Rome Dick introduced me to Lucky Luciano, who was a very likeable guy although I was in awe of him. He had that sort of charisma and made a fuss of me. Albert got on very well and was praising me to Lucky. Later I did a few pieces of work for them.

Dick and Albert had come to visit me in prison when

I was doing the seven years for Spot. At this stage, although Albert was barred from seeing me he could always come in another name. A visiting order would just go out as Mr Smith or Mr Brown. There were no security checks. But if I'd sent out the VO in Albert's name it would have been knocked back. For instance, Albert sent me a printed Christmas card – from Mr and Mrs Dimes – at Dartmoor, and they wouldn't give it to me so I had to petition for it. This was all over the ban the Home Office had made after the incident at Liverpool when Albert and Tommy Falco had tried to see me.

Eventually Dick went back to America and had to leave the machines in legitimate hands, but he also arranged that when people like me wanted to buy a machine I wouldn't be charged an exorbitant price. I had had them before in the 1950s with Albert and a man called Henry Cohen, a street trader with shops and businesses. He was a very rich man, but Albert and I had dropped him out. Now in the 1960s Albert was a proper licensed bookmaker and didn't want to be involved with machines again. He was committed to his shops and it looked better if I drifted away from working with him. I was on a pension from Bill at the time but I kept in touch with Albert even if I didn't work with him. Machines were quite simple then – you didn't have to have a licence; in effect any Tom, Dick and Harry could go into the machine business without breaking any regulations in any way whatsoever. To get the machines we used a big firm over Ladbroke Grove as well as other places and generally they were only too pleased to do business with you, especially people like myself who they knew would pay them spot on and they could trust. They wouldn't get knocked for their money and we'd promote their machines. This was a company originally set up by Dick, but now in the bit of time before Rogers, when I was working with Joe Wilkins, there was trouble over the deliveries. So I put a bomb through the letter-box of a repair and store shop for the machines in Ladbroke Grove. It was a small one but it went off. This was to let the people there know they weren't playing the game. That speeded things up. When I was on the run over the Rogers affair, I couldn't do anything about the machines and the business fell away.

I didn't make the bomb of course. I knew someone who knew someone who could do it. If I wanted something made like this, I would know someone who was in the electronic line of business and I would go to them – people I'd known years. They might say, 'It's a bit beyond me but I know a man who could.' Just like the ad on telly. 'Is he all right?' 'One hundred per cent.' 'Tell me more, I don't want to know his name, just so's I can check.' In the world I was in, once a man was recommended – whether he was to nick a car or make a bomb – and investigated and he was all right, you didn't even want to know his second name. Your contact would then introduce you to the man and that would be his part finished. He would fade away. You'd carry on with the man. You'd tell him what you wanted, where and what time. He would do what he was paid to do and he'd disappear after he'd done the contract. You would be there when it went off to make sure it was done properly, and then you'd shake hands

Me, Stan Baker, Eddie Richardson and friends at the Astor Club.

Charlie and Eddie Richardson.
© Popperfoto

Tommy and Renee Wisbey, Marilyn's parents.
© Syndication International

Battles Rossi (left), convicted with me of the Spot slashing, at the Italian procession in Clerkenwell in the early 1990s.

Me leaving prison at the end of the twenty years.
© S&G Press Agency

1980s. Me and Charlie Richardson's
father and members of his family.

Me in 1993.
© H. McCormack

I explain a point to Marilyn.

The funeral of Arthur Thompson, who helped
Andy Anderson after his escape.
© Glasgow Herald and Evening Times

Me at the preview of the Lou Gent v Nigel Benn
World Title Fight,1993.

My good friend, boxing promoter Alex Steene (right).

The death of Jimmy Moody.
© S&G Press Agency.

Me and my lovely Marilyn.
© H. McCormack.

and away. You'd never see the man again until there was another needed. We'd pay anything from £200 to £1,000, plus the materials, or more depending on how prominent it was, how necessary, or how much you'd get yourself at the end of the day. You would charge a fee of a bit more than double. You wouldn't be greedy so everyone would be content.

As for finance for the machines when I started with Eddie, I put up some and I went to Billy Hill who gave me £5,000 on the condition that I paid a friend of his £100 every week – to build up to £1,700. I kept that up and at the end of the period Bill said, 'Good luck for the rest.' More to say, 'I've treated you to that.' Plus Eddie put so much in himself – a couple of grand. We started with about ten machines at about £300 odd then. They went into the Astor and the Stork, the Log Cabin, the Society, Pigalle and ordinary afternoon clubs like Charlie Chester's, the Cabinet and Modernaires, both owned by Aggie Hill. Charlie Chester's was now a casino owned by George James and his son. The same man whose caravan I'd gone to screw at Rhyl. Remember anyone could open a casino then; they only had to have a licence if they sold drinks. Strangely enough, I think the end of that was the Mr Smith's case. It took another couple of years after the fight there, but that was really the beginning of the end.

The split on the machines was then 50–50 between the club and us. We maintained them and all the rest. If they were damaged we replaced them; if they weren't working our mechanics repaired them. They were 6d a go then, and so we'd take about £40 as our share. £80 for the two machines. An exceptionally good club could come to £200. As time went on they brought out change machines in which people could put half-a crown and get their sixpences instead of keep going up to the barman, and we bought them and put them in clubs as well.

We did so well we decided to expand all over the country. Wales, Manchester, Newcastle, Liverpool, Staffordshire, the East Coast – all points. The expenses were quite hefty, but still worthwhile. In the sticks the machines didn't earn the money they did in London. You had to have staff out there. If the machines broke down, then others had to be rushed from London at all hours of the day and night. I should emphasize that although machines have a twang about them, as if there's something hooky, this was a straight business. There were one or two places where we had to exert a bit of pressure, a bit of muscle – Southport and Manchester – but generally everything went well.

One trouble was at the King's Head club on the front in Southport which was owned by the Jameses. The top floor was a disco, the next one down a casino, the one down from that was a night-club where there was a smart cabaret. They had a bit of luck when they booked Tom Jones just before he went to the number one spot on the hit parade with 'It's not Unusual'. He kept the engagement and it was standing room only. The basement was all machines, pinballs and our one-armed bandits. We had just put our machines in when hooligans from Liverpool tried to smash them up. They were given a warning by the Jameses and when they never took heed of that, action was taken.

I went up specially to sort it out, and about 4 o'clock one morning I did three of them with a big lump of lead outside the club. One was a great big geezer and he fell on the pavement. I was just going to give him another when I felt an arm. I hadn't seen the blue serge, and I didn't realize it was a copper and I thought it was just one of the people who worked for the Jameses saying, 'Turn it in, Frank.' I turned round to say 'Don't worry' and saw who it was. I went, 'Thank God you've arrived, get an ambulance quick.' He said, 'I've seen you hitting him,' and I said, 'How dare you?' He blew his whistle and I said, 'You've got to get an ambulance.' Like an idiot he said, 'All right. I'm going to the phone box to get one. Wait here.' The casino was all locked up, with the Jameses the other side of the door watching. As soon as the copper went across the road I said, 'Let me in.' I went down into the basement, out into another street, off to my hotel, picked up my car and went straight back to London.

The Law nicked John James for helping me escape, but I got in touch with the three guys – one of them had been in Wandsworth with me – and they dropped it out. James was slung at the magistrates' court. The poor copper got put on point duty after that. I'd wave to him when I was up there. That incident made us very strong with the Jameses. We'd already had one bit of trouble whilst the club was being built. Eddie and me went for a drink in the Horseshoe in Southport, which was a little drinking club. It was there we had a little row with Peter Joannides, 'Peter the Greek', who thought he was Jack the Lad and as a result got a right-hander. There was an Alsatian running after us as we got out the club, so we kidnapped it and a mile down the road we let it out to run back. Then we drove to London.

About a week later, if that, we found Joannides had got the number of our car and had gone to the police and nicked Eddie and me. Eddie had parked his car in Store Street near what was the Court of Protection, in one of their parking spots, and when we went back the police were there. Eddie was arrested, taken to Southport and charged. He got bail and eventually the case was dismissed at the magistrates' court. I'd had a word with Joannides. He realized he'd been out of order, and when Eddie was acquitted they just dropped it out against me.

After the incident with the geezers at the King's Head there was never any more trouble with other people trying to move their machines in. This was a standard problem for operators but not with us. Our reputations were, shall we say, leaping ahead of us before we even got there. Or the owner of the clubs who were having troubles with their machines from the local people who'd installed them knew that wasn't good enough. It was a good source of income, most probably better than they were getting from behind the bar. They didn't have to work for it, didn't have to maintain it, but what was the good if the local people had it and the local thugs were smashing them and trying to cheat them – putting buttons and duff coins in them, ruining the machines. They would have heard of the efficiency of our firm and the organization and the extra muscle, so the owners would come to us, not us go to them. They'd phone us up and ask if we would be prepared to come up and install our machines. We'd make enquiries behind the scenes from people in the town whom I'd most probably met in prison or Borstal over the years, who would tell us everything about the local scene and who would also see the local thugs and say these machines are going in, drop it out or you'll cause yourself a lot of headaches. That nearly always worked. Then we'd get in touch with the owner of the club and say we'd be only too pleased to accept your offer, and we'd fetch the machines up immediately. In the meantime the local man would be contacted and he'd take his machines away. Probably he'd have got fed up with it by then and wanted his machines out. Nine times out of ten they were never working.

The working directors were me and Eddie, but we also had Sir Noel Dryden on the Board. He was a figurehead on the company notesheets to give it a bit of prestige, rather like the Twins had a peer or two on the boards of their companies. I think we got him through Captain Mark Hewitson. He was a bit of an alcoholic, a very nice man, but all he was interested in was keeping his elbow working. He committed suicide after the Mr Smith's affair. I remember reading it in the papers whilst I was serving my sentence.

Atlantic Machines lived in Windmill Street, off Tottenham Court Road, just round the corner from the police station. The building and shops are still there to this day. We used to keep shotguns and thunder-flashes in the cellar. Flashes could only be held by the Army, and by film producers with permission from the War Office. We were raided. It was just one of them sort of raids which would take place at that period. Machines were being stolen from clubs all over the country, and anyone who had machines would be raided periodically for a check on the numbers. The guns weren't found but the thunder-flashes were. They were really stun things: if you slung them at anyone they would be knocked unconscious for a few seconds. I think Dryden was charged but I'm not sure. One of the directors was. If it wasn't Dryden it was Bert McCarthy's brother, Leslie, although neither he nor Dryden would have known what was going on behind the scenes. Billy Hill went to see Ernie Millen about it, and we got Stanley Baker to put up a film producer who would have had permission to have the flashes. The producer was to say he'd had a delayed flight to South Africa, and rather than cart the explosives round London with him for the three or four hours until the flight went he'd asked permission to store them in the cellar, and it was in that period the premises got raided. The director was acquitted, and I think got his costs from the magistrate.

You had to have a bit of security. In that type of a business you did have a lot of unruly elements who would try to steal the machines or break them. Forewarned is forearmed if it had to be like that. Not that you wanted it, but it was a business where you had to be prepared. It was also nice for the mechanics to know that there was some protection there. Some clubs would be open all night, so the mechanics would have to go out all hours of the day and night.

Eddie and I never emptied the machines – this was done by mechanics along with someone who worked for us, such as Jimmy Andrews. Also the machines were programmed to count the sixpences, to save counting by hand and to stop any skimming. We paid our men good wages, treated them well, and that way you had more chance of getting their loyalty and good workmanship. We weren't foolish to put temptation in people's way by giving them a lousy wage. Half in joke, Eddie and me would pat our collectors' ankles saying, 'Gosh, aren't they thick.' But it kept them honest. We had about a dozen mechanics and other people, depending on how busy we were. Others would come in on a part-time basis. A phone call and they would be happy to get a day's work. It was all cash; no one was paid by cheque in those days. The club owner never had the keys to the machine, so he couldn't do anything he shouldn't. Roy Porritt worked for us. Alfie Fraser, who I'd tried to help those few years ago, did so as well. He was no relation, although when we were in prison we made out we were cousins to get visits to one another. He was the first successful tunneller when in 1955 he tunnelled into Martin's Bank in St James's. He got caught with dirt on his shoes which, the police said, could be traced to the bank.

I was working at Atlantic in July 1965, the day Ronnie Biggs escaped from Wandsworth along with three others. One of them was Robert 'Andy' Anderson who, in fact, was the first up the wall. The men at the top laughingly told him, 'We ain't come for you, we've come for someone else,' but they got him away with Ronnie, Eric Flowers who was from East London, and Doyle, the fourth man. The others on the exercise never knew until seconds before it actually happened, so that way it couldn't be leaked. There weren't many there, but they were all escape-risk prisoners in yellow fluorescent patches. Category A didn't exist then. Doyle was only doing four, which by the standards of Biggs doing thirty years and Flowers and Anderson each doing twelve, wasn't anything. Flowers already knew of the escape plan but Anderson and Doyle just took their chance.

A screw in the mailbag shop who had been there about thirty years kept empty the seat where Biggs had been sitting the day he escaped with the mailbag half sewn. His ambition was that one day he'd be back to finish the bag. Years later in 1974, when Biggs had been recaptured in Brazil, he was delighted, saying, 'I've got his chair ready for him.' Then one day it came over the tannoy that Brazil had refused to extradite him. We all cheered and shouted out, 'Anyone can sit in that chair now.' I went and sat in it and there was nothing he could do about it. In the end he accepted it and began to grin himself.

Meanwhile, I didn't know Anderson myself but Patsy Fleming – who I'd known for years and who had escaped with Alfie Hinds and was now working at Atlantic as a mechanic – had been on remand in Brixton with him for an offence for which he, Fleming, was acquitted. Whilst in Brixton Anderson told Patsy he was going to try and escape. Patsy laughingly had said give us a ring at Atlantic Machines if you do and you want some help. He wasn't sure whether Anderson was serious. But Anderson did take it that way and remembered the phone number and address.

Andy told us when they got on top of the wall, the people who threw the ladders down took off the boiler suits they were wearing, and give him and the other man the suits and £2 each, as well as one of the getaway cars. Anderson and Doyle drove off, but after half a mile along the road the car broke down so they left it there, shook hands and split up. Now all that distinguished Andy was the striped blue shirt prisoners wear, so he went to a men's outfitters and bought a white shirt for about £1 10s. and changed in a pub lavatory. Then he made his way to Tottenham Court Road. I was coming out of Atlantic with Patsy to get the van and go and have a look at a site. We'd heard four men had escaped from Wandsworth, but we didn't know at that stage who they were. I remember it was a nice summer's day and as we went into the yard there was a man spreadeagled across the bonnet of the van. At first I thought he was a drunk and shouted at him to clear off, but he wouldn't move. Fleming looked up and seen who it was and recognized him, saying, 'It's one of the men who's escaped.' I immediately took him into Atlantic. Stanley Baker and various other people were there. One of the men, who was about the same size as Anderson, stripped down and give Anderson his clothes. We then had a collection which was worth a few hundred and I asked how old he was. He said twenty-six, and that he'd only been out three months from a five-year sentence at Dartmoor before he'd got the twelve.

A complication was the police would be on the lookout not only for Biggs but the others, and this would only draw attention to all of us. You couldn't afford to have him wandering round London. People could expect swoop after swoop and it would be quite likely we'd be in the frame for one of them. I got my car and took him up my mother's. I told him my parents were getting on a bit so when they went to bed not to have the TV too loud, but that I would stay the night there with him in any event. I then asked would he go back to Scotland if I could arrange it and he said he'd love to. I asked how long ago it was since he'd last lived there and, when he said the last time was when he was fifteen, I knew the prospect of the police recognizing him would be slim. He had a very broad Scots accent and so he'd stick out like a sore thumb down here.

I got in touch with Arthur Thompson, who was the King of Glasgow in those days, and he was wonderful. He told me not to bring him to Glasgow because it was King Billy Day – one where there was all parades and there would be one-way streets and a lot of police – instead to take him to Waverley Station in Edinburgh.

A friend of a friend had a Rolls-Bentley and he dressed up as a chauffeur. At 4 a.m. on 12 July we left my mother's house at the back of the Old Kent Road with sandwiches and a flask of tea. I sat in the back with Anderson, and except for stopping for petrol we went straight through to Waverley Station and there was Arthur along with his partner, Mendel Morris. They had a flat all ready for Andy and they were really nice. They wouldn't take a penny from me. I'd taken some money up with me for his expenses and Andy had his whip money. They looked after him like a son and gave him a job up there. After three or four months, to give them a break I had him transferred to Manchester before I could think how to get him abroad. Bobby MacDermott, King of the Barrowboys, then had a flat for him and had him working on the barrows. Every weekend Anderson would go back on the long-distance coach to Glasgow and come back on the Sunday night. I didn't know this – he wasn't my everyday responsibility now, Bobby was in charge of him – and one evening as he was waiting for the coach in Manchester he was arrested. He'd been out seven or eight months. It was no fault of anyone's but it must have leaked out; he may have told someone who shouldn't have known. I didn't see him again until I was in the security wing at Durham two years later when a broad Scots voice shouted out from the cells, 'Hello, Frank', and it was Anderson.

Later we had a benefit and whip at the El Morocco for the kids who'd helped Biggsy by holding the screws back. Eva sent the money in to the prison and the Governor must have told Tommy Butler because he went to see Eva, saying it was Great Train Robbery money. She told him it wasn't and her husband, who was a bookmaker, and his friends had felt sorry for the men and had had a collection. She told me about it and I went to see a solicitor in the Tottenham Court Road to make a statement. Fortunately nothing came of it.

Atlantic Machines was running perfectly well until the fight in Mr Smith's. When we were arrested for Mr Smith's, Tommy Butler and other top policemen such as McArthur, the head of No. 9 Regional Crime

Squad, went to the clubs over the country and not one owner complained in any way whatsoever. I'm sure they were given every chance to say if they'd been forced to have the machines in their clubs, and been threatened with a beating if they wouldn't accept it, but not one of them would have it. If there'd been the slightest complaint of that type there'd have been a charge somehow or other. It was never mentioned by the prosecution in the Mr Smith's case or in the so-called Torture trial. Of course we couldn't mention it either – as it never came up there was no point, and no matter what you say machines always leave a smell. It would have been putting my character in as well.

After the fight I was in the hospital in Wandsworth with the broken thigh-bone and Eddie was also nicked. Others on the staff wanted out and because there was no one strong enough to carry on, the machines just disappeared. I had enough on my plate without worrying about them. My visits were watched. There would be two or three officers in a little room with you. You could talk about your case and that was it; it was impossible to talk about anything else. That would be the same for all of us. Remember before that I was in Brixton on a murder charge. Then I'd been in the room and at the same table where all the people on murder charges from Crippen onwards had had their visits.

In the days before our arrest George James and his son, John, were running Charlie Chester's casino in Archer Street. Before it became a casino it had been a pretty low drinking club, Dummys, where there were awful fights. I don't suppose, for a minute, Charlie Chester knew a thing about it, but when it became a casino, George James approached Bert Wilkins as to how to keep out the mugs who'd ruined it before, and he introduced George to us. It was in Bert's flat off Marylebone High Street, curiously enough the same block where Donald Urquhart, the man who was shot in January 1993, lived. In return for our help it was suggested Eddie and me should have a share of the profits, but Bert was smart. Don't go for profits, he told us, go for a weekly wage. And so Eddie and I had £100 a week each.

Then Eddie and I opened a club in Cardiff with George and we had a drink out of that; then the one in Southport. They closed down after a bit but the Charlie Chester money continued right through until Eddie came out of jail after the Richardson case. By the time Eddie finished his sentence Charlie Chester's had changed hands a couple of times, but we still got our money. Then when Eddie came out, long before me of course, he was asked if he wanted a lump sum. He came to see me and we agreed to take it.

10

I'd known Georgie Cornell for some time and found
him very likeable indeed, and brave. He was a fearless
character but, in drink, he could get a bit quar-
relsome at times. I personally never saw it to be
so, but this was the reputation he had. People did
try to avoid him when he'd had a drink. I met
him mostly in prison. Some books have said that
Georgie left the Kray twins and came over the water
because of his friendship with me, but it's not true.
He'd married a very nice girl, Olive Hudd, whose
father and family I knew; that's how he come to live
south side of the Thames. I'd have bumped into him
anyway because of his being with Olive, who was
a good friend of my family. It was inevitable we
should meet. He was probably more friendly with
the Twins than with me because he grew up with
them. He'd been part of the Watney Street mob
of dockers at one time. George wasn't frightened
of anybody and the Twins may have been a bit
overbearing with him. The status and the power
may have gone to their heads, but it wouldn't carry
no ice with him. He'd want people to treat him

as a friend, not as an underling to be trod over when it suited them. It may well have been in the case of the Krays and George. I think that's how it come about he fell out with them, and I also think they were a bit frightened of him. After all, when he was growing up with them he knocked them about over the years. He probably found that with Eddie, Charlie and me he was treated as a person and not as a hireling, and that's why he liked us better.

The Twins could be a bit difficult. One day they could be plotting to kill that glass on the table because it didn't shine. Next day it'd be something else. Ronnie could take umbrage at anything. For example, he cut up little Johnny Dew from Islington just because he said he'd put on weight. That's another reason George liked to be with us because you could take things in the manner it was intended and no one would take offence in any way whatever. If someone got silly drunk and was told, 'Here, you did make an idiot of yourself last night, you did get silly drunk,' the person would say, 'You're quite right George.' But if that was said to the Twins they wouldn't accept it was said in an ordinary, nice way. George did a bit of work for Atlantic whenever he wanted to.

I think the Krays got upset over machines. They wanted to put machines in clubs and those clubs were ours. There was also something to do with blue films. What used to happen, people would rent flats, preferably on the fringes of the West End, Holborn, Tottenham Court Road, where they have quite big rooms, and they'd have 'Brussels Sprouts' – touts – who would go round looking for men on their own and invite them to see blue films which were then all the rage and very daring. It was all done with a projector and a screen; there were none of them videos in those days, and the films were pretty mild by today's standards. The punters used to have to pay about a tenner – it wasn't cheap, but there was nothing of the corner game. Once the punter said yes, it was a genuine show he saw. They got value for their money.

It was Billy Stayton came to Eddie and me and put a proposition. He was working with Bernie Silver and the Maltese at the time, and he said the police had been straightened but only for a short time. Would we give them protection so they could run blue movies for three months? That was the period of time they'd got on licence from the police. We would get £2,000 a week. If punters complained to the police, they would warn Billy and his mates of a raid and they'd move flats. If there was no complaint, they could stay in the same place until the three months were up. One or two people tried to open up in competition and we raided them and closed them down. That was the end of that. Bernie Silver and his friends knew that without us the Twins would have muscled in and they would not have been powerful enough to withstand it.

So when Alfie Gerard and a couple of others asked if a man acting on their and the Twins' behalf could open up, we said we were very sorry this was a one-off three months' deal, and until then the answer had to be no. The Twins also came to Atlantic Machines to ask for themselves. They took the information as it was given, but it rankled with Ronnie and he asked George again, this time in the Stork Club, if he could do something for them. George knew they'd been politely and firmly told what the deal was and he couldn't see why they should ask again.

'I wasn't in the Stork Club that night but I know George had a big row with Ronnie and was insulting to him. By all accounts he told him to get on his bike. Whether he actually called him a poofter as the story goes I really don't know but, as I say, George could be unpleasant when he'd had a drink. There were all types of women who were keen to be with us – actresses, showgirls, secretaries – so the word poofter didn't come into our world. They kept strictly to their world. I never even knew Ronnie was a poofter. I'd heard rumours but I didn't believe it. Nearest I'd come was what Billy's tame M.P., Captain Hewitson, had told me about Tory politicians. After the quarrel George didn't go round talking about it. Personally I never had a row with the Twins in the Stork Club as people make out. We went regularly to the Stork and the Astor on a Friday, but I don't recall seeing them there about that time.

I think too that perhaps the Krays were jealous, most probably that we had a better edge in the West End than they did. Looking back that was possibly the case. They were quite pleasant when I spoke to them. If I had a drink with the Twins, it wasn't above a dozen times. I can remember Ronnie sending a message in October 1965 – would I meet him in the Grave Maurice. I went with my nephew, Jimmy. Ronnie had heard a whisper from a crooked copper that the police were looking for me for a G.B.H. and to watch my step, and I thanked him and had a drink. Nothing came of it but when James Taggart gave evidence in the Torture trial he said he'd made a complaint in 1965, so the information Ronnie had must have been good because it was a secret hush-hush enquiry. Ronnie must have known the bare bones. If he'd known it was Taggart and told me, it could have made a remarkable difference to the case.

But there was nothing of this great rivalry that people have made it up to be. Certainly not on the part of Charlie and Eddie, they were above it. They had their own businesses and the Krays didn't enter their heads. I don't mean they disliked them or anything like that, but I can see how the Twins might think a row with Eddie and Charlie might be a stepping-stone to bigger things.

There was a fight in the Astor one night but the Twins weren't there. I was down there with Eddie Richardson when it erupted at about 2 a.m. This would be the beginning of 1965 or the end of 1964. It was nothing to do with Eddie or me and we just left – paid our bill and went. I wasn't involved, but people I knew were. The police were called and as Eddie and I got out of the back door we bumped into Eric Mason, who'd been a good man in his time, outside on the pavement. Although I'd met him in prison, really I hardly knew him but he wasn't a bad guy. That night though he started off by saying, 'I'm not standing for this, nor will the other people stand for it either.' By this he meant the Twins. He was like threatening me. It was nothing to do with them, but the way he said it was like a threat as if they would be upset enough to take retaliatory action against me.

So I kidnapped him and bundled him into a car with another man doing the driving. I took him across the river and I really see to him. I did him with a chopper over the head and everywhere, and slung him out in his underclothes wrapped in a blanket outside the London Hospital in Whitechapel.

As I say Eric wasn't a bad fellow, but that particular night he was bang out of order. You can't go around saying things like that and not expecting anything to happen. I know it sounds as if it was a bit rough, the punishment, but it wasn't excessive although it might sound it to people who didn't understand the rules. What he was saying is that he would see that I'd suffer. You can't go round threatening people without putting it into reality or pay the consequence for uttering such a threat. If he wanted to say such things, he'd have to be prepared to accept what happened and do whatever he liked afterwards. He swallowed it. I understand he went to the Twins after he came out of hospital. In his book Leslie Payne, who was the Twins' accountant, says he was present and I said, 'Take this back to them.' I never said that to him. It was nothing to do with the Twins and I understand, when he went to see them about it, they gave him £5 and slung him out.[1]

I was always closer to Eddie than to Charlie, who'd got irons in the fire all over the place. He was involved in mines in South Africa and goodness knows what else. What I didn't know, and I don't think Eddie did either, was just the trouble being stored up for us. Now Eddie thinks it may have been Charlie's involvement with the secret police in Africa which didn't do us any good. But certainly the trouble was Charlie was getting diversified into so many things he was handing out tasks to people who weren't equipped to deal with them. When they were interviewed they'd say whatever the police wanted. Charlie had been a professional boxer. I never saw him because I was away at the time, but he was very good I hear, and

[1] Payne says that, 'Fraser came over and pulled him out of the Astor, took him to their offices in Tottenham Court Road and simply set about him with an axe. First he cut a great slice down Mason's forehead. Then he chopped away at his left knee so there were cross-gashes all up his left thigh. Then he had a go at his left arm, and nearly cut it through. I supposed he failed because – unlike a tree – the rest of Mason didn't offer enough resistance.

Still Mason spent months in hospital and when he came out he naturally put his troubles before the Twins because it was, in theory, an unwritten rule that if one mob had a go at a member of another mob, then he had to be revenged in style. But in practice neither side wanted out-and-out warfare. They'd each pick off the other's men on odd occasions, knowing it was all going to be straightened out. But in the end 'straightening out' would have needed the deaths of half the East End of London. When Mason turned up at Vallance Road – I was sitting next to Ronnie – in a terrible mess, all twisted up where he hadn't healed properly, with one leg trailing, and his left arm hunched up under the shoulder, and said, 'Look what they did to me,' Ronnie replied, 'Yeah, well, Fraser took a bit of a liberty with you, but it's not really our problem now, is it?' From that moment he was off the firm. They had a whip round and gave him £40.' *The Brotherhood*, Leslie Payne (1973) London, Michael Joseph, p. 115.

so was Eddie although he was an amateur. Charlie had about three fights in his own name at halls like Manor Place Baths, but then he gave it up. He realized he could make money easier without having to go through so much suffering. He had a pretty wicked temper and most of the time he didn't suffer fools gladly. He does now, but not then. I think he had a few bare-knuckle fights. In the profession of scrap-metal dealers that would be quite common – disagreements would be settled like that.

Once I went to Charlie's office and Charlie said, 'There's a guy who just escaped from Bristol Prison.' I asked when and he said, 'Yesterday.' There had been nothing in the newspapers. If people escaped from a closed prison there'd have been a mention at the very least. I questioned the man and it turned out he was on the hostel, a scheme where men worked and came back to the hostel at night. This meant he'd absconded, which is very different from escaping. I mentioned a couple of men in racing circles in Lambeth. 'Do you know them?' He didn't. I conveyed this to Charlie, saying the man was a liar, but Charlie would go and put him into a business, a wholesale warehouse thing. One morning it's locked up and the guy's gone. The trouble with Charlie was he was a kind man. He hadn't done proper bird, just like Spot hadn't, and so he never really appreciated how the low life thought.

11

If I'd have thought there was going to be trouble that night at Mr Smith's I wouldn't have gone. It was a no-win situation. If there were ordinary members of the public involved the police must get involved also. It's something to be avoided. You'd know the people at the club you were going to have a row with and you would sort them out at times and places when no member of the public was about. You'd probably see them first and try to talk to them. If they wouldn't listen, then there'd have to be some other way. But you wouldn't go to a club and do it – there could be no winners. In that situation there's more than a great possibility that someone's going to be arrested.

Within two days of the fight at Mr Smith's Georgie Cornell was dead. He was in the wrong place at the wrong time. He'd gone over the water to see Jimmy Andrews, who'd lost a leg in a shooting over a domestic matter and was in the London Hospital. On the way back he had stopped off in the Blind Beggar in the Whitechapel Road for a drink, when Ronnie Kray heard he was there and went and shot him dead.[1]

[1] There are numerous accounts of this incident, including John Pearson's *The Profession of Violence* and in Reg and Ron Kray's *Our Story*.

I was in the prison hospital in Brixton charged with Dickie Hart's murder at the time, and visits were very difficult. If you were on a murder charge you sat at a big table about 10–12 feet long: you sat on one end and your visitors sat at the other, with screws between you. So there was no way any message could be passed through visitors to me. Stan Baker came up with Albert to see me whilst I was on remand, which was good of him, but I wasn't getting much news of the outside world.

Eddie Richardson, Billy Hayward, Jimmy Moody and the rest were all committed for trial on an affray charge, and I was sent up the road for the murder as well. There was to be a separate trial for me on the murder charge, and this would take place before the others had their affray heard. After the committal I got a message to say that no one was going in the witness box in the affray trial, and would I not do so at my hearing. The reason was that whatever I'd have said other people would have been stuck with that. That was the impression I had anyway.

After the murder was slung, then maybe if I had given evidence I would have been acquitted of the affray. The evidence was now much weaker against me. Henry Botton, who'd said he saw me shoot Hart, had changed his evidence but they used his original statement as one of the main planks against me. I was completely innocent of that murder. I did chin Hart and get the gun off him. As I say, I hit him with my right hand, I got his wrist with my left and as it pushed down a shot snapped my thigh-bone. It was a chance I had to take. The gun went to the floor and rolled away; it was someone else picked it up and shot him.

Tommy Butler wasn't in charge of the Mr Smith's case at first; he came on it three days later. Butler, as head of the Flying Squad, knew the strength of me from the Train Robbery. He had asked to take over the case as it had publicity value, and he got a patrol squad man from Southwark to say he found the gun in the garden where I had been laying. In fact the gun was 100 yards away, hidden in a little courtway. The police had obviously found the gun and now an officer said it was by my hands. It all fell apart for them because the evidence of another policeman was that he had made a note of officers who were present, and that the one who spoke of finding the gun in the garden wasn't there at any time. By today's standards that officer would have been arrested, and even now I regret that I didn't press against him. They might have dropped the Torture trial out. Even if they hadn't, it could have caused tremendous inquiries and embarrassment involving Butler downwards because it was such blatantly false evidence.

After the other officer had said the one who 'found the gun' wasn't there, my counsel, Charles Lawson, made a submission that there was no case for me to answer and the judge agreed. But I was slung to the wolves on the affray even though I'd only been defending myself. I suppose that's because I never went into the witness box. I got five years for it and went to Wandsworth for treatment on my thigh.

It was when the Canadian physio who'd been treating me in the hospital at Wandsworth had gone on holiday for six weeks that I was transferred into the hospital at Wormwood Scrubs. At first I was put in the end of A wing, but then the Chief Medical Officer said I would be put in the hospital to save them wheeling me about. 'Don't let me down,' he said, and I told him I wouldn't. I did seventeen days of the best prison I'd ever done. There was a radio and you could make a cup of tea; you could bath every day as well.

That's when I met George Blake, the spy. He came over the hospital a couple of times and I chatted with him. Blake knew which prisoners he could talk to; which he could trust. Even then he was talking about how one day he'd be gone. I said it would take a long time. He'd only done about three years of the forty-two, but he said he had it in mind to leave earlier. I thought yes, it would be quite easy, because prisons weren't as secure then as they are now. Security was nowhere near like today. Category A prisoners didn't exist. On reflection it's a miracle they kept anyone in. I wasn't at all surprised when he went in October 1966. There was no great celebrations when we heard he'd escaped – he was a spy and a dangerous one – but if people like Frank Mitchell or Ronnie Biggs got out, it went round the prison like wildfire and everyone was absolutely delighted.[2]

Charlie Richardson and the others, along with my nephew Jimmy, were nicked on the day England won the World Cup. My wife Doreen visited me on that day and told me. Doreen and Francis, my youngest

---

[2] After the escapes of Blake and Frank Mitchell the Government instituted the Mountbatten Inquiry into prisons. After that security became a lot tougher.

son, came up from Brighton to Victoria Station where Jimmy 'the Stick' Goldstein was to meet her and take them with my nephew Jimmy to Wembley. I'd got four tickets for them. Unbeknown to her, Jimmy had been arrested at 5 o'clock that morning and his wife was in such a panic she didn't know where he'd put the tickets. When Doreen turned up on the visit she was nearly in tears. News of the arrests had been on the radio, but I never dreamed of Charlie being nicked. It never entered me head. And the last thing I dreamed was that my nephew James was in it. Fortunately Francis, my boy, was able to go to a relative to see the football on the television – black and white, it was then.

In the next few days Albert Dimes came to visit me again. He was now back allowed to see me. Where they failed on the murder charge, it would be a long shot to rope me in, he said, and I agreed with him. Fool that I was, I didn't look further than my nose. I thought I was all right until 12 August 1966, the day three policemen were shot just outside Wormwood Scrubs. McArthur, the Assistant Chief Constable, could see a good publicity move here and about 7 p.m. mobs of prison officers come into the ward with handcuffs. 'Get your stuff, you're being moved.' At first I thought it was back to the wing and so I said, 'Are you jealous that I'm having it too easy?'

'No,' was the reply. 'You're being transferred.' Away we went to Wandsworth.

That night it was said on the radio I'd been moved as the shooting of the coppers was thought to be part of an escape attempt to get me out of Wormwood Scrubs, but I knew then I was going to be in the dock along with

Charlie and the others. It was a good publicity coup. I didn't have to have the brains of Lloyd George to guess that one out. A few days later I was taken before the Governor, who said I was to be taken to Clerkenwell Magistrates' Court and would be charged there.

Although there were dozens and dozens of charges against all of us, basically there were three charges against me of grievous bodily harm. I was meant to have assaulted James Taggart, Christopher Glinski and Benny Coulston. It was a put-up job and it got my poor sister, Eva, a three-year sentence.

I didn't know that Glinski knew Charlie. I'd never met him before the Spot trial when he gave evidence supporting Basil Andrews. Glinski was later done for perjury over that case and was found not guilty. Later he sued the police and won damages. He genuinely owed Charlie money, and I had gone over to Victoria with Johnny Longman to Glinski's offices in Vauxhall Bridge Road to ask what he could pay and when. The trouble was he got saucy and acted as if Charlie should give him the money, which was outrageous. There wasn't really even a fight. He got one punch and we left him in his office chair half knocked out. At the committal Glinski said my nephew, Jimmy, was there. I don't know why, because he genuinely wasn't. When the trial came this put me in a spot. I couldn't say there was just two of us and my nephew wasn't there. I had to say there was no incident at all or, if there was, it wasn't us three.

James Taggart was the one who started it off and went to the police. He was a very brilliant fraudster, a con man into long firm, and he was also a karate expert. He was very friendly with another conman, Frank Prater, and at one stage they invented a very clever trick with their own football pools but Prater got three years for that. He believed that Taggart had shopped him and got out of the case. This would be in the early 1960s. I had met Prater because Charlie had been very good to him. Charlie must have known him before he served the three-year sentence because, after he was released, I think Charlie gave him £25, and £100 to set him up in a business, get his 'phones on in an office and the like. Charlie was very good helping to put him on his feet.

James Taggart said Charlie, Tommy Clark and I attacked him in the street, punched and kicked him and then bundled him into a car. Back at Charlie's he said that I hit him with a two-inch-thick pole until it broke. He said that Alfie Berman, another defendant, had brought in some sandwiches and a beer and then the three of us had attacked him again. Each time he'd been obliged to clean up the blood with his underpants. A bit later he had seen me in Wigmore Street, and had called a cab to get away from me and next day went to the police.

It simply didn't happen like that. For a start, I wasn't in the room when he was done up. It all came about because Berman came to Charlie saying Taggart owed him a lot of money. Then, by accident, Charlie and I bumped into Taggart at traffic lights in the East End somewhere. Charlie asked him to go and see Berman, who was at that time a friend of his, and he took Taggart to see him over at Berman's premises which were not far from the Jamaica Road. I waited outside in the car, and later I'm told Taggart had got very aggressive with Charlie. I understand Charlie give him a punch and Taggart had a bloody nose as a result. They came out and shook hands. Prater was there as well – he was in Berman's at the time and Taggart just drove home. That was that. It's absolute rubbish that I beat him with a pole. He didn't go to hospital and he allegedly had a doctor come to see him, which I don't believe for one moment. By the time that doctor give his evidence it was about eighteen months later and he had no notes of any kind. Prater jumped on the bandwagon on that evidence. The thing was Prater and Taggart hated one another. I remember Prater saying Taggart had shopped him when he got the three years over the pools. But it didn't stop him becoming a prosecution witness.

Taggart rowed Berman out at the end. What people didn't know was that at the time of the trial Taggart was running a long firm almost around the corner from the Old Bailey, £10,000 in one go. The long firm was in clothes and materials in Bishopsgate, but the deal was Berman had given Taggart money, so he would get Berman out of it when it came to it.

It's also true we did see Taggart in Wigmore Street. Taggart was running a fraudulent bank around the corner from there, I think it was in Manchester Square, and by sheer accident we bumped in to him. I think Charlie then reminded him, 'Have you settled that up with Alfie Berman?' That was it. My mind boggles at the unintelligentness of it all. Taggart says he jumped into a taxi and got away – all very dramatic – and the next day he went and saw McArthur. No one ever dared ask how he came to see McArthur then; he was Assistant Chief Constable of Hertfordshire, and was head of the No. 9 Regional Crime Squad. You couldn't just go to him like that. Taggart had to be McArthur's man. Normally, to meet a police officer of his rank and standing it might take up to a week to get to him. You couldn't just go to him like that, without injuries and a story of an alleged assault which has happened months before. He must have been an informer of some type and was already working for him.[3]

It was in this period, October or November 1964, that Ronnie sent a message to see me and to meet him down the Grave Maurice in the Whitechapel Road. I took Jimmy, my nephew, with me, and Reggie was there as well. What he wanted to tell me was that someone was about to grass me. He never gave me a name but he said he'd heard that someone had gone to the police with a whisper. He was very vague in his information, but he'd obviously got hold of it from some crooked copper. I thanked him because it was good of him to bother to tell me and we had a drink. It didn't enter me head who it could be. But looking back it had to be Taggart seeing McArthur.

---

[3] Another explanation appears in Neil Derbyshire and Brian Hilliard's *The Flying Squad* (p. 130) when they quote McArthur as saying, 'Taggart had a girlfriend who had been a witness in a case I was investigating in South London. She had been extremely brave in coming forward to give evidence, and we provided her with a twenty-four-hour protection up to and during the trial. When Taggart found himself in trouble with Charlie Richardson, she persuaded him to come to me for advice. It was simply that I was someone she knew and trusted from the past.' This could account for why Taggart had a hot-line to McArthur.

That must have been the incident Ronnie spoke to me about.

The Coulston incident happened on Charlie's birthday, 18 January 1965. Just prior to that Bennie Coulston and another two men were going round with the old con trick of a carton said to be filled with 25,000 cigarettes, possibly even more. When the carton was opened up to a prospective buyer the top layer was filled with brand-new packets of a popular brand of cigarettes; the rest was filled with sawdust and things like that. But the con was that the buyer would never dream of looking through it.

When Harry Rawlings, who had a wholesale business in Lambeth Walk and who was a well respected and very likeable man, went on holiday with his wife he left his younger brother, a kid of about twenty-three, in charge of the business. Lo and behold, when he's away in go Coulston and the others into the shop and do the con on the kid. They painted a picture of a quick profit and he paid out £650. I suppose he was going to sell the cigatettes, packs at a time. He put the carton in another room, and look at the consternation he had when he was unpacking it and see it was full of sawdust. When he had to tell his older brother the boy was nearly in tears. £650 was a lot of money when he'd just started. It was quite a big knock-back.

When we heard about this everybody was upset. If people do them type of things on people with backgrounds and who know the facts of life, they have to be prepared for the consequences. If they do it to straight people, well them poor people have no redress whatsoever. If they go to the police they don't know who the people are because they've given false names and everything. When they do it to ourselves they must be prepared to suffer the consequences that could come back to them. Harry could have done it himself, but we went as a mark of respect.

We weren't just looking for Coulston; we were looking for three men. I'd been with my wife Doreen to see her father in hospital at the Royal Free, and I put her on the train to Brighton telling her I had to go back to the office for a bit of business. Then we went looking and found him in a pub in South Lambeth and from there took him back to Charlie's scrapyard. We asked for the £650 to be put back, and he got a few clumps into the bargain. There was none of this so-called torture.

Afterwards I dropped him home back at South Lambeth, right outside his house. There was nothing wrong with him at all. He only went to hospital because he had one cut on the head and it was still oozing a bit. He was asked to return the money as soon as possible but he never did. He just disappeared.

If he'd gone straight to the police, he'd have had no injuries to show and all I'd have been charged with was assault. The worst I'd have got is six months – if, and it's a big if, I'd been convicted. But he didn't go to the police then. When he went to hospital they just kept him in overnight as a precaution. Today, with the hospitals full up and closed down he'd have been turned out there and then. He'd already jumped bail on a drunken driving charge, and he ran out of the hospital the next day in his pyjamas and disappeared. He re-surfaced again about fifteen months later when he was convicted of theft and got ten months' imprisonment.

His version was that he'd been kidnapped outside the Prince of Wales pub in Wilcox Road and taken to Charlie's offices at Peckford Place. There he said he'd been stripped naked, punched and pushed and then questioned by Charlie who had a gun. Next thing I was meant to have come in and hit him across the eye with some metal object, splitting his eye-lid. He said he was put in a cold bath, and then I'd tried to take his teeth out with a pair of pliers. According to him I'd missed the first time and just got a bit of his gum, and then I'd done a bit better and pulled out part of a top tooth. He said he'd been burned with cigarettes and then wrapped in a sheet with weights, put in the van and driven round again. Later he'd been brought back to the office, where Eddie had said he was sorry and that it was all a big mistake. His evidence was all rubbish.

I remember Jack Rosa – I think it was in 1957 – he got six months for doing exactly the same trick with the cigarettes. If Harry's brother had gone to the police, Coulston would have got some bird in the same way. We'd never have done anything like that but, as it turned out, it makes you think it would have been the best thing if it had happened that way.

They never got Harry Rawlings. He used to have a drink on a Friday and his wife would tell him not to drive home, and so he'd stay at his mother's. When the arrests took place on that Saturday morning, Harry wasn't at home and he had warning that the police had been round. They couldn't charge his wife, and she'd got a message to Harry so he disappeared for two years. He was the main character, it revolved around him. Coulston completely denied the cigarettes allegation. All you could hear was him saying Rawlings was in on the beating. We never mentioned the cigarettes either because obviously we were saying we knew nothing at all. Coulston said he was falsely accused of participating in this fraud and he was mistaken for whoever did participate. The other men with him never give evidence. If they had, there might have been some sympathy from the jury. After he got his clipping from us, he'd said the other men were known only by their first names, and this may have been correct. If you participate in a criminal activity and someone tells you his name is Bill or Tom, you accept it. Like I've said already, you don't ask for the other name if he's been guaranteed by someone else.

Whilst I myself was serving five years for Mr Smith's – at this stage no one had been arrested – I went on an appeal visit at Wandsworth in early July 1966. Visits were in boxes in those days. Lo and behold, who was there but Benny Coulston. It came out in the trial that he'd been put there by the police to identify me as the Fraser who he'd named in his statement. He said, 'Hello Frank.' I didn't recognize him at first although I'd known him and his family for years. They used to have an afternoon drinking club, The Sunset, in Streatham or Brixton. He said, 'It's Benny.' I said, 'Are you all right?' or something like that, and that was the end of the story as far as I was concerned. I went on my visit and I forgot all about it until he gave his evidence. But lurking somewhere near were detectives dressed as prison warders who were watching and writing it all down.

During the trial Coulston said he'd seen me in prison. The jury wasn't supposed to know of my previous convictions, and my counsel made a song and dance. The judge said to the jury that they mustn't take any regard of the bit of his evidence that he'd seen me in prison, and that I might have been there for not paying maintenance or for non-payment of a fine.

After we'd all been charged, Coulston was in the same prison as me although I was in the hospital. A prisoner who was working as a cleaner came up to me and said he could do Benny Coulston, and that might make him retract the lies he'd already told. One of my family sent £350 to an address in Walworth I'd been given. A week later the cleaner told me he'd done him, and sure enough Coulston came to the hospital where I was with a towel with what looked like blood all over it on his head. But a Scotsman who was a librarian in the hospital told me there was something fishy and the bloodstained towel over his head was part of the act, so I ignored it. If he had have been hit over the head, then that would have come out in the course of his evidence. It was an ensnarement, a trap to make things worse for me. It shows the lengths the police were going to. Luckily I had this good librarian who marked my card.

A few years later, in about 1969, a doctor got fourteen years over drugs at the Old Bailey and he was in Brixton. A lot of the evidence against him was from a grass. The same man who said he'd get Coulston beaten up said he could find a man who'd kill the grass for the doctor. But the people who came up to see the doctor to arrange the business were detectives. This same man must have been a professional witness for the police.

Meanwhile Coulston had got my sister Eva into trouble as well. His brother Johnny was now working as a doorman in Billy Howard's club, The Beehive, in Brixton. Billy Howard got in touch with Eva and said Johnny worked for him, and he would like to see her as he might be able to help me. Remember they came to Eva, not the other way about. Johnny told her their mother had died and they were letting Benny go to the funeral under an escort, but that he would be able to talk to him. Was that all right? He then reported back to Eva and said he'd seen his brother and Benny would be prepared to tell the truth. Eva said by all means. It was arranged that when Benny finished his ten months Eva, Johnny and Benny's girl should meet him at the prison. He'd told the police he didn't want an escort, and eventually Eva took him to a solicitor's to make his statement. Eva introduced him to the solicitor, said who she was and what the case was about, and took no further part. There's no disputing that in any way.

Coulston had come to Eva first through Billy Howard, who knew her better than the Coulstons did. She never went to him; she did what any sister or member of the family would do. Charlie's secretary, Louise, went along too. Albie Woods, who was arrested with them both, was just a friend who acted as the chauffeur to pick Benny up to go and see Louise, who prepared an affidavit for him to swear. They even went to the National Council for Civil

Liberties for help, and a member of the organization gave evidence for the defence. It was all open and above board. It didn't stop the police prosecuting Eva, Louise and Albie Woods for conspiracy to pervert.

The next thing we heard was the judge was to be Mr Justice Lawton, and guess whose son he was? I had had a spot of trouble with him as well and as a result I hoped he might stand down. He didn't.

12

My trouble with Lawton had come just about the time of the Coulston incident, when Doreen's father was ill and I was going back and forwards from Brighton to London. It could even have been the day of the Coulston incident but I can't say for sure. It certainly happened one night in early 1965 at Victoria Railway Station.

We'd been to see Doreen's father, who was in the Royal Free Hospital, and were on our way back to Brighton. Before the station was modernized the old W.H. Smith bookstall was just near the rails leading to the platform. Doreen had gone to buy a football magazine for our son and to get something to read on the train for us. I was just standing there when I saw a man with his back against the railings dressed in barrister's uniform – bowler hat, umbrella and grey striped trousers. As I looked I knew immediately who he was. I'd seen him at Pentonville and Wandsworth with his father, and I'd also seen his photograph when he defended Podola and when he'd been elevated to be a High Court judge. I knew his history.

As I really hated his father and I had every cause to do so, I could not resist going up to him even though, in fairness, it was nothing to do with his son. I approached him, excused myself and asked if he was Sir Frederick Lawton. He said he was, and I asked if he would be seeing his father. There was a note of caution in his voice, but he said he might.

'Well, my name is Francis Davidson Fraser . . .,' I began, and I went on to recap that I thought his father was the most vicious, spitefullest, wickedest man who'd ever been in the modern Prison Service. I told him that more men had had bread and water and been flogged as a result of what his father had done than anyone else, and that his father had been the most assaulted prison officer there was. Everything I said I believed was the truth. Sir Frederick couldn't get away. He couldn't go back because of the railings, and he couldn't go forwards because I was in front of him. When he moved to the side I'd do the same. Unbeknown to me, there was a large crowd gathering behind me. I was speaking loudly. I wasn't shouting, but my voice was raised and people wanted to see who was being spoken to. In the meantime Doreen had got her magazine and seen this crowd and come over. She heard my voice, pushed people aside, tapped me on the shoulder and said, 'Come on, love, take no notice, come on.' I think she thought someone was laying into me. I turned round to answer and Sir Frederick ran for a taxi. I chased after him, calling his father names. I can't see how anyone would forget that incident. I made no secret of my name.

Jimmy Fellowes, my solicitor, got Charles Lawson and John Lloyd-Eley to defend me both on the murder and at the Torture trial. At the Torture I had Lloyd-Eley on his own at the magistrates' court. He was very good, but it was an impossible task with Geraint Rees, the magistrate, against him. I paid several thousands for my defence, I can't remember exactly how much. I didn't have legal aid until the end, if I did then. I went on the basis he would try even harder that way. On being found guilty, Mr Justice Lawton also ordered me to pay £2,000 towards the costs of the prosecution. I certainly never paid it.

Eddie and Charlie Richardson knew of my quarrel with Lawton. I made no secret of it, and when Eddie and I had a conference in a room at Wandsworth Prison before the trial started Lawson and Lloyd-Eley were there and so was Eddie's counsel. We asked when the trial would start and they told us. We asked who the judge would be, and they said it was Lawton. I wanted to tell them now about me and Lawton at Victoria but Eddie said to hold on, see if he says anything first. At the beginning of the trial that'll be the time for Lawton to disclose it. If he don't, then you can raise it when you see what attitude he's taking.

Eventually the trial began on 4 April 1967. Ninety-one people were turned down for the jury, including thirty-seven rejected by the prosecution and three who were excused. I objected to the women on the jury. Everyone had seven free challenges to jurors and when I had reached my seven I did give a reason for one more. I knew I'd seen the man who was going to take the oath somewhere before. Then I remembered I'd seen him many times on the Brighton train. I'd travelled with Dave Sexton, who was then the manager of Leyton Orient, and I knew this man through that. The man admitted he'd travelled on the train with me and he was taken off the jury. Instinct told me he knew who I was – Frankie Fraser – and that would not rebound in my interests. It would immediately class me as a villain, and so anything the prosecution said about me would be believable. I was being called 'Mad Frankie' even then. I also objected to another woman. I thought that only one woman amongst eleven men might be subject to pressure, but Lawton rejected it.

The trial was split into bits and the Glinski allegations came in the second part. After two weeks Taggart was giving evidence and it was clear the trial wasn't going well for us. By the seventeenth day of the trial I thought Lawton's attitude was vindictive. It seemed to me far above what a judge should be. I spoke to Charles Lawson, my counsel, and told him I wanted him to object to the judge. As Charlie and I had the same junior, Lloyd-Eley, we could have a conference with both counsel together. I told them exactly word for word what I'd said. They looked aghast. I said the reason why I never told them in the beginning was that I was sure Lawton would declare it. Now I was mentioning it. They went white. I told them they could see my wife and she'll tell them word for word. Lawson made his objection the next day.

Each day, the trial would start at 10 and finish at 4.30, and about 11 o'clock Lawson, he plucked up the courage and said he'd like to make an application in the absence of the jury. Sir Frederick sent the jury out all nice and friendly. Little did he know what was to come.

Lawson began:

He tells me that about the end of 1964, the beginning of 1965, he had arrived at Victoria Station for the purpose of catching a train. He was then, apparently, travelling to Brighton. He saw your Lordship on the railway station standing, he thinks, between platforms 14 and 15, approached your Lordship and asked whether your Lordship was Sir Frederick Lawton. Your Lordship replied, 'Yes.' I gather that he then made derogatory, defamatory remarks about your father and that your Lordship walked away up the platform, I think pursued by my client, who was continuing to make these remarks.

Lawton was furious:

Mr Lawson, there is not a word of truth in this, not one word, and I want to say that at the earliest possible moment. I would undoubtedly have recalled such an event, and I have no recollection whatsoever of anything of the kind happening.

I jumped up and shouted, 'Yes, it did,' and was told to sit down. The jury was recalled and Taggart continued giving his evidence. Taggart was really going for me. The karate expert was saying I was hitting him with a hammer, lump of wood, umbrella, everything bar the kitchen sink. Normally Lawton would have been going, 'Not too fast, Mr Taggart, hold on, I'm writing this down.' But Lawton was now clearly thinking about something. I was sitting behind Charlie and Eddie, and I wrote a note pointing this out and saying something was going to happen. Sure enough it was now about

1 o'clock; time for the lunch break. The jury retired and we all went to stand up. He told us to sit down. I said to Charlie and Eddie, 'You watch.'

Lawton said, 'You made an application to me, Mr Lawson, earlier on. There was an occasion in the winter of 1964–65 on a London railway station when a man was abusive to me. A drunken oaf I took him to be, and he was not your client, I'm sure of that, but even if it was, it does not mean to say I cannot carry on with this trial.' Words like that. He really belittled Lawson. I felt really sorry for him; it destroyed him in a way. I jumped up again and shouted and he told me to sit down. He said he'd no recollection of his father's name being mentioned. I think in the period after Lawson had raised the matter Lawton must have remembered he'd complained to the police, and the record might exist and we might have it. That's why he had to admit it. If it hadn't been me, how would I know the details of the incident?[1]

---

[1] In fact Mr Justice Lawton said, 'There is a matter I want to place on record with regard to your application. You did not do me the courtesy of giving me any warning of the application you were going to make, or of the basis upon which you were going to make it, and as a result I had to put my mind directly on to the problem there and then, and I want to say as emphatically as I can that I have no recollection whatsoever of having spoken to your client.

During the hour or so which has transpired since you spoke to me I have been running through my mind the occasions in my life when strangers have come and spoken to me, and I can just – but only just – recollect one occasion on a London station on a winter's evening when somebody spoke to me and was abusive. I have no recollection of any abuse relating to my father. I feel if there had been any abuse relating to my father I should have remembered it. I have no recollection whatsoever if it was your client, none whatsoever, and I am quite certain if it had been your client I would have remembered . . . in the circumstances it would be no ground whatsoever for my not going on with this trial.'

Looking back, my real mistake was probably not making the application at the beginning; but the only bogey with that was no one would have heard the story. If I'd told the barristers in that room at Wandsworth, Lawton wouldn't have taken the case and it would never have come out. The idea was we would have got an inkling how the case was going, and in a re-trial we could have refreshed ourselves as to how the prosecution was going. We knew what Taggart was going to say, and second time around we'd have had a better chance. That's only my opinion with my little bit, well quite a bit, of legal knowledge. It was a chance which never come off, but in the long run it was the wiser of the two.

Charlie says in his book, *My Manor*, that he was with me that night. He wasn't. If Charlie had been at Victoria it would have been better for both of us. Doreen had to be interviewed, and I'd have been much happier to leave her out. If I'd said it was Charlie with me, Doreen wouldn't have stood for the truth not coming out.

I think whereas Charlie and Eddie in relation to me were very much experienced and able businessmen – far more up front than me – in criminal matters such as this I had much more experience. I was much more realistic. I had my feet firmer on the ground than they had theirs. I don't think they realized what they were up against but I did. I knew that in that day and age it would be nothing short of a miracle which would get us acquitted. The powers that be then were determined you were convicted come what may. Even though the case was shaky and lightweight in many respects, where no reasonable jury now would convict on such witnesseses, then it was different. I didn't tell them because I didn't want to dishearten them. By my reckoning I don't think that now the DPP's office would even have charged us on that type of evidence or, if they had, then they'd have decided not to carry on.

Take Eddie's case with Jack Duval – the incident was said to have occurred six years before and this admitted conman had never made a complaint in the meantime. Would any jury in its right mind accept that today?

Coulston had X-rays for a suspected fractured skull. Those X-rays would have shown if his teeth had been pulled by pliers, but the X-rays were lost. The hospital could produce everything else bar them. To me that smells. Today that evidence wouldn't have been accepted, but then people were naïve. It was just calmly brushed aside by the prosecution and the judge. If those X-rays had been produced it would have completely got me out of that case; it would have destroyed Coulston's evidence completely. If I had been convicted it would have been on a much lesser charge.

Why didn't we have Coulston seen by a dentist? First, it only ever come out eighteen months later and, in those days, solicitors didn't try as much. Then they were frightened of the prosecution. It was such a big case. But give them credit, every point Lloyd-Eley made at the committal proceedings, Geraint Rees, the magistrate, brushed it aside. I'll give you a prime example of what happened at the Old Bailey. Take the so-called black box which was meant to have given people electric shocks, and which was never found because it didn't exist. The prosecution produced a replica of what, in their opinion, the box would have looked like, and they had all the electrical equipment with it. James Fellowes, my solicitor, did well here. He produced a top scientist who said if you were to use this so-called box on anyone, no matter what part of the body you put it on all it would do would be to produce a mild tickling sensation. Today that evidence would have stood up and things would have been different.

But then his evidence was absolutely brushed aside by the prosecutor, Sebag Shaw who, by the way, used to play cards in a Jewish fellow's spieler in Jermyn Street. I saw him there occasionally. He was a very able player and a very able prosecutor, but then he more or less had a licence to say what he wanted.

That's what I'm trying to say. Even if you'd produced a dentist to say, 'No, that definitely didn't happen to Coulston's teeth or gums,' it wouldn't have been accepted. His whole mouth would have been in a terrible state. If he'd been injured as he says, there was no way he'd have been able to run out of hospital the next day or even talk to doctors. There's no denying he did go into hospital but all his medical records disappeared. The prosecution never called any dentist either. Would a jury accept that now?

I did give evidence at my trial. I was quite good but I made a mistake. One of the witnesses against me was Bennie Coulston of course. Part of his evidence was that I, amongst others, had been smoking cigarettes and burning him with them. I'd finished my evidence the evening before, and the next morning when I went to court I said to Mr Lawson that I'd like to go back in the box to say I'd never smoked, and that I wouldn't know how to hold a cigarette even. It was a very small piece of evidence but to me it was important. Anything that would dislodge the evidence against me would help. He agreed, so I went in the witness box that morning and I did so well that the prosecution were really desperate. So they brought up some registered letters sent to my address in Brighton during the five months I was in custody before Charlie was arrested. These receipts were what my family were sending to my wife – £20 and £30. They found the receipts when they arrested my nephew, Jimmy Fraser, but they made out they found three or four of these receipts in Charlie's house. That made it look as though I was more friendly with Charlie than I had said. I think that really turned the case against me, just that one bit. By going into the witness box again I gave the prosecution the opportunity to come up with that bit about the payments, and it did for me in my opinion, although we'll never know. In my heart I think we probably never had any chance. My family had only held on to the receipts in case they were lost. If there was anything to hide, they'd have destroyed them.

In the end Berman was acquitted on the main charges. He gave evidence against us all but he ended up suffering. Lawton thought he was more sinned against than a big-time crook. He was wrong. But if he hadn't altered his evidence to go along with the prosecution, then he would not have had to divulge all his business affairs. As a result, two years later he got twelve months for not paying his tax. That crucified him. He's dead now.

Funnily enough I was very good to Berman. His wife was always having affairs with other geezers, and one of them was with this Irishman. Then she accused him of pinching her jewellery, went to the police and got him arrested. It could have been her turning wicked just because the Irishman was going to leave her. I said to Berman he couldn't allow this, and so Berman got his wife to withdraw the charge. When the Irishman came out of the nick I kidnapped him, held him, got a ticket for him for Australia and put him on the plane. Along the way he'd had a few thumps for his pains. Then she had an affair with a taxi driver and she tried to prosecute him. Berman begged me to do the same for him as I'd done for the Irishman. At the time I thought he wasn't a bad fellow; he was always cheerful and good company, so I gave the man a couple of digs and he promised not to see her again. Then Berman just went against us. He was up on a charge about a man who'd been messing with his wife, but that got dropped out.

The hardest thing was that his wife and sister was very friendly with my sister Eva. Before the hearing at the Bailey, Berman had been moved to Lewes with Jimmy Kensit whose daughter is an actress. When they did things like that the rumours soon got round. Eva asked Berman's mother and sister, was it true that Berman was going against us? They denied it, saying no way, Alf would never tell lies and he liked Frank and Eddie. But Berman's wife and sister knew all the time what he was going to do. Kensit, they just let him go but he'd made his statement. If he hadn't gone the other way his evidence would have helped us get out of it. There was a picture in the papers the other day of Reggie Kray holding Patsy Kensit's baby. Charlie Richardson was very upset and sent a note in to Reg saying he shouldn't mix with the families of grasses.

The trial lasted ten weeks and of course when it came to it Charlie, Eddie and me, along with a few others, went down. Charlie got sentenced to twenty-five years, Eddie got ten for his part on the assault on Coulston and two years concurrently for doing Jack Duval. Roy Hall, who was one of the men in Charlie's yard, got ten. Jimmy Moody, who'd been charged over Benny Coulston, was acquitted.

I don't know. Charlie had been messing with people in high places. He'd been involved with the South African Secret Service. Sometimes Eddie and I wonder whether that is why they made a dead set for us all.

After the first trial was over I said to Charles Lawson, he'll be sentencing me tomorrow, and that's when Lawson said that whatever happened I'd still have to come up on the Glinski case, the other charge. In those days you had the right to make a personal statement from the dock before you were sentenced, and I said I'll be telling Lawton everything of our meeting at Victoria Station. Charles Lawson went white – I think behind the scenes he must have been hauled over the coals over what I got him to say. I was in the cells at the Old Bailey and he came back on the morning I was going to be sentenced and said he's not going to weigh you off today.

When I and my nephew James and Johnny Longman

came up for Glinski about a week later, I objected to the jurors and the three of us objected to twenty-one in total. That was our maximum. After the prosecution made its opening speech and the trial got under way, it was then we see the clerk of the court, Leslie Boyd, give the judge a note. Lawton read it and said, 'A note has come into my possession written by a jury member, and it says his father was a PC for twenty-five years in Camberwell and as he knew all about the "Fraser gang" he didn't think it fair to sit on the jury. What I propose is that the juryman is excused and we carry on with eleven.' All counsel nodded, and so did Jim and Johnny Longman. I wouldn't have it. Lawton asked me why I was objecting, and I asked who else has the juryman told this to? With that, three more jurymen put their hands up to say they'd read the note, and so the trial was abandoned. I was told if I pleaded guilty I would get a very lenient sentence. Jimmy and Johnny Longman would get eighteen months each, and mine would be eighteen months on top of what I got for Coulston and Taggart.

Still I wouldn't have it: I wanted to plead 'Not Guilty'. Lawson came down and said it was down to fifteen months, then to nine, and I still wouldn't have it. Eventually they came down and said the prosecution was offering no evidence against me and it was put on the file. It knocked the ground from under my feet. Jimmy was to be released immediately because of the time he had served. It was the second time he got done for something over which he was innocent. He'd been convicted in the Challenor case all those years earlier, and it had come out in an inquiry that he'd been innocent. Now he pleaded guilty to be able to get out to help his mother and father, who were charged with a fraud at London Airport which was tacked on to the Torture trial.

I then told Lawson again about what I was going to say. He said he was afraid that if I said anything he'd hammer me. Lawson was really worried. Behind the scenes he must have been in trouble.

Nevertheless, I did tell Lawton I'd seen him at Victoria Station and what I thought of his father, and that I took nothing back. When he sentenced me Lawton said, just like Mr Justice Donovan in the Spot case, 'I take the view that you went berserk,' and then he said that he had given Clark, who'd been charged with us and who worked for Charlie, eight years and he had to give me more, so he give me ten. I think he must have had a conscience because he really was lenient with me. Bearing in mind my previous, ten years was a result.

It wasn't the end. Three men were arrested for getting into the jury of the Torture trial. We'd got a tip that one of the juror's brother went into a café in the East End and the owner told one of our friends. It was decided if the truth could come out it should do so by any means. Leslie McCarthy, from Atlantic Machines, Billy Stayton's brother and a friend were all arrested. The caff owner had introduced them to the brother. He said that if it was him there would be no problem but said, 'With my brother I think you're wasting your time. The police sleep in his house.' We'd been told this at the outset of the trial. 'I will ask him but I don't think it'll be any good.' He went to his brother's house, spoke in private and mentioned the possibility of giving a favourable and true verdict. His brother immediately told the police. It never even got off the ground. In fact it was as legitimate as you could have done it. Bill Stayton's brother got twelve months and Leslie got eighteen months. The third man was acquitted. The juror was retained on the jury in the main trial.

I would love to be able to say I'd pulled out Benny Coulston's teeth with pliers. It would make for a better story and I'd have happily boasted to think I'd inflicted that pain. My poor sister Eva served two years when she was completely innocent, and it would have given her some happiness to know it did happen. Coulston named twelve people; all twelve were charged and nine were acquitted. In one period his evidence was so ridiculous people in the dock couldn't suppress laughter. He fingered my nephew Jimmy Fraser. Today that case would have been slung out. Coulston never said a word against Jimmy until the end of his evidence at the magistrates' court, but when Jimmy was laughing at him he suddenly turned and said, 'He's one of them.' I'm not a lawyer or barrister, but in my own layman's way I have a knowledge of law through my lifestyle. I'm quite confident that case would never have stood up in the courts of today. No jury would be so foolish as to tolerate such evidence.

My brother James and his wife were the Frasers charged in the airport frauds. They were both acquitted, quite rightly. It was always said that the Richardson

246

gang were leaning on the people who worked the car park fraud at the airport, and were threatening them. It was ridiculous. Would I threaten my own brother?

13

The day after I was sentenced I was taken to Durham from the hospital at Wandsworth. I was walking properly by this time, although I still had my stick with which I had been hoping to get a bit of sympathy from the jurors. It didn't take long for me to get into more trouble. By the time I went there in the July, I had done over twelve months as a convicted man. Charlie Richardson had only done a week, and the rules then were that you couldn't watch a bit of television unless you had served so many months. I kicked up a fuss and got the other prisoners to join in. As a result the screws had to let Charlie and Roy Hall, who was with us, look at the telly after that.

There was always sheer hatred for London prisoners from the Geordie screws, and in 1967 when I went back hatred was more inflamed than ever. They didn't like the southerners in any event. Tensions built up between prisoners and the prison officers, and I'd only been there about a month or six weeks when a mob of prison officers came and took me to the punishment block. When I got in the cell they came in with escapers' patches. In the security wing at Durham you wore the ordinary prison clothes because it was then considered escape-proof, although later John McVicar got out and Wally Probyn and Joey Martin nearly made it. I refused to wear them. Apart from that time as a kid I'd never tried to escape even once, because when any good escape attempts were being hatched or were ready to go I'd been transferred. I am a very practical person that way. By that I mean I didn't want some fancy scheme which you knew full well would fail. If I was going to try to escape, then I wanted a reasonable chance of success, but I was never in a prison where I could see that chance. The Alfie Hinds scheme was all right, but it was the only one I heard of and as I say he was moved before anything could be done.

I was left in my cell with just my pants on. An hour or so later I heard a voice shouting out from another cell, 'Frank, Frank.' It was a prisoner called Ronnie Piper, serving a sentence for manslaughter, who also had refused to wear the escape outfit. He said he wasn't going to eat either. We weren't on report. Knowing we'd refuse the patches and so would therefore be on punishment all the time, the screws were trying to make an example of us and intimidate the rest of the prison. We were both taken before the Governor for refusing to obey an order, and given bread and water as well as loss of remission and solitary confinement. The bread and water didn't make any difference because we weren't eating anyway. We were then put on report again for refusing to sew mailbags in our cells. We got more punishment. After three or four days I had a visit from Doreen, and Piper asked if she would make a complaint on his behalf as well when she did for me. I said I'd do my best. She went to see his wife, and went to the Home Office and protested. After seven days a prison officer came and said my friend was now sewing and had put on the patches. I burst out laughing, I thought he was kidding me. When he shouted out that evening, I told him what the screw had told me. He said it was true. I said he shouldn't have started in the first place if he was going to give in. He said the Deputy Governor had promised him he'd go into the wing, and that when his wife visited he'd get a much better visit – not just twenty minutes. I said yes, but you knew all this before you started and you'd have to suffer. Why do it in the first place? I said he was weak, and he more or less started crying. A day later they let him up. I carried on and after about twenty-eight days they took me to the hospital. I had refused to go and so I was strapped down and was taken over in a body belt. I was forcibly fed. They forced my mouth open, put a block of wood in and put the tube through the wood. After a day or so the doctor said, 'You've won. You'll go back on the wing and you don't have to wear the escape patches.' My wife came to visit me in the hospital and I was told I'd get a two-hour visit.

On the previous visit I'd asked Doreen to write to Mr Bainton as he was now Director of the Prison Service. She went to see him and he told her it would be best if I was transferred. I was now eating and three days later I was put back on the wing. People cheered and shook my hand. After two days my door was opened and there was an escort from Leicester to take me to the security wing there. What Durham never said was that my wife had told them that she was coming to visit me that day, so she came all the way for nothing.

So in October 1967 I went to Leicester. The screw who took me had had a straightener with Jack Rosa in Birmingham in 1948 or so. Jack got eighteen of the Cat for attacking him with a weapon, but it had been a straight fight. He knew I knew this, and that I didn't like him for it. He was the type of screw who fancied he was a street fighter who could hold his own, but he'd underestimated Jack. He'd come to Jack's cell and got done. That was a bad start for me and Leicester in a way. A straightener with a screw wasn't common but it wasn't completely unknown. For example old 'Dodger' Mullins, after the Dartmoor mutiny, had had a straight fight with a screw and then the screw had said he'd attacked him. The same thing happened with Jack McVitie, but no one ever offered me one. I'd have taken the chance it was genuine if a screw had offered it.

When I got to Leicester it was a shambles; only the main part had been built. The security wing was on the ground floor. People in the basement couldn't look up, and you were separated from the first floor as well. Workmen were still putting doors and electricity in. Tommy Wisbey, Bobby Welch, Jimmy White from the Train, Joe Martin who'd been in Durham and had tried to escape with John McVicar, and Frank O'Connell who was doing fifteen years for manslaughter, were all in the security block.

After Buster Edwards arrived I can remember him telling me that Tommy Butler and Frank Williams had been to see him in the cells at Nottingham to say they never went crooked on him. Williams had given evidence to say that Buster should have burned the Farm down and that he hadn't been on the Train Robbery proper. This supported Edwards' evidence and the judge, Milmo, who'd acted for the *Empire News* in my libel action, must have half believed him. By getting only the fifteen, it did open the gates for the others to get parole.

There was always conflict at Leicester. There were prison officers who wanted to make it hard and tough for the prisoners, and at that stage in the Prison Service they were predominant as opposed to the ones who were intelligent and wanted a liberal regime. They could manipulate the Governor, Clay, who was known as Cassius. You never knew where you were with them. One moment they would be all right and the next they'd want to clamp down. In the meantime, with the works going on the noise was terrible.

One day Tommy Wisbey, me and Micky Morgan, who'd been nicked for murder at Wakefield and was doing life, got into trouble and had a row with prison officers and were put on report for it. We got our punishment and when we managed to get together again we were riled about what had happened. Even by prison standards it was a liberty. I suggested we shouldn't waste time with the officers and rather go for the Governor, and they both agreed. So we did the Governor, rather gently in a way I suppose. You had to take turns at cleaning the submarine, which is what we called our landing, and me and Tommy and Mickey would do it once or twice a week between us. We would leave five buckets spread discreetly round the wing. These buckets would be full of filth, dirt, urine, dog-ends, and it was the Governor's luck on that happy day to fetch round the Chief Probation Officer for Leicestershire. There would be a chief officer, possibly with eight or more officers clustered round him. You'd hear him saying proudly, 'I've got the Train Robbers,' because they were world famous. Out of the blue came the three of us with buckets. We pushed everyone aside and tipped them all over the Governor. Tommy Wisbey was magnificent. As he was taller, he could tip the bucket actually over his head and ram it down. It had to be pulled off him. It may read or sound terrible to people who don't understand prison life, but to prisoners it meant a lot. You were only doing things the prison officers do to you down the punishment blocks. We were jumped on and locked up. The Governor had to have a shower and a suit brought over for him he was in such a state. It was wonderful fun. We lost remission, were given bread and water by the magistrates, and we did it happily. We weren't transferred immediately. I was the first one to go, and I was sent to Brixton three weeks after the arrest of the Twins.

It was the day Manchester United won the European Cup and I remember being driven down the M1 and seeing all the scarves and pennants flying from the car windows as they passed us. Shortly after I arrived in Brixton, who came in but Tommy Butler who'd arrested me over the Mr Smith's fight. This time along with him was James Earl Ray, who was later convicted of shooting Martin Luther King. I shouted out abuse at Butler – the screws had to fight to get me away – as he had fitted me up for the murder of Dickie Hart.

They had Ray in a room which had been used as an office and which in effect was two cells knocked into one. They'd cleared the office out and had him with two officers. Now it really was rather like he was in the condemned cell, with the one slight difference that you could actually speak to him whereas in the condemned cell no other prisoner could speak to or even see that man.

He was on the landing underneath and occasionally I could nip down and have a word with him. It wasn't permitted but the screws turned a blind eye. The officers would tell me to go away, but they didn't want to enforce the order. Their main role was to see that he wasn't assassinated rather than to prevent his escape. There was a big black population in Brixton itself, as well as a high percentage of prisoners. In fact a black civilian worker, a stoker in a boiler house, was, I think, suspended until Ray was sent back to the States. They were concerned in case there was a riot. Once the officers realized I wasn't trying to attack him they weren't too worried about me talking to him. As I had been in so much trouble prison officers, for once, weren't tempted to rock the boat. Ray wasn't fighting the extradition; he didn't deny his involvement to me or anyone else that I knew. All he did was run down the black people in the south of America, seeming to try to justify his action. He called King a man who stirred up trouble for the whites.

I was only in the wing for three months. I could also see Reggie or Ronnie to get a parcel of food sent in. They were already there, and I used to have the odd conversation with them. First, they asked me about Charlie Mitchell who was charged along with them. They had a gut feeling he was going to give evidence against them. Mitchell was a good dog doper, and he had been a good thief in his time. Did I think he would give evidence? I said I didn't think he would but I wouldn't trust him. He was very rich and he could use as much money as he needed to get himself out of it. He did give evidence at the committal, but he didn't turn up for the trial. He went abroad, where he was later killed in a fight.

What the police were trying to do in the Kray case was to get to as many people as possible, and if a man of Mitchell's standing in the underworld gave evidence that would encourage many others to do the same. That part of the prosecution succeeded. The Twins then asked if I would help with their defence, and I said of course I would. Ronnie had just been charged with Cornell's murder and asked if I would give evidence to say they were very friendly with him. In fact I may have suggested it to them, I can't really remember. We couldn't have really long conversations, just pieces here and there, because with me convicted and them on remand we weren't supposed to be able to mix, but of course we did.

Then in August 1968 I started fighting with the officers in the security wing in Brixton. I was injected, put in a straitjacket and put in the padded cell in the hospital. Twice they did this, and it was on the second occasion after I was taken out of the straitjacket I was moved to Wandsworth down the punishment block. The needle must have been dirty because I got yellow jaundice. If you're on punishment a doctor has to see you every day. Usually they just look in your cell, go 'All right' and move on to the next, but this day a hospital screw looked at me, said 'You've got jaundice', called the doctor back and in no time I went over to the hospital where I was treated.

Some months later I was taken from the hospital to see the Deputy Governor. A solicitor representing the Krays wanted to see me, would I see him? I said of course, but the Deputy tried to talk me out of it. I told him to get on his bike and mind his own business. A solicitor came and took my statement and I was produced at the trial to give evidence.

After completing my evidence, as I went through the dock back to the cells I shook hands with Ronnie and wished him the best of luck, said that I knew he was innocent. It was all a bit of show. It didn't do any good, but I did me best and they appreciated it. It really infuriated the prison authorities. I think that everyone else had been frightened off by them.

I was then immediately taken to Leicester security wing. I rather fancied going back there. However, Eva had bumped into Rene Wisbey, told her I liked the idea, and she passed the message on to Tom who said to tell me to forget it. After the attempted escape, life was murder there and I should stay away. I thought it was just that they had a good number going and they didn't want me messing it up.

What had happened in August 1968 was a very daring escape from the security wing, six of them in all including Tommy Wisbey, Joey Martin, Bobby Welch and Little George Elliott. They tied up the screws, made two makeshift ladders, one to go over the fence and the other to be pulled up and pushed on to the wall – Leicester prison's wall is the highest in the country, always had been. Unfortunately for them they had had to guess the measurement from the fence to the wall. The ladder missed the wall by an inch or two and it crashed. They didn't have time to lift it up and try again. The security wing cameras had seen, and in seconds armed police was in. They were arrested and charged in the prison and were all punished. A new Governor was brought there. He was called Steinhausen.

It was sensible advice from Wisbey, but like a fool I took no notice. Whilst I was in Wandsworth, Beisty – that was the Governor's name – had brought the Prison Director round and I'd asked him if I could go to Leicester. It's unusual to get where you want to go, but sometimes they agreed with what you asked. Plus I'd written a petition about the dirty needle, and I think they may have sent me where I wanted to keep me quiet. Generally wherever they say you go, you go. If you refuse, you get to go in a straitjacket.

I arrived in March 1969 and I'd only been there two days when I arranged to go and see the Governor.

Micky, an Irish guy, agreed to come with me.[1] It was decided we would see the Governor and ask for better visits, because when you had them there were screws breathing down your neck the whole time in case you planned something. We hadn't been there at the time of the escape and we thought it might carry more weight. The screws took us out the workshop into the wing and took Mick in first. Unbeknown to me, Mick had a row with the Governor and he chinned a Principal Prison Officer. I'm marched in to the Governor and I could see everyone was tensed up. With prison instinct I knew something was wrong. The Governor was still arrogant, but he did listen and then completely dismissed the application.

Later when Mick told me what had occurred with him, he said he would attack the Governor the next day. I said that since it had been my idea to see the Governor, on principle I had to do it. I told the rest and they said, 'Don't. Don't get in trouble.' I said, 'No, it's got to be done.' The next day when the Governor came into the workshop I went into the toilet, came out, washed my hands, gently eased my way past a throng of officers and slung him a beautiful punch. Many a prizefighter would have been quite proud of it; he had about eight stitches below the eye. I was engulfed by officers and I shouted to the prisoners not to get involved in any circumstances. They said they wouldn't as long

[1] Some time later, Micky was on a motor-bike on his way home when one of the police cars escorting the Queen when she was visiting Clapham knocked him down and killed him. His wife got a letter from the Queen expressing her sympathy.

as the officers didn't beat me in front of them – all they could do is restrain me. Blood all over him and I managed to spit in his face. It doesn't sound nice, but that's what I thought I should do. I was put in a body belt, and when the screws brought food in they deliberately spat in it and one said he'd pissed in it. I kicked it out of their hands all over them. I was taken in front of the Governor, this time in a body belt, and was charged with gross personal violence to the Governor. He really shouldn't have heard the charge, he shouldn't have taken part. When he remanded me to the Visiting Magistrates, by a superhuman effort I slung myself, dived over the table and nutted him. Half of me is on the desk and half is on him. I got paid properly for that and was back in the strong cell in minutes.

I wouldn't eat or drink for about ten days. It was a miracle how I lived. I was then taken out of the security wing and put into the punishment block of the prison proper.

In the meantime, that bent copper Walter Virgo was head of prison security.[2] I didn't know it then, but Virgo was trying to contact Jimmy Humphries, the Soho porn king, to touch him for a few quid. He knew that in 1951 Humphries had been arrested with me and been acquitted of the burglary of the hotel in the Aldwych when the juror had given Jimmy the nod. Jim Humphries and I had gone a long

---

[2] Commander Wally Virgo, who was head of the Porn Squad, received twelve years' imprisonment. He and a number of other officers had been taking money from Humphries and others in the Soho porn industry. Virgo's conviction was later quashed on appeal.

way back. When Humphries got married to his first wife, Eva and Jimmy Brindle put them up in a room in their house until they could get on their feet; so Jim Humphries had a great regard for them both.

Virgo got in touch with Humphries to say that the authorities knew I was going to have a knife smuggled in on a visit, stab the Governor and smuggle the knife out. Virgo had also told him that all my visits were tape-recorded. Jimmy must have realized all this was complete rubbish. For a start, we were surrounded with screws during a visit and you couldn't pass over a cigarette paper let alone a knife. Anyway, visitors had already been through an electronic survey before they were allowed to see me. I was just the excuse and a cover for him to get in touch with Humphries, and Jim did get a message to me.

When Eva and Doreen arrived at Leicester in early April for a visit, they're marched into the Governor's office where there's a screen. They're told they won't see me unless they strip. Rightly they refused, and the visit was cancelled. They went to the Post Office and sent me a telegram explaining what had occurred and then they went to the *Leicester Mercury*. I was given the telegram the next day and the *Mercury* printed the story of the search.

I had been on hunger strike about twenty-eight days in protest about the treatment of Eva and Doreen when the Director of Midland Region came round. He had one leg and one arm. He slung the screws out and asked me if I wanted to go to Broadmoor, which he said would be much better for me. I wouldn't have minded but I couldn't say yes. Francis, my youngest son, was at school and I couldn't have him being teased that I was in Broadmoor; it was bad enough for him me being in prison. I'd promised Doreen I wouldn't go to Broadmoor again if I could avoid it and so I said I'd like to go to Chelmsford. He gave a very definite 'No'. I then said what about Parkhurst? He went 'Maybe' and that was the end of the conversation.

Away he went and a few days later I was transferred to the Isle of Wight. There had been plenty of trouble at Parkshurst in the 1960s. The prison had been built in 1838 and was really well overcrowded. There'd been trouble with warders taking things home for themselves, and fights between them and prisoners. The *Daily Mail* had published an article the year before I got there, saying that prisoners were being beaten by the screws and there would be a riot if something didn't happen. The laundry got set on fire, and just before I got there prisoners sent out a round robin letter to the *People* newspaper saying they were being beaten up.

I went straight into the hospital and saw Dr Cooper there. He said to me I was to eat little but often, and I did so. I was on the punishment wing, but when it finished they still kept me down there. Alistair Miller was the Governor, immaculately smart but not as strong a governor as some and someone whom the prison officers could manipulate but he seemed the perfect gentleman. A new Deputy Governor, Hawkins, arrived, but again he was a bit weak and not particularly nasty. He spoke to me quite pleasantly. I'd got on reasonably well and it was agreed now I'd done five months down the punishment block I would go into the prison proper. About three weeks or so later, in October, a prisoner engineered a marvellous escape; out of his cell, over the security fence, over the wall and just missed the ferry. He was then running round the Island. He was the first man to get out of his cell in thirty-five years. Everyone was chuffed. Prisoners were tormenting the screws – we should have known better – and there was a lot of news coverage. The officers were fuming.

Right out of the blue the officers got into the Governor and he gave an order that all Category A men would be moved from their cells and on to another landing. A cell is a prisoner's home, and when he has to move home when he'd not been in trouble it's a very important thing. If you've been a prisoner you'll understand. We went to see the Governor and he pooh-poohed our complaints. Added to that, the final straw came on the Wednesday before the riot when a prisoner was taken ill in the recreation area. The screws wouldn't get him a doctor, and so some of us stayed over until medical help did arrive.

We agreed we'd have a sit-in at 7 o'clock at the end of association on 20 October 1969. There'd been a similar one in Durham the year before, and at the end of it everyone had been given a bath and a meal before being sent back to their cells, and the Governor had come and listened to what they had to say. Ours was to be like that. There would be up to twelve officers with us, and we had to do it very quickly so they couldn't stop us. There was to be no violence. That was to be all there was to it.

We asked every prisoner who would be on association if they would join in, and if not would they stay away from association that night. It had to be done, but it was dangerous because of the risk of a leak. As it was, six of the prisoners went to the authorities. They went sick that afternoon, and once they were taken out of the workshops they'd ask to see the Chief Officer. This type of sit-in had been talked about for two years but on each occasion, when it came to it, the prisoners had done nothing. Their nerve had gone. This time, with the reports from the grasses, the screws took it serious. All officers' leave at Albany was cancelled, along with all association at Albany and Camp Hill. Officers arrived from Winchester and Portsmouth. At 5 p.m. everyone was locked up there and groups of prison officers were drafted in, twenty here, thirty there, forty in the bathroom. Riot sticks were issued, but the prison officers on our association weren't told. If the screws had wanted to stop the demonstration they could have done so easily. All they needed to do was to cancel association that night, or the Governor could have sent me and a couple of others down on Rule 43 for twenty-four hours. They didn't do either of these things. Instead they allowed more prisoners than usual into association that night. They were just spoiling for a fight.[3]

[3] Where it appeared desirable for the maintenance of good order or discipline, the Governor could invoke Rule 43 and order that a prisoner should not associate with other prisoners generally or with specific prisoners. This could last for twenty-four hours, after which a member of the Visiting Committee could continue the order which could be renewed from month to month.

I gave the order at 7 p.m. The barricades were up and they was on us. There was tremendous fighting, literally in minutes. There's been riots enough since, but I doubt that even to this day there has been such fighting as that half hour. The order was to go in and get us come what may. Quite a lot of prisoners who did nothing were knocked about. The officers turned it into a bloody, violent confrontation when it needn't have been. They say they were fighting for their lives, but so were we. Inside half an hour it was all over. They had six of us in the table tennis room. We were all unconscious and as we came to, there lined up were officers in riot gear with sticks – tough guys taking the piss out of us. I said, 'I'll have a fight – keep the stick or not.' They all said, 'You're mad.' Then in comes the screws' hero, a big brute of a man built like a barn door – in he come, sleeves rolled up. They told him what I'd just done. He come forwards, and I must admit I was frightened but I had to challenge him. It was the road I'd gone down. When it came to it he was a coward like the others; said I was mad. The officers were stunned with disbelief. As he walked into the corridor someone who hadn't been rounded up threw a billiard ball at him and knocked him out.

As we were walked down the steps from the association room there was a gauntlet with riot sticks – like an arch at a wedding. One screw had got a meat cleaver; others had bars of iron. The officer at the top of the steps was in charge. He would shout out 'Smith coming down' and the inflexion in his voice meant you can give him a clout but it doesn't matter if you don't. If there was a growl it meant give him a few clumps, but if there was a stern voice it meant see to him. Then 'Fraser coming down' meant anything goes. From the association to the punishment cells was about a hundred yards with officers all the way along, so by the time I got to the punishment cell I couldn't stand. Then I was just slung in there. When the doctor came round two hours later the floor was smothered with blood and he immediately ordered I be taken to hospital in a wheelchair. That's where I was kept for six weeks until after the trial. And most of that time I was still in the wheelchair.

Cooper, the doctor, was good to me and to the other prisoners as well. It wouldn't be right to say otherwise. He did have sympathies and asked to be told exactly what happened. Cooper was really my mentor; he wanted me to go back to Broadmoor, and he brought a South African doctor from there to see me. Again I had to say no because of the promise I'd given to Doreen. It was a promise which did me no good. I'd have been much better there. Broadmoor was improving by leaps and bounds. When I was there in 1955 no one got remission. All that now was done away with: they were only too pleased to get you out.

Finally nine of us were summoned over the riot including me, Martin Frape, Tony Blythe, no relation of Billy, Timmy Noonan, Mickey Andrews, Stan Thompson, Peterson, and Andy Anderson, the one who'd escaped with Ronnie Biggs and landed up at Atlantic Machines. I had about eleven summonses including incitement to murder as well as GBH on the screws. There was no point in actually charging us because we were already serving sentences. Eva got me a lawyer – the one who'd defended her over that conspiracy to pervert in the Torture trial – and he briefed Billy Rees-Davies, who was known as the One-Armed Bandit and who was an M.P., and also Ernle Money who was then a Tory candidate. Unfortunately the election came up and they couldn't continue with the case, so my lawyer suggested I got George Shindler. He telephoned me at the hospital in Parkhurst – I was called into the doctor's office to take the call – and Mr Shindler said he had prosecuted my son David when he got seven years for a security van. He was very honest, he didn't have to tell me. He said that one day he prosecuted and one day he defended, but I just didn't feel on principle I could have him and so he defended Anderson instead. To my delight he got him found not guilty, but it was also a bit of dismay because he might have got me a not guilty and all. Eventually I had Richard Harvey, who was known as Don, a big, nice Irishman who wrote *Harvey's Industrial Relations*. He was very good but he was a bit soft when it came to it.

One of the problems, since we were all separated and in solitary, was preparing our defence. Jimmy Robson was a red-band by now, and used to come to my cell window and we could have a chat. I could give him instructions saying I'd like to call this witness, ask him if he'd mind. I wanted their permission to pass their names on to my lawyer. If they said they didn't want to, then I wouldn't get them involved. Out of the blue Eddie Richardson, who was in the security wing, came over the hospital to report sick from a cold. Whilst me and Jim was talking at the window we could hear the dog barking. Eddie would normally wave and I thought he'd do it that day and Jim would get caught. Fortunately no one noticed.

Messages used to be left in the chapel font, but the screws found this out and brought it up at the trial. There was one which was intercepted saying we wanted to get a barrister called Guy Willett to defend, and the message read he was 'shit-hot'. When it came up at the trial Mr Willett stood up and said, 'My Lord, I have to tell you I am not'.

First, we heard the judge was going to be Mr Justice Lawton, and we were very upset and were going to appeal against him, but then we were told we were going to have Mr Justice Bean, and what a difference he made in the end. Then we were told that we were going to have the trial on the Isle of Wight, which was something we didn't want because we thought a jury would be prejudiced against us and favour the screws. What we didn't know was that the screws at Parkhurst weren't generally popular on the island. Mr Justice Bean's son came and watched the trial, and he was sitting near us. We all heard who he was and Timmy Noonan wrote him a note: 'Tell your Dad to see we get a fair trial and to find us all not guilty.' The boy had a sense of humour. He wrote back, 'What's the point. Because if you're all innocent why should my father have to find you not guilty?' We sent him another saying, 'Tell your Dad to do his best.' He turned round and gave a charming smile. He was a nice boy.

It was a funny trial. It was the first they'd ever had on the Island. They didn't want to transport us to Winchester for security reasons and so they converted the upstairs of the Town Hall where they'd held the committal proceedings. There was no room for our relatives and at first there was a tannoy system into a room outside the court, but then when we protested the judge said that our families could come in and sit behind us.

About the second day when we went back to Parkhurst, there on the cell floor was Andy Anderson's radio, the screws had smashed it whilst he was gone. As a result, we stayed away from court. The judge sent a note to all of us saying we would be welcome back any time, and when we heard the trial was being fair we did so. But what was best was all the barristers in the case, including the prosecution, had a whip for a new radio for him. It was terrific what they done. Another time the prosecution, Sir Tim Molony, treated one of the prisoners to a pack of twenty cigarettes. We used to break in the morning for coffee and there was no time to send us back to Parkhurst and no room to separate us from the barristers outside the court, so they used to give cigarettes to those of us who smoked during the adjournment and then go straight back to cross-examining us afterwards. And that included the prosecution. Patrick Back, who was for Martin Frape, was especially good. He used to come and spend hours with him in an evening calming him down because Martin was really on edge. At the end of the trial when Mr Back came in to see Martin we all sang, 'For he's a jolly good fellow.' I would say, for that time and day I've never seen barristers and solicitors work so hard and diligently for the people they were representing. I think they felt, 'Yes, there is something wrong here.'

Every night when I came back to the prison hospital Dr Cooper would come to see me, and the day he gave evidence for the prosecution he told about our injuries. That night he showed me a card he'd received from the wife of a prison officer saying he would be killed, and another one saying he was a dog. The next day I told my counsel and when it was put to Dr Cooper he never denied it. The night after he was cross-examined I apologized, but he said it didn't matter and it was the truth. He was very very good.

In a way the judge summed up for us. He told the jury that we had been hit by the screws after the riot. 'Injuries to prisoners in the Parkhurst Jail riot permitted no other explanation than the excessive use of riot sticks,' is what he said.

When it came to it the jury was decent. I was acquitted of incitement to murder but convicted of the main charges. I got another five years added on to the fifteen I was already doing. But if I'd gone down on the incitement to murder I don't think I'd ever have come out. In its way it was a result.

14

I went straight from the court and off the Island. This time it was to Wakefield. Five or six officers from that nick were at Parkhurst a few days before the trial ended, waiting for me and having the time of their lives because no one could be exactly sure when it would finish. From then on life was going to be a misery for me. The whole story came out when a Wakefield officer was arrested. Of course, I didn't know this at the time. On the ferry to Southampton, I saw the *QE2*, and from there I went to Leicester, had something to eat and then on to Wakefield. I was taken straight to the hospital and then began the most unbelievable experience that I ever had in prison.

From the word go, from the moment I arrived in July 1970 the screws were very clever. Every evening I was allowed to go and watch television. My cell would be unlocked at 6 p.m. and then I would go to a ward and watch for a couple of hours. My cell door was locked behind me and it would be opened in front of me when I came back. One day when I went back I noticed that a bar of soap I'd bought in the prison canteen was missing, and I wondered when I had a bath could I have left it in the recess? I never dreamed someone could have stolen it. On my landing there were only five cells. No other prisoner could have crept in my cell, and so I put it down to my forgetfulness. Then another day my toothpaste was missing, and so on. The doctor would come and see me every day about dinner time, and eventually when he asked if I was all right, I said no. I told him about the shampoo or whatever had gone this time. The doctor looked at me as though I was imagining things. When could it have gone? I said it was a prison officer. I didn't have the slightest bit of evidence and that made it worse, but I stuck to my guns.

Now I kept all my gear in a pillow-case, and when I went to watch the TV I used to take everything with me. In the meantime I was getting on well with a hospital officer whose name was Jim. He told me to watch my step; he said when I first went there I had been discussed and it had been suggested that I should be beaten, but one screw had said, 'Do him my way, I'll send him round the bend'. Jim knew full well I wouldn't go to the doctors or governors because he wouldn't substantiate it; he wouldn't be that game. After a bit, though, he said he'd had enough; he was disgusted and was resigning. He was going to work on his wife's market stall in Leeds. I knew then I was going to lose a friend. I was going to have to put up with it.

Then in the recess at Wakefield, on the middle landing the walls were all dusty where the cleaners hasn't washed them. On the wall was the name 'EVA' written in the dust. I complained to the Chief Officer

271

and he had it washed away, but he looked at me as though I'd done it myself. When I came into my cell – to reach a window I'd have to stand on my locker – I could see on the windows EVA BR. I didn't say a word. All this was because in May 1971 Eva had arrived with her solicitor at Wakefield to take part in a Yorkshire TV programme called *Calendar*, and the M.P. for Grimsby was the presenter. Eva hadn't visited me because she wouldn't have her photo taken. It would be after the 6 o'clock news that she come on and she was really good. Her sincerity shone through. She'd come over terrific and the screws had a meeting and, so I heard, Hamilton went off alarming, calling me and her all the names under the sun.

But it's right I had got to him a bit, even though it was only in retaliation. Prison officers in the hospital wing wore a white coat, and in those days you got ice cream about once a week. As he was giving it out I was at the back of the queue. I'd be going, 'Get your ice cream from the salesman in the white coat.' Everyone laughed. I was getting him down. I was coming back even stronger. He would go red in the face. He'd creep to my cell door, and I'd see his shadow and so before he got there I'd shout out, 'Got you, Duggie, seen you looking through.' Bit by bit it was getting to him. The tormentor was being tormented. The difference was he couldn't take it.

Now he was getting desperate – I was getting on top of him. It reached a crescendo in July 1971. An officer has to sleep in the hospital, and when it was Hamilton's turn he must have got hold of my record and dug out the juicy bit which in essence said provided I behave myself leave me alone, but if I didn't, make life difficult and then send me to Wandsworth. He left it out of the file and, by chance, it got put on the floor and a cleaner found it – an Irish prisoner doing five years. He gave it to me, saying I must have dropped it. When I went on exercise I showed it to a friend of mine who was en route to Broadmoor. He said, give it in. I said that the Irish kid would get into trouble, but my friend said I ought to. So next morning I asked to see the Chief Officer. I gave it to him and told him where I'd got it. That dinner time forty officers were called over and they searched the hospital, me and my cell and everybody else. I kicked up murders. I had a visit and told my wife to go to the Home Office.

Right out of the blue, the security P.O. came to my cell and told me that there were two police officers here to see me and the matter was out of the prison's hands. I was taken to a doctor's office and there they were – a D.I. and a D.S. They said they weren't from Wakefield but from the Regional Crime Squad, so there could be no suggestion there was any collusion. Did I want the security P.O. to stay with me? I said no and so they asked me to tell them everything that had happened. There were visitors waiting so that day my wife, who'd come from Brighton, got only half an hour. I told them in my cell Eva's name was written in the dust on the window. They had the fingerprint guy to photograph my cell. With this news I was running round the hospital saying the screw would soon be nicked. I was being premature. Then the coppers came again and said at first they hadn't believed me, but then they'd tracked down the screw at the market.

The officers had said I'd made a key and given it to the Irish guy who'd opened up the record in the office, but Paddy was dead honest. He stuck strictly to what had occurred and they realized Paddy couldn't and wouldn't have done it. By a sheer miracle everything come my way.

Recently P.O.s have come a tumble over and over, but back in the 1970s it was outstanding to be able to prove such a thing. A month later Bainton returned to the prison, and as I came down at 8 p.m. there he was watching me. It must have been him who authorized the police to be called in. The police saw me yet again, and they said they'd interviewed just about every officer in Wakefield but that they hadn't interviewed Hamilton yet. He should have gone on holiday on the Friday, but he stayed on until the Monday and they had left him until last. They said, 'You're making life difficult because you're letting them know what we're doing.' Now the Chief Officer was cocksure nothing would happen and, in fact, Hamilton had been promoted.

What Hamilton did next was get a Christmas card and send it to my sister, and wrote filth in tiny writing inside the card. Eva got it on Christmas Eve. You can imagine how she felt. My family never told me. I'd have had to have killed him if I'd seen it. By September 1971 the investigation seemed to have petered out. My wife got in touch. Eva still had the card and went to a solicitor, phoned up the Home Office and kicked up a fuss. The police from the

Regional Crime Squad came down the next day, saw her and signed for the card. They told her to tell Doreen to tell me to keep quiet. Now Hamilton had been transferred to a Young Offenders' prison. At first he denied everything, but then they brought the card out. When they asked for a handwriting test he broke down and confessed. He even told them how the plan had been hatched, and he named five or more other officers who were involved. He was arrested, fingerprinted and photo'd. The prints matched those on the panes of glass. They came to see me the next day.

They said they would be arresting other officers provided I keep my mouth shut and didn't tip the screws off, but I said I didn't really want them nicked. As soon as I was let out from the interview I was dancing round saying, 'Hamilton's in there.' Bainton came and walked round the exercise yard with me, saying I would have to go back to Wandsworth. That was September 1971. In the meantime Eva got something stuck through her letter box. It was on official paper and read like, 'This is where we intend to see he spends his twenty years.' She went to see the police. She gave the police the document and was allowed to come and see me on a special visit. She made me strip to ensure I wasn't bruised. Hamilton came up at the magistrates' court, pleaded guilty and made out that I had driven him to do this. He even produced a certificate saying he'd had a breakdown. He was given two years' conditional discharge and he was dismissed the service on 2 November 1971.

When Hamilton was convicted it made history. It

was the first time anyone had ever had a screw done, and it was the card proved it. Hamilton hadn't time to put the record back and never dreamed I'd hand it in. It was the most disturbing experience I or any other prisoner has had. I think it was my finest moment that I came through it all right. Miles away from home, everything against you. The police did say, 'Look, we've done very well. If this had been the Flying Squad they'd have taken a few quid, pooh-poohed what you were saying and dropped it out.' I said, 'No, they'd have done it better,' but in my heart I knew they were right. They did a good job. Who was I? A tuppenny-halfpenny prisoner making allegations.

Meanwhile, after Parkhurst a whole lot of us had sued the Home Office and the screws for our injuries. Most of the others settled and got between £100 and £150 but I hung on. Eva arranged a benefit night for me at the Astor, to put up money for the exes. There was no legal aid on offer. Eventually I settled for £750 and costs. I gave it to Francis, my youngest son, for his twenty-first birthday. That was one of the reasons I called the action off. I really didn't see Francis outside until he was seven and then, when he was nine and a couple of months, I went away on the twenty years. By the time I came out he was a man of twenty-eight. He always came and saw me. Doreen brought Francis up very well. He was born in 1956, about four months after I got the seven years. He was a schoolboy boxing champion and played rugby and cricket for Brighton and Sussex Schoolboys. But he was best at football and was captain of Sussex Schoolboys. Later he turned professional with Brighton, but then he did his knee. He was training at Sussex University training ground, went into a sliding tackle and cut his leg on a piece of glass. After that, just about every time he played it opened up. He went and played part-time for Maidstone, and then he went into insurance. It makes you think that if you're brought up in a good environment you may not turn to crime. But that's not knocking my other boys.

A few years later a Scot, John Quincey, who'd been with me in Parkhurst, even cut a disc about me and the Parkhurst riot and the song got played in London clubs for a while. The words went:

Oh they tried and they tried and they tried.
They tried, they tried, how they tried
They tried to murder 'Frankie'
But his spirit never died
No, his spirit never died.

He was doin' bird in Parkhurst on the Isle of Wight
A peaceful demonstration turned into a bloody fight
All the prisoners wanted was their basic
human rights
But the guards they disagreed and charged
from left and right.

Frankie Fraser's the ring leader, so the Junte said
They rained blow after blow upon poor old Frankie's
head
Then someone gave the order 'Let the blood flow
thick and red'

They battered Frank unconscious – believed
they'd left him dead.

I was taken down to Wandsworth, and whilst I was
there I was involved in an incident where a screw got
shot in the leg. Around Christmas 1971 one of two
men who were serving a sentence of ten years for a
bank robbery at Birmingham now had to face a charge
of GBH on the police. Whilst at Wandsworth they
both had visits for their appeal, and for their defence
on the other charge. They were both Category A
prisoners. You went into two little boxes; prison
officers sat behind you and your visitor. Because the
men didn't confine the conversation to their appeals,
the officers said that's the end and dragged them out.
They got bread and water for talking on the visit. They
were very upset and told me and said they were going
to arrange to have a screw shot, what did I think? I
said good idea, and they went about getting it set in
operation. In early March 1972 a prison officer was
shot in the leg either going on or coming off duty at
Wandsworth, I forget which. The prison authorities
immediately put the Angry Brigade[1] prisoner, Jake
Prescott, in the punishment block. He was happy
enough to let them think it was him, but in fact it
was nothing to do with him at all. It was just a random
screw who was shot. It hits home even more that way.

[1] The Angry Brigade was a group of anarchists who in 1971 carried
out a series of bombings particularly in the London area, including
one on the Barnet home of Mr Robert Carr, then the Minister for
Employment. On conviction members received heavy sentences. The
attacks led to the founding of the Anti-Terrorist Branch (C13).

Years later Lennie Osborne, who was one of the people on report, turned supergrass. In his time he'd been a good man. In fact, in the late 1950s at Wandsworth he was doing two or three years and there was a grass on one of the landings. Someone had made a key, before they had the new locks, gave it to Osborne to do the grass, but he went to a cell and cut the wrong guy. He was nicked for it and he got another two or three years which made him up to five.

He did the five, was out three weeks and got ten years for robbery at a Christmas Club share-out at the back of the Old Kent Road. He was the only one nicked. There were another six in it, and they knew they were safe and he wouldn't grass them. They never give it a thought. He kept his mouth shut then. He wasn't out long, and then got another ten for the bank robbery in Birmingham. That's what he was serving when the screw got shot.

When he come out of that he lived with Tony Baldassari's sister, and when he turned supergrass he mentioned that she was in the plot to shoot the screw.[2] She immediately denied it, and so did the other man he named. The prison officers couldn't remember what the people looked like and she and the man got off, but one of the men who did it later admitted it and ended up with eight years sometime in the early 1980s. They'd done this out of the kindnesses of their hearts.

---

[2] Tony Baldassari later committed suicide. He was on the run wanted for armed robberies when he barricaded himself in a house in Streatham, burned all the money rather than let the police have it and killed himself.

Before the war Osborne's step-father, Johnny, got five years' penal servitude for stabbing a copper when he was completely innocent. The comedian Monty Modlyn's parents had a dress shop in Lower Marsh. Some people were breaking in when a special copper by the name of Skeggs came by. He got stabbed and Johnny was nicked for it. The guy who actually did the stabbing got six months for the shopbreaking. Johnny was a lovely guy. He'd only one eye. If he hadn't died, I don't think Lennie would have turned grass.

In 1971 when I went to Wandsworth a prisoner Roy Grantham came in serving eight years. He told me he was waiting to go up on GBH charges on screws in the security wing at Brixton, and he was calling prisoners as witnesses. I said, call me. He said, 'Impossible, you were in Wakefield.' I said, 'Don't worry, I'll come up with something', and I came up with the cute little story that at Christmas 1971 – when you always got an apple and an orange – I went to give mine to Grantham and the Chief Security PO tried to stop me. I said, 'There's nothing to stop me. He's innocent.' 'Yes, I know, but we're going to get him convicted.'

I was at Gartree down the punishment block when I was told a solicitor wanted to see me. I couldn't think why, and then they mentioned Grantham and I remembered. Sure enough, in November 1972 I was taken from Gartree to give evidence. He must have called every prisoner from every prison he'd been in. There were twenty or more escorts. One of the recent prison charges of mine was slinging boiling tea over a prison officer, and it was also one of Grantham's.

When he was found guilty his defence was that I'd only had six weeks loss of remission, and as a result he got only three months.

Grantham was a Liverpool man who'd lived in London and became a supergrass. Thankfully he committed suicide not long after he gave supergrass evidence against Johnny Hasse, a Liverpool man, who got fourteen years. Grantham had been a good man in his day. He and Freddie Sewell cut through the wire in one nick and nearly got out. Then he became a dog. He'd been to Broadmoor, and he was a bit loose in the head and couldn't handle bird any longer. He wasn't even facing a big sentence; he went in for six months for drunken driving. It's no excuse. When he became supergrass he couldn't handle that either. I wouldn't have bothered to help him if I'd known he would become a grass.

There's no doubt the shooting of the screw did do a lot of good. When I went back to Wandsworth on 5 November 1972, there was a subtle change in the attitude of the screws. Now they weren't so cocky. Later on they went back to being spiteful, but at that stage it was rubbing off just a bit.

The story that I only wore slippers got in the papers by the end of my sentence. It started in Hull at the beginning of 1973. I was up in the strong cell in the punishment block. When they let me out on exercise I was only allowed in slippers; they had taken my shoes away. I complained that it was cold, but I was told I couldn't wear boots or shoes. When I was transferred I was given shoes and told to put them on. I said, 'No, I'm wearing slippers.' The screw said, 'Now you're being transferred you can wear shoes.' I said they had made me wear slippers and that was what I was going to wear. After that I never wore anything else but slippers in rain, shine, slush until the end of my sentence, and it caused unbelievable scenes. They said I could wear trainers or be measured for shoes. That was the order. I was saying it's all right for you to make rules, but when I say I want slippers it's not OK but you're stuck with it.

It didn't always work out to my advantage. In the bad prisons in the north, like Durham, Leeds, Manchester – there the officers took a delight when the snow was melting and you could go out in the exercise yard on slush to call out, 'Exercise, Fraser.' Normally they'd have a yard party sweep a path, but with me I wasn't ever sent out on a clean yard. The screws hoped I would say it was too wet. But I wouldn't. I would go round the yard going slosh slosh slosh for my full hour, or whatever I was allowed. And I never wore a jacket either, just my blue sweater. My feet would be freezing and soaking. At the end I would complain I hadn't had my full hour; that would take the grins off their faces. Then instead of getting warm, usually it was back down the punishment block where it was freezing cold. But it was a decision I'd made. I'd saddled myself with it and I had to put up with it. It's a miracle I didn't suffer some serious illnesses doing this. How I never got pneumonia or very bad colds I'll never know.

My blue sweater was special. It was a lovely dark blue, and good by the standards of its time. It's so long ago I can't remember which prison I was in when I had it first, but only about twenty were issued. Then for some reason or other the prison officers got jealous of prisoners having them, and went round collecting the sweaters and issuing others. But by then I'd been moved to another prison and I had taken it with me. I hung on to it for fourteen or fifteen years. At every prison they tried their damnedest to get it off me, but I fought them off. Eventually they slung the towel in and I still had it. By the end it was frayed at the elbows and in holes, but it was my way of having my little dig at them. It was a big event by prison standards.

Towards the end of my sentence the screws tried to get me to help them once. Michael Waight, who was doing life, had got on the roof at Winson Green Prison, Birmingham with a banner and had slung notes over to the media. At the time three prison officers were appearing at the magistrates' court charged with murdering a prisoner; they were discharged, re-arrested and discharged again. This time the prosecution asked for a Voluntary Bill of Indictment and later the officers were acquitted by a jury. This incident was on their first occasion at the magistrates' court. Michael was protesting about their acquittals.

He had punched a prison officer on the way to the roof and, so it was said, he broke the officer's jaw. I'd been locked up in my cell when this took place because we were on different exercises, otherwise I'd have been up there with him. Now the Governor of the prison, James Green[3], asked me if I would go up and talk to Michael and ask him to come down as the man respected and would listen to me. I refused, saying he believed what he was doing was right. Eventually he did come down after he thought he'd achieved his objective. He was taken to the punishment block beneath me and we had a word through our windows. A day or so later I was taken to Lincoln and he was sent to Long Lartin, but before then he was really knocked about. Long Lartin refused to have him because he was all cut and bruised, and he was taken back to Birmingham.

Months later I was at Leeds Prison and I was asked to make a statement about the case. I saw a solicitor and I appeared at Birmingham Crown Court. By now Green had retired on medical grounds. I'd gone in my famous blue jersey and the slippers, and when I told the jury my evidence there was an uproar. I was told to be quiet by the judge but I wouldn't stop. There was an outcry. I wouldn't budge from telling exactly what happened.

I never got asked by the screws to help again.

---

[3] In December 1981 the Governor, James Green, who had been on indefinite sick leave since October, retired five years early because of ill-health. He had allegedly asked Waight to stage a re-run to demonstrate additional security flaws and had been the butt of criticism by local officials of the DOA.

15

As best I can remember, the sequence in which I went to prisons over those twenty years after the Mr Smith's case was Brixton – Wandsworth – Wormwood Scrubs – Wandsworth – Durham – Leicester – Brixton – Wandsworth – Leicester – Parkhurst – Wakefield – Wandsworth – Bristol – Canterbury – Chelmsford – Wandsworth – Leicester – Norwich – Exeter – Durham – Shrewsbury – Canterbury – Exeter – Durham – Shrewsbury – Canterbury – Lewes – Dorchester – Strangeways – Bedford – Wandsworth – Exeter – Durham – Birmingham – Cardiff – Manchester – Lincoln – Wandsworth – Exeter – Durham – Lincoln – Wandsworth – Gloucester – Leeds – Bedford – Canterbury – Gloucester – Strangeways – Birmingham – Lincoln – Norwich – Bristol – Manchester – Birmingham – Canterbury (where they refused me and I went straight on) – Wandsworth – Cardiff – Manchester – Birmingham – Wandsworth – Winchester – Manchester – Leicester – Canterbury – Wormwood Scrubs. I was being moved with my van load of stuff every few months, sometimes every few weeks and, of course, I got into trouble in most of

285

them. I can't remember all my moves, but I've read that by 1983 I'd been moved a hundred times.

When I used to go from Exeter to Durham – and you can't go much further in the English prison system – the screws would stop at Nottingham and then stay at Durham overnight. It would be a four- or five-day holiday. They would say, 'You've earned our holiday money.' Once it was the Queen's jubilee year. When we got to Yorkshire the Queen must have been visiting and all the motorway was sealed off. The escort had the police and we went all the way along the hard shoulder. From the van you could look out, but no one could look in. I could see the crowd were peering at us thinking it was something to do with the Queen. The screws loved it.

But very little was jokes. Twice I lost around 500 days' remission.

The first time was in April or May 1975 when I was at Bristol. The screws had just got this brand-new uniform which was light blue. Although it was probably nicer than the old dark blue, they looked like doormen on a strip club in Soho. The uniforms were laughable. I was on Category A and I was exercising with other Cat A prisoners who were all IRA men. All of a sudden two of the dog-handlers came on the exercise and they were wearing the new uniforms. The IRA guys started taking the piss out of them, wolf whistling. But the screws couldn't prove they were doing it at them.

Every weekend the prisoners had to wear grey rather than the blue Monday-to-Friday work uniform. With the Cat As they didn't bother; we could just wear the blue. About a week after the incident the screws came onto our exercise and said, 'Change into the greys.' We all refused so more screws were brought up. This was obviously a retaliation for laughing at them. They started pushing and shoving everyone; sticks came out, and with that I knocked one of the screws down. All the IRA boys cheered and went in satisfied. I still wouldn't go and, of course, I was dragged in. Then whilst in punishment waiting for the Visiting Magistrates to sentence me, I had a row with another screw and chinned him. A few days after that, again in the punishment block, I had a fight with a third screw and so I was on three separate assault charges.

In the meantime my family had got to know about this, and they got a solicitor and counsel to go to the court to get an order that I have legal representation at the three magistrates' hearings. By now it was June 1975.

I was marched into the Visiting Magistrates who told me my case would be postponed indefinitely on the assaults – hadn't a clue why and they wouldn't tell me. This meant I could rot down the punishment cells until kingdom come.

All of a sudden, about a day later I was brought in front of them again and the three charges were heard without representation. The Divisional Court had turned down my family's application. Lo and behold, the IRA prisoners had been down and insisted they give evidence on the first charge over the exercise. They were too good in a way, calling me 'Mr Fraser', and I could see the Governor and the magistrates stiffening their backs at me getting a title instead of being called 'Prisoner Fraser'. Anyway it was a formality. No one ever got found not guilty in those days. I think I lost somewhere between 450 and 500 days' remission. A hundred here, two hundred there, all consecutive.

Almost immediately I was transferred to Canterbury. They never told you where you were going until you got in the motor, and sometimes not even then. You had to ask but I wouldn't.

In those days with Cat A prisoners the police forces in a county took over the escort of the van in which the prisoner was travelling so, say, as you come to the border out of Somerset and into Wiltshire, one force drops off and the next lot takes over. The Principal Officer in charge of me was waving to the escort thanking them as they dropped off. He had to be daft, because it had one-way windows and although you could look out of the van no one could look in. On an escort I very rarely spoke, but on this occasion I was sitting handcuffed and I asked him if he was mad. He got very aggressive and said, 'Why do you say that?' I told him no one could see in. He was waving at the time and he tried to ring it by pretending to rub his nose. All the other screws burst out laughing at him. But it didn't do me any good because I suppose it made him mix it up even more than he usually would have done.

As we went into Surrey we lost the escort. Now they had no security so they drove into the Met area without one. First police car they saw they waved him down and drove us to Wandsworth Prison to contact the Surrey police. So I got twenty minutes in Wandsworth for a cup of tea when I could tell the prisoners in the reception about the P.O. waving to the escort.

In Canterbury I lost another 500 days for chinning a screw in about the November. Canterbury at that period was a cunning little nick. I was the very first Cat A prisoner, so they were keyed up for me and I had a special cell. A Cat A man is known as being on the book because a prison officer goes with you all the time, and when he hands you over to another prison officer he signs a book as to the time and place and gives it to the next officer. Once I came out of punishment I was told I was having two screws with me all the time. One always had to be a senior officer, which was very unusual. I should think it was the first time this happened. This made me a target prisoner to the screws. It was a little country nick where the screws – and some of them were very flash as well – had it their own way. It hurt them to see such a fuss was being made over their safety, particularly since I was so small. Eventually it inflamed them and it led to me being on another assault charge. I just lost patience with them. It seems as though I say it repeatedly, but I never ever wanted to chin any screw. I'd do my best to avoid it. There was only going to be one loser at the end of the day, and that was going to be me. There'd be more prison, and I'd be very lucky not to be knocked about by screws either there and then or later. That was another 500 days gone. If I'd had a two-year sentence from a proper court, I'd have got out quicker.

There were also other losses: 168 days in Leicester for hitting the Governor; 200 days at Lincoln for tipping slops over the Governor, and 300 days at Wandsworth for joining a protest about new productivity rates for sewing mailbags. In 1984 my family went to the Divisional Court again to try and get a loss of 356 days for assaults at Lincoln quashed, but they didn't win.

After a third of my sentence I was entitled to be considered for parole. You don't have an interview with the Parole Board, nor do the individual members of the Board see the prisoner like they do in the States. Here a probation officer comes and sees you and assesses you. It was a complete farce. When it kicked off in 1968, one in a million was getting it. It was the perpetual carrot in front of a donkey. The prisoner could never get parole, but he thought he could.

If I thought I'd have a chance I'd have tried for parole, but I never thought I'd have a fair hearing. How can you have one when you never see the Board? A couple of times a screw give me a form or left it on the table in my cell. I didn't touch it and no one ever asked me why I hadn't completed it.

And so at the beginning of 1985 as I neared the end of my sentence, I was moved to Canterbury from Leicester. There was great rejoicing amongst the screws when I was moved. A few weeks earlier the Governor, Bob Mole, had refused to let Charlie Richardson come and visit me. He said I hadn't completed the forms properly. Now I had about three months of my sentence to go and it was in Canterbury that I had my last lot of trouble.

I'd only been there a month, still in my carpet slippers, when I done the Deputy Governor who was Acting Governor. This would be in the March. It seemed to me that Canterbury was determined not to let me out. My wife Doreen and my son Francis had come to visit me and travelled all the way from Hove. I had done nineteen years by this time, and the prison authorities wanted to give me twenty minutes' worth of visit. It was a repeat of the incident which had happened at Leeds a couple of years before. Doreen and Francis had got there bang on time, and they asked to see the Chief Officer as there were a lot of things to do about my release. I never had any home leave in all those years. I was never even asked. So I had to do everything I could on a visit to prepare myself for release. Whatever people say, nineteen years is quite a long time particularly in the conditions in which I had to do my time; all in closed prisons – no semi-open, no working outside, no home leave, nothing. One may say I brought these conditions on myself, but nevertheless the prison authorities made no attempt to break that deadlock. At the end of those twenty minutes on the visit in April 1985, I refused to go and my wife and son staunchly supported me. This was at a table in a visiting room. At this stage I wasn't on punishment of any kind. My wife asked to see someone higher up to discuss it.

I wouldn't leave. Mobs of officers were brought in and stood around in intimidating attitudes, but I still wouldn't go. It was a point of principle now. Doreen and Francis held firm as well. We were also surrounded by prisoners doing three, six and twelve months – nothing sentences in comparison with me – and here they were getting longer visits. Their families had travelled from around the corner so to speak, so it was a blatant act to create the situation. They knew full well I would respond and so get myself into trouble.

Eventually, when I thought I had as long as I should, I went in. But once I got inside the prison proper, the entrance was right by the side of the punishment block. Officers jumped on me and dragged me into the punishment block. I was slung in a strong cell and there was another fight there. Next morning I was placed in front of the Acting Governor on a charge of assault and refusing to obey an order about the visit. He remanded me to the Visiting Magistrates, and a couple of days after that I attacked again. In full view the prison officers had spat in my food; blatantly. They knew I'd respond in the usual manner and I did. I'd flung it over them and refused to eat anything from that moment onwards. How could you? It's such a distasteful thing. It's not as if prison grub is that good, but you do have to eat nevertheless. But when they're spitting in it in front of you, well, you can't. I went on hunger strike.

Meanwhile, my wife and sister and friends flung themselves right into my cause and in fact all hell was breaking loose on my behalf. On punishment I had no radio or newspapers, so there was no way I knew what was going on, but I was also getting a few letters of support from people outside who I'd never heard of. Harriet Harman, the M.P., was very good. Eva got in touch with her and she asked a question in the House of Commons. Pressure must have been getting to the prison authorities because they then let me have another visit whilst on punishment. Eva and a friend came up to see me. This time there was no interference whatsoever. I was given the visit I was entitled to. If they'd done this in the first place, all this would never have happened.

They still had their last kick. Bobby Welch, one of the Train Robbers, and another friend came to visit me with a proper visiting order which I had sent out. Right out of the blue the screws opened my door about 1.30 p.m. and said, 'You're being transferred'. I was taken out of the punishment block, handcuffed to prison officers and put in a prison van. Another had all my gear; the officers had packed it all up in advance. As we went out of Canterbury Prison, who's coming in but Bobby Welch and my other friend? The officers knew they'd arrived because it was official visiting time. I shouted out through the bars but the van was away. There were smirks on the officers' faces. This was their last little dig at me.

I was taken to Wormwood Scrubs. I had only a month to do because the Visiting Magistrates hadn't made any order for further loss of remission against me. Things were better there. I was out of the punishment and there was a South East London pair, the Pitts, Charlie and his son-in-law, and various other long-term prisoners to talk to. The screws at the Scrubs leaned over backwards to make sure there would be no more trouble. So life wasn't too bad for that last month. In fact, Bobby Welch was allowed in a few days later.

Two days before I came out of the Scrubs my eldest son, Frank, and one of my nephews, Jimmy, turned up by arrangement with two vans and took all my gear away. The day before that I'd gone down to the reception and checked everything. The authorities went mad, but it was my turn for once. There was birthday cards, Christmas cards, letters, old scrubbing brushes, floor cloths, and a few suits from the trial at Parkhurst where we were going to court every day for nearly three months. I'd had suits and shoes brought in, and I'd never had them sent out. There were boxes and boxes of gear; they had to have two vans. Frank and Jimmy had a good laugh about the gear, and later they hung my famous jersey up in the Tin Pan Alley Club they had at the time in Denmark Street. It's now a wine bar. The sweater was there in the club for ages – and my slippers hung with it, one on either side as a mark of respect for the jersey.

I checked all my property as well, but they had done me clever. There was no wrist-watch – a present from Billy Hill – no fountain pens, no chain, really good ones. All had disappeared from my property. I couldn't believe the prison officers would be so blatantly vindictive in stealing them. These articles didn't go in property at reception, if you were a Cat A man they went in a Chief Officer's safe. Once you came off Cat A, if the property was really valuable it would go to reception for safe keeping. If it was really, really good it would go back in the Chief's safe. My chain and pens and watch were there on record, but they had just disappeared. For years I was a Category A prisoner, and right to the end I was always transferred on my own and never knew when and where I was going. The special property was sent on afterwards. When it's missing, it's not simply missing, it's been stolen. There can be no two ways about it. I know it was there for ages because I would never sign and that's where I was foolish. When I wouldn't sign, that gave them the chance to take the gear. It was about 1979 when I discovered it was missing. The officer I asked said it would be in a safe in a prison somewhere and it wouldn't be any problem, but it was. I never got any compensation. That was my fault. I did ask, but I was still hoping it would turn up.

My youngest boy, Francis Jnr, collected me from prison in a Rolls Royce. He'd visited me the day before to tell me that Frank Warren, the boxing promoter, was going to lend him a Rolls, but his had some fault, so Francis hired one from Jack Barclay for £1,500 for the day. He had to let the prison authorities know because they had to let it inside the prison to be searched. As we left there were a number of reporters at the gates and they chased us. I had intended to go and see Eva first, but we couldn't shake them off and we went straight to Brighton. They were still following us, so we pulled up at a petrol station on the way. Francis got out, locked the doors leaving me with a newspaper over my head, went over to them and said, 'I appreciate you've got a job to do but, please, my father doesn't want to speak to you.'

They turned round then. Later that night they traced us and rang up, but I didn't speak to them.

I stayed with Francis for a fortnight in Brighton. I was white as a ghost from all those years inside, and I was still in a bad way from the hunger strike and one or two bashings I'd had in Canterbury, so I needed a fortnight in the sun to recuperate and get some fresh air inside me. I wasn't on parole; no one had given me an after-care officer. They never said, 'Here's someone to talk to if you want.' There was no probation officer saw me in the last month at the Scrubs. As I say, I hadn't had home leave although I must have been entitled to it. I didn't have to report to anyone. I must have been the only prisoner treated like this, but I was on my own and that was good.

After that fortnight I came up to London and saw Eva. Funnily I didn't have any trouble in adjusting to life on the outside, even though I'd never had even an hour outside during those twenty years. I found that to be the case on every prison sentence I ever done. I've read and heard so much in the media when men have come out of prison and found how difficult it is to acclimatize themselves, especially men who've been away a long time. I can only speak for myself, but in a roundabout way I would say to a man who goes to an open prison where there's a lot more freedom, and who goes out to work on home leave, it might seem irksome and tough that he isn't out properly. It might affect him when he is finally released. I've never been to any of those kinds of prisons, and in any sentence I never had any home leave, but I've found that the moment I left, even after those twenty years, inside seconds of leaving prison I've completely forgotten about the sentence. It's as if I've never been away. Twenty-four hours after leaving prison, if you were to ask me what I was doing this time the day before I'd have a struggle to remember. It doesn't affect me in any way. People say they have trouble with the noise, but not me. All those horrendous days and nights and weeks, and year after year of solitary and bread and water, punishment, the real vicious things the authorities did to me – from the moment I was out it seemed as though it never ever happened. I do understand that with most people they have trouble adjusting, but not with me. In a way I wish it did, because at least it could make me think twice before I got in trouble again. The change in coinage, fashion, music, motor cars, didn't matter to me at all. It was as if I'd never been away.

I never started to hate people myself – although I had cause. Perhaps I had the strength of mind not to let anything like that get to me. It would become an obsession and do me more harm than good. In a way, having the prison officers and the authorities to fight may have stood me in good stead. So anyone who I thought might have let me down outside took second, third, even fourth place. Men in prison have felt let down and it has become an obsession with them. At the start they may have been right thinking that friends of their families haven't been doing enough for them, but it's eaten them up.

My friends and family arranged two benefits for me. The first was one at the A & R Club, off Charing

Cross Road, which by now was being run by Jimmy and Frank, who along with a couple of others had bought it from Ronnie Knight. There was a running buffet and people came up, bought drinks and just give me money. That was worth quite a lot, quite a few grand. Some would give £10 or a fiver, some gave a grand, plus I got a share of the bar takings. I was stuffing it in my pocket and giving the rest to someone to mind for me.

There was a much grander benefit at a club in Holborn at the top of Chancery Lane and each ticket cost £50. I got all the money. Some people would buy four or five tickets and never came. They'd done their bit. That was their way of saying, 'Good luck, Frank.' There was a little live band and a gorgeous running buffet. That was worth a lot more money to me. It was jam-packed. I had been going round selling tickets in advance, and friends from all over the country had been doing the same. This was par for the course. It was a terrific night. Charlie Kray, a few of the Train Robbers, Charlie and Eddie Richardson, and Johnny Nash and many more came. So many I can't really remember.

I just took me time, but I was content with what I'd got. I had to get a car. I'm not into flash cars and so I got a little second-hand Allegro. I was still living with Doreen in Brighton, but I was up London quite a lot and it did take time to settle back on my feet. I never drew social security. The media were getting in touch on various occasions wanting to write my story, and I wasn't responding. I didn't take any notice of it, but one or two including the *Sunday Mirror* really were persistent. I arranged to meet them in my solicitor's office, Blackburn Gittings, because I wanted to say that I wasn't interested in person. The journalist who came said he'd like to do it as a book. I said I wasn't interested. I didn't know whether I could do it justice at that stage and, at the time, I didn't think I could work with him.

That December I was arrested in Spain. I first went there in the November to collect some money for Charlie Richardson. He had invested in property out there, but the deal had fallen through and now he wanted his money back. He asked if I would go and get it, and said it would make a little break for me as well. I said certainly I would. I saw the people involved down in Puerto Banus where I met them in a restaurant. They said they didn't have the money but they'd have it in a fortnight's time. I rang Charlie who said, 'Fair enough. Come home and then go back.' There was no point in staying there the whole time. Then I got a call from them to say they'd paid the money to Ronnie Knight and I could collect it from him. I rang him and he said yes, that was right he'd had the money, but now he'd given it to Freddie Foreman.

Out I went with a friend, Steve McGoldrick. I saw Fred on a Sunday. He and his friends all used to collect together and have Sunday lunch in this English pub near Fuengirola. We'd stayed in the Hotel Angelo nearby and had had our lunch there. Afterwards we went down to the pub on the road to Marbella and had a couple of drinks. Fred give us the money and we came back to the Hotel Angelo. Next morning we went to the airport and as we went through Customs armed police pointed guns at our heads – it was unbelievable. We'd already checked in our luggage. They took us in an office; searched us. In the luggage they found the £18,000, not a great sum of money really. Where did you get it? We told the truth. We'd got it from the property deal. We'd just gone for a nice little three- or four-day break, collect the money and come home. Unfortunately it didn't turn out that way.

They separated us then and handcuffed me to the wall. Later I was taken to the prison down the coast past Tarifa. I think they missed about £20 on Steve and he sent out for food. We were in separate cells and I ate the Spanish stuff. I thought the prison was better, more informal, than the British ones. It wasn't as strict and I didn't have any trouble with the screws. The strong point was the incommunicado. If you were up to nonsense you'd have a hard job getting your act together to get out of it.

Two days after that I was taken to court. By now people were waiting for us at Gatwick. They found out what had happened. Blackburn Gittings had got in touch with an attorney in Fuengirola by the name of Francisco Madrid. We met him at the court, but before the hearing they wouldn't even let us talk to him.

I was being told I was a murderer, bank robber, what Scotland Yard must have said about me is nobody's business. Then we went into the court – really a room – one at a time. You just sat in front of the judge. The prosecutor was on one side and us on the other. Madrid spoke excellent English. I came out and they took the handcuffs off. All of a sudden the police drifted away, two and three at a time. Then all at once there's no one with us at all. Was this a ploy to get us to make a run for it and then shoot us down? Then Madrid came out beaming and said, 'You're free.' 'Where's our money?' 'That's another story. That's a civil action, but it'll take months. You'll get it.' We were penniless, but he gave us some pesetas. We went down to see Ronnie Knight and he bought us some more flight tickets, put us up in the hotel, and gave us £500. Suddenly, who arrives but Gittings? He flew back with us the following day and we gave him a lift to London.

A few months later me and Steve McGoldrick flew to Madrid itself, where we met Francisco. This time not only was he our defence but he was the interpreter. They'd had a proper one in the criminal trial. I remember him saying, 'Don't start saying in English, "How's it going?" because although the judge may say he can't understand English he probably can.' We went in separately and we won and got the money.

Now I was buying and selling cars. Eddie had a very nice club, J. Arthur's, in Catford. A big place with good acts such as the singer, Joe Longthorne. The building's still there to this day, but in 1986 a man was killed in a fight there. No one was convicted, but when the licence came up it wasn't renewed. I never had a financial interest, but that same year Charlie Richardson and I did have an interest in Bentley's, a disco club mainly for black kids in Canning Town. Charlie and I were silent partners. I used to go quite regularly and I took Lord Longford and Dennis Andries, when he was the world champion, down there to let people know I was doing my best. It was a nice club which we'd had done up. Then one night in the early hours of the morning there were helicopters all over the place and van-loads of police who raided it. All they found was a couple of joints of cannabis on the floor, but in the office they found a couple of bullets and an empty gun licensed to the holder. In the safe they found the partnership agreement, so they knew we were involved. At the end of the day the only person arrested was the licensee. It had a devastating effect; the licence was suspended and the club collapsed.

That was the year I was arrested and charged with dishonest handling. It is the only charge I've had in England after the twenty, and it was over some antique coins said to be worth £30,000. I bought them legally exactly as was described in court. They were antiquities and Roman coins. A man had come over from Joliet near Chicago, where funnily enough there's a prison, and had attended an antiques fair in the Marriott Hotel in Mayfair with his wife. He was in the lounge sitting round the table having coffee. He put his purse by the side of his chair, and the next time he looked it had gone. He reported it stolen. This was whilst I was inside. Two years later it was offered to me in Caledonian Market; I bought it for £500 off a stall. I wasn't sure if I had a bargain. I was then making arrangements to sell it, and in the process one night I was driving in Queen's Road, Camberwell, from Charlie's car site, going towards my sister's.

For about three days it had been the coldest weather of the century and I was driving very slowly and carefully about 7 in the evening. A police Landrover was coming in the same direction, and with the slowness I was driving and signalling once when I didn't turn, I suspected at the time he thought I was drunk. I was stopped. As soon as they realized I wasn't drunk they got on the radio to the station with my particulars and said, 'We're going to search your car.' The box with the coins was by the side of me. They searched the car and at the last moment came up with the box. A policeman opened it up and asked, 'What's this?' 'Some old coins.' He opened it up and he went to put it back when another copper came up and asked what he had. I repeated they were just old coins. The second copper looked at them and said they were antiquities. There were twenty-seven of them. I told them where I'd bought them; I said I'd given £500. He asked if I had a receipt, and I said not on me but that I could get one. They'd already been on the phone for reinforcements. When a van arrived they didn't lark about and I was taken to Carter Street and then on to Kennington Road. I was searched, and I then saw the policeman who was in charge of the Brinks-Mat. I thought what's going on? They wouldn't let me get in touch with John Blackburn Gittings, my solicitor, and when they tried to interview me I wouldn't say a word. After all, I'd told them all about the coins. I couldn't improve on it. After twenty-four hours they let a Gittings representative see me and the next day I appeared in court.

I now had both the trouble to trace the guy I had bought them from, and to try to get bail. I appeared in front of Sir Bryan Roberts. The ordinary uniformed coppers at Horseferry Road court said he was known as Bail'em Roberts and I had a good chance of getting bail, but I was remanded in custody for about nine days over two weekends. So much for Bail'em Roberts, I thought.

On the remand hearing I appeared in front of Eric Crowther and he was very fair. The prosecution vehemently argued that I shouldn't have bail under any circumstances, but Gittings fought long and hard and Crowther over-ruled them. He said he had appeared as junior counsel in the so-called Torture trial all those years ago. Alex Buxton, the one-time British and European boxing champion, stood bail for £40,000. He got a bit mixed when he was explaining who he was, but Crowther helped him. Another bailee mentioned Arsenal, and Crowther said he knew I supported the Gunners. It was unbelievable.

As soon as I got bail I found the man who'd sold the coins to me, a publican from Finchley way, a Welshman who I'd known at the boxing and who'd had them on the stall. I think he was once a special constable. He produced the brother of the man who'd sold them to him. The man who he'd bought them from had died, but the brother had been there when he'd sold them. So not only did I produce the man I'd bought them off of, but I near enough produced the man he'd bought them from as well.

I was amazed how I was found guilty. The jury disagreed and the judge directed that he would take a majority decision. Back they come and I was found guilty ten to two. He was extremely vicious to me and I was given three years. The judge said something about the publican being prosecuted, but he never was. I think the prosecution was in a bind. What would have happened to my case if he'd been acquitted? As I work it out now, I think I should have put my character in evidence and told them all about myself before I was found guilty. That would have explained my reticence once I was arrested and in the police station. I think if I'd brought my character out it would have helped. I think I might have made a mistake there.

Charlie was very good. Unbeknown to me he saw Canon Diamond, who had a big church in Deptford, on my behalf and told him the circumstances. Diamond said he would do what he could. He drafted a very good letter, got in touch with Blackburn Gittings and sent it to them. Gittings had come to see me at Wandsworth and said on appeal he didn't think there was too much chance against conviction but, on sentence, he was quite confident there was a prospect. I heard no more until about the February 1988, three months after I'd been convicted. Then I got a note saying I had leave to appeal. This was the first time ever I'd been given leave to appeal, and instinct told me that I was in with a decent chance of getting something. In April 1988 I went to the Court of Appeal with Andrew Trollope as my counsel. I think he was related to the novelist. He came to see me in the cells at the Law Courts and said immediately that of the three judges, two of them were OK but one could be a bit difficult. Even so, he was confident he would get something off for me. Before a word was said on the appeal, the senior judge said there was to be a reduction to two years but that if Trollope wanted to try for more they would listen to him. The letter from Diamond, who was well respected, was read out. He painted me out to be a saint, in fact I was looking round wondering who they were talking about. Parts were true about the club, but I'd never met him in my life. It's possible I'd been in his company but that's all. It was enough to fetch tears to your eyes. It clinched the appeal for me, but they wouldn't be budged on any less than the two.

I had two rows during the time I was away. The first was in January 1988 when they wanted to put me two in a cell at Wandsworth and I refused. They said I had to, and I was put on report straight away and put down the punishment block. I was quite happy to be going in a single cell down there anyway, and I was charged with refusing to obey an order. The doctor had to see me to see if I'm fit for punishment. I said I wasn't all right, and I was entitled to a single cell because I'd been certified insane three times. The doctor didn't know me, but the senior hospital officer who he had with him did and said I was telling the truth. He said I shouldn't be two in a cell with my history, and the doctor said he would look into it.

About an hour or so later I should have been in front of the Governor, but I wasn't taken. After the punishments are handed out, the Governor has to see the remaining prisoners in the cells. He didn't come and see me and so, after dinner, I asked why I hadn't been in front of the Governor. They said I'd probably go tomorrow. The next day I was taken in front of him and he said the charge was dismissed as I was unfit to plead, and I could go in a single cell.

The second time was in May 1988 when I was told I was being transferred to the Island the next day. They didn't say whether this would be Albany, Parkhurst or Camp Hill. I said I wouldn't go. They said I had to. I said no. Parkhurst was the last prison I should be going to. They said that was an order. I said 'Bollocks' and walked out. They took me back to me cell and half an hour later there were mobs of screws and I was taken down the punishment block. There I was told I would be forcibly taken to the Isle of Wight. This meant in a body-belt. I said, 'You'll have to have a right fight for it,' and I got meself all ready. This would be about 11 a.m., and about 3.30 in the afternoon the door opened and there was another mob of screws. I squared up and they said, 'No, you can stay. You'll be going back to your cell. If you get in trouble you'll be moved but if you behave no one will bother you.' They swallowed it. Then I had no more trouble. I was left severely alone and I did my bird the easy way. But I still didn't get home leave or even get put up for parole.

Charlie met me at the gate in the spring of 1989 and I got another whip in the Tin Pan Alley Club, obviously not the same size as after the twenty but still not bad. When I came out I went to thank Canon Diamond with Charlie. The Canon was having a tea-party and the Bishop of London was there along with various other dignitaries. This was the only time I ever met him. He was quite a character, an absolute raving top of the roof. The Bishop of London seemed quite pleased that the Canon was reforming me.

Looking back, when I was first arrested over the coins they said they knew I was Frankie Fraser and had to search my car for drugs. This was ridiculous. I don't even smoke or anything. They said they stopped me because my rear number-plate top bulb light wasn't on. In the December I'd spent over £500 on the car, having it re-sprayed and serviced and the electrics done. I'd only picked it up the day before the night I was arrested. I remember I was so pleased with the job the garage had done that when I parked it I walked round looking at it. That light was there; it was on. The bulb must have been taken out between my going in Charlie's office and coming out.

Whilst I was doing my two years, Charlie discovered a bug had been planted in his office at the top of the car site. In 1986 Charlie and the girl he was with at the time, Sue, were both arrested on some pretext. Charlie was held for twenty-four hours and Sue for twelve before being released. Charlie and the others were of the belief that the bug had been put in there behind a big long cabinet in the office when the police had it to themselves. In 1988 it was found by sheer accident. It had both a battery and an activator. I'd shown Charlie and Sue the coins whilst I was there. They were admiring them, and I told them I was now confident I'd found a buyer. It makes me think that some police knew about them before I even got back in my car.

Doreen was wonderful to me in the times I was away. She never missed a day in all those weeks of my trial at Parkhurst, and along with Eva she came all over the country. I can't speak highly enough of her and her support for me. But life has its sad times and we just drifted apart. The hard bit was that in 1978 her mother, a lovely lady, died whilst she was round our house. Doreen was upstairs when she heard a thump. She thought her mother was having a joke and shouted down, but no reply. She rushed downstairs and found her mother had had a heart attack and was dead. They were very close and it really upset her a great deal. I think that was a turning point in her life. She always thought if she had been downstairs it wouldn't have happened. I was in Cardiff Prison at the time, and when she next saw me she was really upset. Of course her mother had been a great help to her. Doreen was an only child and they were very close. The trouble was she was a straight girl. If you're a criminal, it's better that you marry a girl from a criminal family who knows what the rules are. If a man has a criminal background, then he really is better to marry or go with a girl who, even if she hasn't 100 per cent criminal past, somewhere along the line has a father, grandfather or older brother who's been in prison. When this is the case she'll understand and be much more helpful than if she's lived a completely straight life.

I thought I was likely to have a spot of trouble with the police over a matter in South London in 1989. To use a police term, I suspected they might want to see me to 'help with their enquiries' and it seemed a good idea to leave for a bit so I went up North. Whilst up there staying with friends one of them was telling me about a big fraud case which was going on. He knew one of the defendants very well, as he'd worked for him a few years previous. I didn't say any more at the time but I thought it through and next time I saw my friend, a few days later, I said I was confident I could get his friend out of the charge. I thought I could straighten the jury. At worst there would be a disagreement and there would be a great chance of an acquittal. It was at a non-secure Crown Court.

I was taken to see the defendant in London about 6 o'clock one evening. He'd just been at court, but it was a trial which was going to go on for weeks and probably months. I was shown into his office because his friend had insisted it was a personal matter. When we went in the defendant opened his coat, saying, 'Look, I'm not bugged up.' My friend put the idea to him and he listened very attentively. He said he thought it was a good idea and he appreciated what was being said, but that he was absolutely confident he would be found not guilty. My friend had impressed that this wasn't a con or a trap. He just didn't need the help. He was oozing confidence and I thought that made sense, but nevertheless with his money he should have taken the offer up and made it a certainty. I'm quite confident it could have been done. We shook hands and I left. History shows he went down. When I spoke to my friend recently, I heard the man bitterly regretted not having a bit of help.

It wouldn't have come cheap – it would have been real money. Remember you have to have three jurors, and in a case of that magnitude you couldn't give them peanuts. You'd have to drop everything else. It takes dough and time to find which ones; you'd have to look at them all. The friend would have put the money up to start with, but it would have been cheap for the money he had. You had to make the rainbow tempting. You'd have had to find people who knew people, and they would have had a drink. But I still reckon I'd have come out with £100,000. Say you met the cousin who agreed to introduce you, you'd have to give him £10,000 or even more, then you'd have to pay the person who introduced you to the cousin. You're not going in rash or blind. With a long case you'd got time to do it. It sounds a lot of dough, but it's not really. You're not talking about someone who's nicked for a security van or drugs where that type of money isn't available. After all, you are only balancing things with what the police do. The difference is they can do it much better.

I met Marilyn Wisbey in the spring of 1991 when she was singing 'Crazy' in a pub. And a bit later I met her again in my nephew Jimmy's Tin Pan Alley Club. Obviously I knew her father very well through the years and I'd known her really as a child. She said her father Tom, who'd got ten years for conspiracy over some cocaine, would like to see me, so I arranged to meet her at Waterloo Station and travelled with her to the Isle of Wight to see him in Parkhurst. Our relationship sort of took off from there. We're planning to marry but I'll have to get divorced first. On the other hand it might be worth going for bigamy – I do my best to get most of the crimes on the calendar in. I haven't been convicted of that yet and there's no violence involved.

I'd only been seeing her for a few weeks when I was shot. It was at Turnmills, a large night-club in Clerkenwell. We'd been out with a number of people and someone suggested going. It was the first and only time I'd ever been down there. In fact, it was the first time I'd ever even heard of it. I'd been drinking all that day and I'd had far too much to drink. I wasn't being a nuisance but I wasn't my normal self. It was very late – it must have been 3 in the morning when we went. We had a drink or two there for a couple of hours, and as Marilyn and I were leaving there was a cab across the road. I went over to it and I can vaguely remember seeing someone approaching as I was waiting to get in the cab. I took no notice. I wasn't staggering about, but I was well drunk. The next I know is that there was a tremendous explosion. It hit me in the side of the head but it didn't knock me off my feet. Drunk as I was, instinct told me what had happened. I had to go for where the noise had come from. Marilyn stuck her arms around me to stop me and then there were two more shots. The person who was firing panicked when he saw me coming to him and the shots missed. Sober, I might have got nearer to him because I'd have seen the approach. They couldn't have crept up like that. Marilyn certainly saved me. If she hadn't put her arms round me I'd have been right on top of him and it'd have been point blank. It more or less was anyway. Then he ran and I didn't see any more.

I wanted to chase after the gunman and I got in the cab, telling the driver to follow him, but he wouldn't drive. Then we were surrounded and people were calling for an ambulance. All I was interested in was getting after him. In no time an ambulance was there, and by now Marilyn wouldn't take any answer but to put me in it. I was still thinking of getting after him and patching meself up later, because although there was a bit of blood it wasn't as much as you'd expect. In a way the drink may have saved me; I don't know. The bullet was a .22, but they're as dangerous as any of them. Bullets will usually exit, but these are not powerful enough to go right through so they travel round looking for an exit and then they can do a lot of damage if it's near your heart or your brain. It came in by my right eye, went all round my face under my nose and lodged by my left eye. Fortunately it was travelling downwards. If it had been the other way I'd have been gone.

Off I went in the ambulance with Marilyn. By now all my clothes were wringing with blood, but I was never unconscious. All I wanted to do was get out of it. The police were here now as well. There have been a lot of stories about who did it to me. There was a suggestion it was part of a feud from South East London. Two boys, Tony and David Brindle, were charged with the murder of a man called Abby, and it was said that my shooting was in revenge for that. This was rubbish. There are literally hundreds of Brindles in South London, and I'm not even related to those boys. It was nothing to do with any South London fighting. Whoever they were having a row with – if they were – those people would know there was no connection with me.[1]

Then it was said it was over drugs. That's rubbish too. From the word go I've always said, and I always will do, that it was undercover police. I've never made any secret of that. At the time there was a lot of talk about my writing this book which some people thought would uncover a lot of police corruption. Who can tell? I said that from the word go when I'd had no time to think about it.

I never said I was Tutenkhamun. That was all newspaper stories. I didn't give any name. Marilyn said 'Frank Tompkins' and I just said, 'Yes, that's right.' I was never even asked for a statement, and I certainly didn't volunteer one. Once I said the word undercover, they kept well away. I was only in the hospital for two days. I tried to discharge myself, but they said stop and we'll take the bullet out. Later I was moved from a ward into a private room. When I realized there were armed coppers in the hospital I complained. The copper in charge was brought in and the men were moved. I said, 'You've already shot me once. I'm not having you here.' I didn't mean him personally of course. He didn't deny it nor did he admit it.

Whoever did shoot me, it was a complete botch-up.

[1] On 11 March 1991 Ahmet Abdullah, a suspected drug dealer and friend of the Arif family, was shot in a betting office in Bagshot Street, Walworth. On 3 August David Brindle was shot in the Bell Public House, also in Walworth. His brothers, Tony and Patrick, were acquitted of Abdullah's murder on 16 May 1992.

I know if things had been reversed and I had been doing the shooting they wouldn't have been alive. The gunman had to be a right mug, a right coward. He had it all his own way. He had me at his mercy and two point-blank shots completely missed. But it was good fun, good action, it makes a good night's drink after all. That may seem bravado, but the shooter couldn't have had it sweeter. The undercover cop – bet he got a right rollicking off his superiors.

It was the first time I'd ever been shot at in my adult life, apart from that time when Dickie Hart shot me at Mr Smith's. In the War I'd been in a fight with some Yankee soldiers when shots were fired, but this could have been at anybody who was in the fight rather than me personally.

I came out of the hospital on the Sunday or Monday, had a rest in the flat and then just carried on. No one has ever tried again since that night and I've been carrying on normally since. I haven't been hiding. People know where to find me.

In June this year I had a telephone call telling me to go away for a few days. I didn't ask why, because it was a friendly call. So I packed a bag and caught the train from Euston to the North. I was really keen to make sure people knew I was gone. I was at the station with a friend, and someone left a bag on the stairs leading down to the tube so there would be a bomb alert. I was making sure I spoke to people so they would remember me. Luckily I spoke to a photographer who'd reported the bag. He said he'd seen it and a man hanging about. I couldn't help laughing. Just before they cleared the station they said if anyone had lost the bag would they please report it. I don't know what happened – my friend just left it.

I took the train to Stockport and stayed with friends who have a hotel up there. Later that evening I got a call to say Jimmy Moody had been shot. I stayed up North another couple of days and then came back.

Jimmy had given evidence at Parkhurst in the riot trial and then, when he was up for a series of armed robberies, he broke out of Brixton in December 1980 along with Stan Thompson, who was also with me on the Parkhurst case, and an IRA guy. Stan was on trial at St Albans and the jury was out considering its verdict overnight when he escaped. They came back the next day and found him not guilty, so he surrendered himself a couple of days later. He was charged with escaping from legal custody and got a sentence of eighteen months, but he'd served most of that on remand. I used to get a Christmas card from him just saying 'Jim'. You could get as many cards as people wrote, although you were entirely at the mercy of the screws as to how many you actually saw.

I never saw him after his escape, but I heard of him from time to time. I don't think he went abroad. He realized that if he kept a low profile, which he did, he could succeed in keeping out, which he managed for nearly thirteen years. Remember it was an extraordinary escape. Having been in that wing, as I was with the Twins and James Earl Ray, I can honestly say I could see the possibilities of an escape because when they came out of their cells they got on to a flat roof. The screws were so confident with TV cameras and the security fence they never dreamed anyone could do it. Daring and hard work and the sheer boldness of it won the day. Very few people heard from him, even people who were close.

Last year there was the shooting of David Brindle, who was no relation of Eva's or mine, but I heard what had happened a few days later. It now turns out that Jimmy Moody was working in a pub at the back of Walworth under the name Tom. He'd been in the area for ten years. He wasn't an out-and-out night-clubber, so he could have been there and very, very few people would know who he was. He'd done quite a bit of bird, and now he took it as a personal thing to keep out. It was a personal challenge for him. There's a lot of other guys been in that position and they've been out night-clubbing it and soon got caught. Jim did have that determination and single-mindedness to keep that low profile and trust no one. He could be stubborn and obstinate, a good man but a loner. He'd be content to do his work and watch the telly, knowing that every day was a winner. That's how he would look at it. I think David had had a row with the publican and Jimmy had crept behind him and done him with a baseball bat. David was badly knocked about and told Jimmy it wouldn't be forgotten. Next night, or a couple of nights later, Moody and another man went into the Bell in East Street and shot David and a bystander. Immediately afterwards he went over to the East End.

No one has been to see me about the Moody killing nor, as far as I know, have they seen any of David's relations or indeed anyone who you'd think they'd latch on to. Much as I knew Jim well, I can understand the feelings about David's death, and that it was one that had to be done. I suppose if someone who knew it was going off had really pleaded for him it might have made some difference, but I doubt it.

16

What happened to everyone? Well, starting at the beginning, Derby Sabini died in Hove in October 1951. He and 'Harry Boy', along with 'Pasqualino Papa', better known as Bert Marsh, had been interned at the beginning of the War. Derby, he never really recovered after his son Johnny was killed in the Battle of Britain. He went to live in Hove in Sussex, and in the end he was just another small-time bookmaker.

Bert Marsh was a great friend of Jim Wicks, Henry Cooper's manager. In fact Jim gave evidence for him in his trial for murder in 1936 when he was acquitted of stabbing one of the Montecolumbo brothers at Wandsworth dogs. Bert became a street bookie and later opened betting shops in Soho. He died of a heart attack about ten years ago driving home one night. He was a very wealthy man.

After he was finally released, Alfie Hinds played for our football team, the Soho Rangers, run by Stanley Baker. The team played various matches for children's charities, and in the very first one after he won his action against Bert Sparks he was left back. I think the papers had 'Alfie's first away game'. Later he went to the Channel Islands where he was secretary of Mensa. His friend, Tony Maffia, who had helped him in his second escape, went into business with him. Maffia was killed in May 1968 by Stephen Jewell, who during his trial unsuccessfully tried to implicate Hinds. There were allegations of smuggling and a swindle over forged notes. Hinds hired counsel to appear after Jewell's trial and make a statement denying his involvement. Jewell died in 1990 after his release from prison. Bert Sparks, who'd arrested Hinds for the Maples robbery, died in 1992. After Hinds' death in 1992, he had written to the *Police Pensioners* magazine warning ex-officers about publishing their memoirs.[1]

Jimmy Essex settled down in Wallington. He resurfaces for a drink and a chat from time to time. He's had a couple of heart attacks and he's retired now. He had the birch at Dartmoor in, I think, 1955. At the time he was doing seven years for breaking and entering. Then he did eight years' preventive detention. That was for thieving too; just broke into a store. It was a ferocious sentence for really nothing. Today he might have got probation for it.

Spot's man Teddy Machin was shot dead in a domestic dispute. His family were involved in the Tibbs–Nicholls feud of the early 1970s. Jimmy Andrews died of cancer very soon after the shooting when he'd lost a leg in 1956. Jimmy had been a very good amateur boxer and had a few professional fights, but then he went to Borstal. He'd been out for a Friday night and was

---

[1] Hinds wrote his memoirs *Contempt of Court*, and there is an account of the Maffia killing in D. Thurlow's *The Essex Triangle*.

shot as he was walking home. He'd just got married and I think his wife was expecting.

Henry Botton was shot dead in July 1983. He took a blast from a double-barrelled shotgun in his throat when he opened the door at his home in Shooter's Hill Road, Greenwich. It was lucky I was still inside. I was in Durham Prison at the time and I wasn't too unhappy at hearing that piece of news. It made that evening in the punishment block that little bit more joyful. Along with everyone else, he'd got five years for his part in the affray at Mr Smith's, and when he'd come out he had gone into antique dealing. He'd also given evidence in a recent trial which had upset some people. Two men were convicted of his murder. One of them, a nineteen-year-old, said Billy Clarkson had given him a shotgun and told him to go out and do it. Apparently he'd dressed up as a policeman and had gone and shot him. Billy was recommended to serve a minimum of twenty-five years.

The last I ever heard of Bennie Coulston was when I was in Leicester in May 1968. The Krays had just been arrested, so I can place the date. There was an article in a Sunday paper about how Bennie Coulston, who'd given evidence in the Torture trial, now had a twenty-four-hour armed police guard and had been moved to a provincial town. What it looked like to me was that they were trying to brainwash the public. 'Look what they've had to do here in the Richardson case to a witness – God knows what they'll have to do to the witnesses for the prosecution in the Kray case.' That's the last I ever really heard of him. I did hear rumours, as the years went by, that he and his wife were running a social club in Essex, but I never had confirmation of it. I haven't seen Taggart or Prater, but I hear they're still around.

I'd never met Bunny Bridges before the Torture trial case. He'd been a witness for the prosecution, but not against me. However, I did see him when I was driving around the back of New Cross a couple of years or more ago. I pulled up the car and chased him on principle – I had to. But by that time he'd got a very good start and managed to get away, so I lost him. It's the last I saw or heard of him.

Olive Cornell, George's widow, died at the end of July last year. She was a great woman and had struggled against cancer for some years.

'Battles' Rossi is still around, still playing cards. I see him quite often and we go out and have a drink together. Billy Howard was a character in his own right. In 1968 he was arrested for demanding protection money from various casinos. It was said he was taking over from the Krays, and indeed it started off as though they were going to make a new Richardson –Kray thing of it. Fortunately for him it all blew over. The prosecution must have lost interest because he wound up with twelve months. Years later he gave an interview in one of Paul Raymond's magazines. By then he'd married the daughter of Archie Macauley, who'd been an Arsenal player and became manager of Norwich. Bill deteriorated and died after she went off with a milkman. I think he was really cut up about it, and went down and down. But in his day he could have a fight. Later on one or two people said he was a wrong'un, a police informer. I never had evidence myself although a lot of people said so.

Roy Hall's had a couple of heart attacks. He was addicted to weight training in prison, and I think he kept up with the heavy weights instead of dropping down as he grew older.

Billy Hill came to visit me in Dorchester Prison in 1980. That was the last time I saw him. The doctor had told him that if he quit smoking he could live another seven years, but if he didn't the best was five and more likely three or less. 'Can't you turn it in, Bill?' I asked. 'I can't, Frank, I can't,' he said. Although he still kept in touch with Gypsy he was living with a black girl who said she was the daughter of a Nigerian chief. One day he woke up and the black girl was dead in bed beside him. He was convinced that she'd committed suicide because he wouldn't leave Gypsy full time. I was in Cardiff Prison when it happened. He sent me a Christmas card and then only a week later he died, on New Year's Eve 1983. Gypsy organized his funeral. There were only seven or eight people there, which was Bill's wishes. I was right in touch with him to the very end, by which time he was mostly on his own. Percy Horne, who'd been at Borstal with Billy, had got very big in the scrap metal business but had stayed close to Bill. After Percy's wife died he more or less looked after him. Aggie Hill is still living in Jersey where she's been for nearly thirty years.

Percy Horne was one of the few people who

made real money. Anybody who was anybody then knew him. Eventually he went to live in Spain. Before he did that he came to Cardiff with Eva, and brought a letter Bill had given to him for me. It said that Bill had given Albert Dimes £50,000 to look after for me, but that Albert had squandered it. I didn't believe it. He was always jealous of Albert and I think he wrote it to damage Albert's image in my eyes, although Albert had been dead eleven years, as well as to excuse himself for not leaving me any money. As I understand it, he left over £1 million. What he did do was leave most of his money to the son of the black girl. His wife Gyp was to bring him up as her own son and she did send him to college. One of the conditions was for Gyp not to let her story be told until after she dies. She wrote me a nice letter in 1984 when I was in Bedford, sending me a picture of the stone on Bill's grave. I haven't heard from her since.

Spot's still around, I hear, but I haven't seen him since the slashing.

Albert Dimes died of cancer in 1972. I was being driven to prison and we passed University College Hospital where, though I didn't know it, he was at the time. Albert was a good thief, mostly in the War. Once it was over he was able to go back to full-time racing, which was what he really wanted. But occasionally he would do something worthwhile. By the time of the Eastcastle robbery he wasn't that thick with Bill. Bill was a manipulator, he was made that way. He was jealous of Albert,

although he would never admit it. Albert had everything Bill didn't have. Albert was such a lovely,
easygoing, happy-go-lucky man. Everyone liked him,
they couldn't do anything else. He'd give his shoes
away to someone to help them out. There wasn't
a greedy bone in his body. He was a delightful
man, and that was the one thing Bill couldn't be;
he couldn't be like that. To get him to smile and
laugh wasn't easy. Bill was a lovely man, don't get
me wrong, but he wasn't a natural like Albert,
although he could be a very charming man if it
suited him. He would be like a very great snooker
player, thinking not of the next shot he's going
to take but of four or five shots after that. He
would put people in brackets. 'That Albert could
be very useful to me, although I don't particularly
like him and I'm a bit jealous. Nevertheless he's
a good man and I'll keep him for a move or two
ahead.' Bill had a great brain; there's no two ways
about it.

Joe Wilkins is in Spain. I bumped into him in
Marbella when I went over for the currency. He
loves champagne and bought a couple of bottles.
When I had to go to Madrid to contest the civil
action, I flew back to Malaga and had a drink in
Port Banus with him. When in July or August 1988
I read his trial was on in Lewes, I was amazed that
he'd named me as a South London drug dealer, which
I'm not and never have been. I would have liked it
better if he had let me know beforehand. Nobody
ever approached me about his evidence, but it would
have been courteous. If Joe had approached me I'd

have said by all means. It couldn't do me any harm; after all, I was in prison.[2]

Jack Rosa died in a car accident going up to Manchester at the end of 1962. He'd taken up with Fay Richardson, who was known as the kiss of death.[3] He was a disqualified driver and had Ginger Ramsey's brief[4] with him. Game boy he was, when the police came just before he died he said, 'I wasn't driving.' His brother, Ray, had a heart attack less than twelve months ago as he was opening a window. He just collapsed and died. Johnny Longman also died of a heart attack; he was found sitting in his chair at home whilst I was still in prison on the long sentence. On the other hand Patsy Fleming is still around.

Joey Cannon had a bit more trouble up in Hull when someone done him with scalding water. Then he went and gave evidence to the Visiting Magistrates, something which was unforgivable in our circumstances. After he came out, he's made a great success of himself writing books.

Arthur Thompson, who looked after Andy Anderson

---

[2] In 1976 Wilkins was sentenced to three and a half years for living off immoral earnings. He had been running a high-class escort agency with his wife, Pearl, and an old friend Wally Birch. His sentence was cut to two years by the Court of Appeal because, they said, the trial judge had been prejudiced by information which linked him to Fraser.

On 17 August 1987 he was caught sunbathing on a boat, *The Danny Boy*, which was carrying £1.5 million in cannabis. At his trial at Lewes Crown Court Wilkins named Fraser as one of the bosses behind the Costa del Sol drugs racket. He escaped from prison after a visit to the dentist.

[3] All her men seemed to die young. Tommy Smithson, shot by Maltese hit men, was the first. Selwyn Cooney was shot in the Pen Club in 1961, and then came Rosa. She later emigrated to Australia.

[4] Driving licence.

after his escape, and who was the 'King of Glasgow', died in the March of 1993. Marilyn and I went to his funeral and took our wreath – 200 and more roses in a heart form – with us on the plane. Of all the funerals I've been to it was the most impressive I've seen. Even Churchill would have been proud of it.

Eddie Richardson is serving twenty-five years after being convicted in what the prosecution said was a £78 million cocaine drug-smuggling conspiracy. He was sent to prison in October 1990. He has taken up painting and recently won an award. His appeal is coming up soon, and I'm convinced he's innocent and will win.

I still see Charlie Richardson quite often. He has a gold mine in Uganda which takes him out of the country a lot. He wants me to go out on a visit with him. He's now happily settled down with Ronnie, his new wife. His daughter Michelle has just had a baby boy who's a ringer for his grandfather. John Blackburn Gittings, the lawyer in my last case and the one who came to Spain to get me out of prison there, has become Attorney General in Gibraltar.

As far as the Train people go, they haven't done so well in the long term. Bobby Welch has been ill for some years and it looks as though his legs will have to be amputated. Charlie Wilson was shot at his home in Spain and, of course, Tom Wisbey is still inside, but is getting home and work leave. Jimmy Hussey, who was done with Tom over the cocaine, is out now, he did seven years for that. Ronnie Biggs is in Brazil and likely to stay there. Gordon Goody is in Spain somewhere. I don't really see any of them now, except Tom of course.

I'm afraid my three elder sons, Frank, Patrick and David, have all done some heavy bird but they're all out now. My nephew, Jamie Brindle, has a gymnasium at the Henry Cooper pub down the Old Kent Road, and is doing well. Eva's daughter, Shirley, had a bad time some years ago. She was arrested for murder, but I'm glad to say she was acquitted and she's getting on better now. Eva herself is well.

Marilyn has made a demo record which I hope is going to do very well. When I went to the funeral of Arthur Thompson, I met up with the boxer, Lennie McLean, who introduced us to a man who had a recording studio. It turned out the man was the nephew of George Cornell, his mother was George's sister. Of course he was pleased to meet me, knowing I knew his uncle so well. Marilyn did her recording there with synthesizers. She sang an old Sinatra number, 'You and Me'. It's a gorgeous number.

I've got a little import/export business now – glass, fancy goods, mostly from Hong Kong, Taiwan, places like that. Funnily enough it's in a building which I did in 1943. It was a high-class tailor's then and it was stuck up for me. We just cleared out all the cloth. The man we sold it to was ecstatic. There were four of us, and I think we got about £300 each. It's funny how things turn full circle.

The old police officer 'Nipper' Read, who arrested the Krays, gave an interview to a newspaper the other day. I'd met him at a boxing tournament a bit earlier and I wouldn't shake hands with him, although Marilyn did. I think she felt a bit sorry for him with my refusing. In the newspaper he was asked if I'd ever reform, and he said he didn't think so.

All I can say is that others must agree with him, for I've had a fair number of offers these last few years. The police must have thought so as well, because on Thursday 12 August last year, Marilyn and I got turned over. The police arrived at Marilyn's and my place in Islington about 8 o'clock, saying they had a warrant to search for cocaine. Of course they found nothing of any description. Drugs has never been my scene. They turned the place over, and the garage, and then the copper said he was on the Murder Squad and started questions about the murder of Donald Urquhart in Marylebone in early January 1993 and Thomas Roche down near Heathrow in the summer, as if I was involved. I said I didn't know anything about either the murders or the men. In fact, apart from reading about them I'd never ever heard of them. They were at our flat about a couple of hours, and they waited until a solicitor told me they could take away my address book. Marilyn made them tea and I told them about doing this book, and the work I've been doing for a television programme on the underworld scene of the last fifty years. It was really quite friendly.

I must have served forty years or even more, out of my seventy in prison. I don't regret my life at all. The only thing I regret is that I was caught, but outside of that regret I have none whatsoever. It sounds daft, I know, but that's the decision I made and if you kept thinking about what you'd decided, you'd go through life regretting. It hasn't done me any harm. I've got my hair. If I'd become some poor harassed hard-working man, I most probably would have regretted I didn't carry on thieving instead of taking the straight and narrow. Because of the type of person I am, in the life I led, you learn to shrug off adversity better than people who've worked hard all their lives. It affects them very deeply. With my life, you have so many hardships and knock-backs you learn to brush them aside and enjoy life. It would be very hard for the ordinary man in the street to understand. It may not even sound sense, but it's the truth as far as I see it.

Index

A & R Club 297–8
Abdullah, Ahmet 313, 314n.
Adams, Freddie 72
Albany Prison 263
Allen, John 107, 127
Allpress, Alfie 132–3, 184
Anderson, Robert 'Andy' 201–5, 265–6, 268
Andrews, Rev. Basil 109n, 221
Andrews, Jimmy 153, 156–7, 158–9, 160, 177, 216, 320–21
Andrews, Mickey 265
Andries, Dennis 302
Angry Brigade 278
'Annie, Dartmoor' 5
Anthony, Eddie 112
Appleton 101
Army 26–9, 37–9, 114
Arndale school 16
Astor ix, 195, 211, 212
Atlantic Machines xi, 84, 85, 192–6, 199–203, 205, 211

Back, Patrick 268
Bainton, Governor 150, 250, 274
Baker, Stanley 200, 203, 217, 319
Baldassari, Tony 279
Barclay, Jack 295
Barnett, A. see Dimes, Albert
Barrett, Jackie 16
Barry, Johnny 18
Bass, Harry 50–52

Bean, Mr Justice 267
Bedord Prison 96
Beehive Club 230
Beisty, Governor 257–9
Bellson, Sammy 119, 120, 140, 171
Benstead, Billy 98, 176
Bentley, Derek 96
Bentley's Club 302
Berman, Alfie 222–3, 242
Biggs, Ronnie 201–2, 203, 327
Binney, Captain Ralph 44, 45n.
Birmingham Prison 155, 161–3
Blake, George 219
Bloggs, Patsy 177
Bloom, John 189
Blythe, Billy 72–3, 89, 107–8, 110, 137, 138–9
Blythe, Tony 265
Boal, Billy 181, 182
Bolsom's 91
bombs 176–7, 178, 194
Bonsoir 85, 178
Boothby, Robert 85
Borstal 19, 21
Botton, Henry, ix, xi, xii, 217, 321
Boyd, Leslie 244
Boyle, Jimmy 33–4
Bradford Prison 36, 38
Bradshaw, Alfie 152n.
Bravingtons 17
Bridges, Bunny 322

Brighton 119–20, 139, 180, 187–8, 295–6
Brindle, Bobby 110–11
Brindle, David 313–14, 317–18
Brindle, Eva (sister) 3, 9–10, 41, 44, 45, 63, 81–2, 86–7, 102, 111, 160, 166, 178–9, 221, 230–31, 242, 246, 260, 272, 328
Brindle, George 110
Brindle, Jamie 328
Brindle, Jimmy 3, 65, 72, 80, 86, 90–91, 92, 107, 110–11, 121, 162, 260
Brindle, Shirley 328
Brindle, Tommy 71, 86, 110
Brindle, Tony 313–14
Brindle, Whippo 86, 110–11
Bristol Prison 286–7
Brixton Jock 108
Brixton Prison 18, 206, 253–5
Broadmoor 41, 60, 102, 103–7, 260–61, 265
Bruno, Angelo 192
Burnett, Al 67
Burns 81
Bushell, Ted 131n.
Butler, R.A. 148n.
Butler, Tommy 139, 182, 205, 218, 252, 253–4
Buxton, Alex 304

Cabinet Club 76, 84, 87, 91, 107, 195
Calendar programme 272
Cane Hill Hospital 64
Cannon, Joe 124–5, 164, 326
Canterbury Prison 288–93, 296
Cardiff Prison 309
Carr, Robert 278n.
Carter, Buey (Hughie) 110, 113, 117, 141
Carter, Harry 113, 117–18, 141–2
Carter, Johnny 96, 110–14, 116–18, 141–3

Carter family 96, 110; *see also previous entries*
Central Club 107
Challis, Wally 93
Charlie Chester's Club 195, 206–7
Chelmsford Prison 23–48
Chester, Charlie 206
Clark, Tommy 222, 245
Clarke, D.I. 82
Clarkson, Billy 321
Clay, Governor 252–3
Cohen, Henry 71, 193
Cohen, Moisher 175
Comer, Rita 109, 138, 142
Cooney, Selwyn 326n.
Cooper, Dr 261, 265, 269
Cooper, Henry 151, 319
Cordery, Roger 181, 182–3
Cornell, George 177, 178, 208–9, 211, 216, 255, 322, 328
Cornell, Olive 322
Cortesis, the 13
Coulston, Benny 141, 221, 225, 226–30, 239, 246, 321
Cowans, Harry 147, 151
Craft, Huggy 76
Cromford Club x–xi
Crowther, Eric 304

Daniels, Franny 30n., 67, 89
Dartmoor 146–9, 154–5, 165
Davey, Jimmy 144–5
Davies, Dodger 53–4
Davies, Jimmy 28
Dawson, George 175, 176
de Antiquis murder 44
Delap 99
Dennis, Ginger 137, 151, 166
Dew, Johnny 209
Diamond, Canon 305, 306, 307–8
Diamond, Alice 176
Dimes, Albert, 16, 109, 112, 113, 118–20, 123, 124–5, 134,

150–51, 160, 167, 169, 189, 192–3, 220, 324–5
Distleman, Hubby 119n.
Docker, Lord and Lady 130–31
Donovan, Mr Justice 138
Dorchester Prison 323
Dove, Johnny 75–6
Doyle 201–2, 203
Driberg, Tom 84
Drury, Kenneth 37
Dryden, Sir Noel 84, 199–200
Durham Prison 99–103, 248–51
Duval, Jack 239, 243

Eastcastle Street 108, 176, 183–4
Edwards, Buster 5, 179–80, 252
Elliott, Little George 257
El Morocco 178
Emery, Lennie 130, 145–6
English, Johnny 4–5
English, Liz 4–5
Essex, Jimmy 16, 46, 169–70, 320
Evans, Jimmy 173
Exeter Prison 154–60

Fairns, Duncan 98
Falco, Albert 150, 193
Falco, Tommy 137, 150, 193
Fellowes, James 187, 233
Feltham Prison 18, 21, 32
Fidler, Governor 21
Field, Brian 151, 184
Fleming, Patsy 16, 17–18, 38, 126–8, 185
Flowers, Eric 201–2
Ford, Jimmy 72, 112
Foreman, Georgie 173
France, Gilbert 178
Frape, Martin 265, 268
Fraser, Mrs (mother) 1–2, 3–4, 10, 27–8, 39, 47
Fraser, Alfie 137, 170
Fraser, David (son) 266, 328
Fraser, Doreen (wife) 120, 155,

174, 186, 219–20, 250–51, 260, 276, 291–2, 309
Fraser, Eva *see* Brindle, Eva
Fraser, Francis (son) 219–20, 276–7, 291–2, 295–6, 328
Fraser, Frankie: shootings of ix–xiv, 312–15; family 1–3; childhood 3–12; first nicked 15–16; meets Billy Hill 23–4; deserter 29; psychiatric history 34–5, 38, 39, 59–65, 102–3; cat 46, 48–50; meets Lawton 55–6; bank jobs 68–70; wages snatch 86–7; and gang feuds 109–14, 117–25, 135–8, 141–3; petrol bombings 176–7, 178; Torture trial 206, 212, 218, 233–47; sequence of prisons 285–6; benefits for 297–8; handling charge against 302–5; shot 312–15; present business 328; 'turned over' 329; *for prisons served in see under names of prisons*
Fraser, James (father) 1–4, 10
Fraser, Jim (brother) 3, 47, 86–7, 246
Fraser, Jimmy (nephew) 219–20, 221, 224, 243–4
Fraser, Kathleen (sister) 3
Fraser, Patrick (son) 328
Fraser, Peggy (sister) 2–3
Fred, Fearless 131–4
French Lou 171
Frett, Dickie 'Dido' 87–8, 136

Garrett 161
Garrett, Johnny 'Little Legs' 152
Garrett, Lennie 28–9, 73
Gartree Prison 280
George Carters (store) 130
'George, Little' 23, 36
Gerard, Alfie, 73, 173n., 210
Gerard, Nicky 152n.
Gillies, Bernard 141

333

Gittings, John Blackburn 299, 300, 303–5, 327
Glasgow 204–5
Glinski, Christopher 109n., 221, 235, 243–4
Goldstein, Jimmy 'the Stick' 220
Goller, Billy 66, 68
Goody, Gordon 179, 327–8
Grantham, Roy 280–81
Great Train Robbery 151, 178–85, 187, 191, 192, 205, 251–2
Green, James 284
Greeno, Ted 29, 122
Gregory, Alf 144
Gregory, Ernie 144–5
Grew, Major 22

Hailsham, Lord 141
Hall, Roy 243, 248, 323
Hamilton 272–6
Hardy, G.L. 94
Harmon, Harriet 293
Harris, Bennie 117, 141–2
Harris, Johnny 141–2
Harris, Mikey 75–6, 82
Hart, Dickie xii, xiii, 217–18
Hart, Edward 131n.
Harvey, Richard 266
Harwood, George 2–3
Harwood, Harry 2–3
Hasse, Johnny 281
Hawkins, Deputy Governor 261
Hawkins, Charlie 116
Hayward, Billy xi, xii–xiii, 217
Hayward, Harry x–xi
Headley, Bobby 44
Hennessey, Peter xi, xiii, xiv
Hewitson, Mark 83–5, 160, 199, 211
Hideaway Club 168, 178
Hill, Aggie 74–5, 83–4, 109, 124, 323
Hill, Archie 131
Hill, Billy x, 23–5, 38, 41, 45, 67–8, 73–6, 78–9, 80, 85, 88, 89, 107–8, 109, 121, 124–5, 127–9, 130–31, 134, 135–7, 150–51, 160–61, 162, 163, 166–7, 168, 176, 182–5, 189, 195
Hill, Maggie 25, 30, 75, 176
Hinds, Alfie 3, 125–7, 144, 319–20
Hogg, Quintin 141
Holford, Harvey 188–90
Horne, Percy 323
Horricks, Governor 50–51
Household, Geoffrey 127
Howard, Billy 192, 230, 322
Hudd, Olive 208
Hume, Donald 128–9
Humphries, Jimmy 92, 259–60
Hurst, 'Nippy' 20
Hussey, Jimmy 179, 327
Hutchinson, Leslie (Hutch) 17

Ireland 135–6, 139
Isaacs, Johnny 152–3

Jackson, 'Spindles' 46
Jack the Rat 172, 182
James, George 89, 196–7, 206–7
James, John 196–7, 206
James, Roy 179
James Clarke's 40
J. Arthur's Club 301
Jeffreys, Ronnie xi, xiii
Jenkins, 'Harry Boy' 44
Jenkins, Tommy 44–5
Jewell, Stephen 320
Joannides, Peter 197–8
Jockeys' Fields 108, 109
'Jock the Fitter' *see* Robinson, Jock
'Johnny No Legs' 51–2
Jones, Brian 88
Jones, Raymond 130
Jones, Taffy 130
juries 91–2

Kensit, Johnny 242–3

Kensit, Patsy 242–3
Kimber, Billy 13
King, Bobbie 108
King, Martin Luther 254, 255
King's Head Club 196–76, 198
KLM bullion raid 108n., 184
Knight, Bogey 106
Knight, Ronnie 152, 299, 301
Kray, Reggie 11, 163, 165, 224, 243, 255
Kray, Ronnie 11, 165, 167, 209, 211–12, 216, 224–5, 255, 256
Kray Twins 68n., 84, 167–8, 176, 208–12, 255–6; *see also previous entries*

Lane, Johnny 36–7
Lawson, Charles 218, 233–4, 235–7, 241, 243–5
Lawton, Governor 55–7, 58–9, 89–90, 98, 116, 158–9
Lawton, Sir Frederick 231, 232–8, 245, 267
Lee, John 21
Leeds Prison 284
Leicester Prison 251–3, 256–61
Levine, Harry 192
Ley, Thomas 5n.
Lincoln, Ellis 139–40
Lincoln Prison 290
Lithgow 149
Liverpool Prison 47, 50–53
Lloyd, Dr 175
Lloyd-Eley, John 233–4, 235
Log Cabin 195
London Airport 25, 30, 110
Longford, Lord 302
Long Lartin Prison 284
Longman, Johnny 221, 243–4
Longthorne, Joe 301
Lowery, Joe 172
Luciano, Lucky 192
Lucy, Alf 39
Lyons, Patsy 42, 81, 97, 136

McArthur, A.C.C. 220, 223–4

Macauley, Archie 322
McCarthy, Bert 200
McCarthy, Leslie 200, 245, 246
McCarthy, Tommy 178
McDermott, Bobby 136, 205
McGoldrick, Steve 299–300, 301
McGrath, Paddy ix–x
Machin, Teddy 30n., 67, 121, 167, 320–21
McLean, Lennie 328
McVicar, John 249, 251
McVitie, Jack 'The Hat' 155–7, 159, 160, 251
Madrid, Francisco 300, 301
Maffia, Tony 146
Maloney 19
Manchester 135–6
Mancini, 'Babe' 119
Maples 125, 126
Marrinan, Patrick 118, 121, 138–41
Marsh, Bert 74n., 88–9, 131–4, 170, 319
Martin, Joey 249, 257
Meaney, Thomas 15–16
Mella, Tony 112–13
Millen, Ernie 83, 200
Miller, Alistair 261
Miller, Dickie 19
Miller, Max 120
Mills, John Platts 151
Milmo, Judge Helenus 151, 252
Mr Smith and the Witchdoctor Club ix–xi, 205–6, 216, 218
Mitchell, Charlie 255
Mitchell, Frank 146–7
Modernaires Club 74–5, 84, 195
Modlyn, Monty 280
Mole, Governor Bob 290
Moloney, Sir Tim 268
Money, Ernle 266
Moodie, William Ernest 100n.
Moody, Jimmy xi–xii, xiii, 217, 243, 316–18
Morgan, Micky 252–3
Morris, Mendel 204

Mudie, John 5n.
Mullins, 'Dodger' 75–6, 93
Murdoch, Dr 61
Murray, Bill 11–12
Murray, Billy 12
Murray, Michael 12

New Cabinet Club 75
Nicholls 49–50
Noble, Eddie 108
Noonan, Timmy 265, 267
North Riding Mental Hospital 38–9
Norwich Prison 28–9
Novello, Ivor 35
Noyes, Bill 168
Nut-House 67

O'Brien, Harry 23
O'Connell, 'Holy Joe' 19
one-arm bandits 192–201, 209–10; *see also* Atlantic Machines
O'Nione, Paddy 77, 144
Osborne, Johnny 280
Osborne, Lennie 279–80

Paris 171
Parkhurst 261–9
Parry, Gordon 40n.
Parry, John 40–41, 71, 72, 110
Payne, Leslie 213, 214n.
Pearson, John 216n.
Pentonville Prison 55–9, 115–16, 144–6, 151–4, 164–5
Piaf, Edith 171
Pierrepoint, Albert 96, 97
Pigalle, 167, 195
Piper, Ronnie 249–50
platinum 184–5
Plumley, Red-Faced Tommy 163
Podola, Gunther, 154n.
Porrit, Roy 201
Porthcawl 88–9
Portland Borstal 21–2
Post, Mrs 77–8

Power, Eddie 130, 177
Prater, Frank 222–3
Prescott, Jake 278
Probyn, Wally 249
Purdy, D.S. Ray 154n.
Pye, Dominic x
Pye, Jack x

Quincey, John 277

Raimo, Eddie 38
Ramsey, Bobby 123–4
Ramsey, Ginger 326
Ranch House 188
Ransford, Charlie 46
Ratcliffe, Owen ix
Rawlings, Harry xi, xiii, 225–6, 227–8
Ray, James Earl 254–5
Read, 'Nipper' 68n., 328–9
Rees, Geraint 234
Rees-Davies, Billy 266
Reform Club 168
Reynolds, Bruce 182
Reynolds, Jackie 121
Reynolds, Johnny 28
Rice 115–17
Richards, Governor 100–101
Richardson, Charlie 11, 168, 170, 182, 187, 191–2, 209, 212, 214–15, 219, 221–3, 225, 226–7, 234, 238, 241, 243, 248, 298–9, 305, 307–8, 327
Richardson, Eddie x, xi–xiv, 11, 168, 170, 182, 187, 191–2, 198–9, 206–7, 209, 212, 214–15, 217, 227, 234, 238–9, 243, 266–7, 298, 327
Richardson, Fay 326
Richardson, Supt. Gerald 126n.
Ridge, Charlie 120, 122, 139
Riley, Gipsy 109, 121, 323–4
Robinson, Fred, 'Yocker' 129
Robinson, Jock 77–9
Robinson, Stuttery 85
Robinson, Wally 129–30

Robson, Jimmy 266–7
Roche, Thomas 329
Rochester Borstal 19, 98
Rogers, Bert 39
Rogers, Harry 171–2, 176, 178, 182, 185, 186–7
Rogers, Ted 39
Rosa, Jack 73, 80–81, 87, 103, 168–9, 227, 251, 326
Rosa, Ray 136, 150, 168, 326
Rosen, Jimmy 56
Rossi, 'Battles' 107, 137, 138–9, 322
Rundle-Harris, Governor 158–9, 160
Russo, Victor 'Scarface' 150

Sabini, Darby (Charles) 13, 14–15, 66, 120, 319
Sabini, 'Harry Boy' 186, 319
Sabini, Johnny 66
Sambridge, Johnny (Happy) 122–3
Seaton, Reginald 140
Setty, Stan 128
Sewell, Freddie 126, 281
Sexton, Dave 234
Shaw, Sebag 240
Shillingford, Georgie 120, 172, 186
Shindler, George 266
Shrewsbury Prison 46–7
Sibbett, Angus 123n.
Silver, Bernie 210
Silverman, Sidney & Wally 33
Simmonds, 'Milkbottle' 169
Sims, Chopper 5
Skeggs, P.C. 280
Smith 5n.
Smith, Mrs 10
Smith, George 30–31
Smith, Hoppy 111
Smithson, Tommy 326n.
Society club 195
South Africa 243
Southport 196–7, 207

Spain 299–300, 301, 325
Sparks, Herbert 122. 319
Sparks, Jack 'Ruby' 32–4
Spot, Jack 30n., 39, 67, 107, 109–10, 118–21, 122, 123, 124–5, 131, 134–5, 137–8, 142, 150, 324
Spot, Rita 135
Stafford, Dennis 123n., 165
Stafford Prison 150
Stayton, Billy 210, 245–6
Steinhausen 257
Stork Club 195, 211
Stuart Surridge company 2, 3
Stubbs, Billy 40
Sullivan, Slip 130
Sullivan, Sonny 130
Sunset Club 117, 141
Swaffer, Hannen 184

Taggart, James 212, 221–4, 235, 236, 238
Thompson, Arthur 130, 204, 326–7, 328
Thompson, Stan 265, 316
Tibbs, Jimmy, Senior 187
Tin Pan Alley Club 294, 307, 311
Titmuss, Cherry 132
Trollope, Andrew 305
Turner, Jim 33
Turnmills Night Club ix, 312

United Dairies 82
Urquhart, Donald 329

Venables, Prison Director 149, 154, 163
Virgo, Walter 259–60

Waight, Michael 283–4
Wakefield Prison 2, 270–74
Wales 174–5
Walker, Billy & George 176
Wallington, George 73
Walters, Charlie 59–60, 63

Wandsworth Common 89, 116
Wandsworth Prison 18, 22–3, 24–5, 32, 33, 34–6, 49–50, 59–64, 90, 96–8, 99, 116, 256, 257, 278, 280, 281–3, 306–7
War, crime and 26–7
Warren, Bobby 137–8, 140
Warren, Frank 295
Waterloo Hosiery 18
Webb, Duncan 109, 121, 127, 128–9, 130–31, 184
Welch, Bobby 168, 179, 182, 293, 327
Wheater 184
White, Alf 66, 68
White, Alf (Jnr) 68
White, Billy 68
White, Harry 66, 67–8, 131, 167
White, Jimmy 179, 182
White, Johnny 68
White, Sandra 167
Wicks, Jim 319
Wilkins, Bert 74n., 172–3, 175–6

Wilkins, Joe 172–5, 185–6, 325–6
Willet, Guy 267
Williams, Charlie 30–31
Williams, Frank 252
Williams, Lou 30
Wilson, Charlie 179, 182, 327
Wilson, Harold 84–5
Winson Green Prison 283–4
Wisbey, Marilyn 311–13, 314, 328, 329
Wisbey, Rene 256
Wisbey, Tommy 178–9, 182, 252–3, 256–7, 311, 327
Wood, Georgie 110
Wooder, Jimmy 118, 137, 170
Woods, Albie 230–31
Wormwood Scrubs 18, 34–5, 293–4
Wyatt, Jock 25, 66

Yahuda, Joe 94

Zomparelli, Tony 152n.